I0709727

Be Extraordinary

PHILOSOPHICAL ADVICE
FOR PHOTOGRAPHIC
AND OTHER ARTISTS

GUY TAL

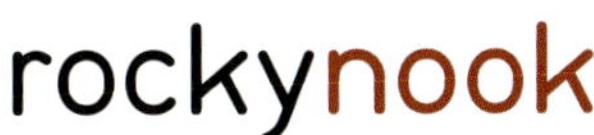

Be Extraordinary
Guy Tal (guytal.com)

Editor: Jocelyn Howell
Project manager: Lisa Brazieal
Marketing coordinator: Katie Walker
Layout and type: Anthony Paular Design
Front cover design: Frances Baca
Cover production: Anthony Paular Design

ISBN: 979-8-88814-204-2
(1st printing, November 2025)
© 2025 Guy Tal

Rocky Nook Inc.
1010 B Street, Suite 350
San Rafael, CA 94901
USA

Distributed in the UK and Europe by Publishers Group UK
Distributed in the U.S. and all other territories by Publishers Group West

Library of Congress Control Number: 2023952036

Cover image: Photographer Michael E. Gordon (michael-gordon.com) in a desert canyon. Photo by author.

It's all so meaningless, we may as
well be extraordinary.

—FRANCIS BACON

In truth, the work itself is the
adventure. And no artist could go
about this work, or would want
to, with less than extraordinary
energy and concentration. The
extraordinary is what art is about.

—MARY OLIVER

TABLE OF CONTENTS

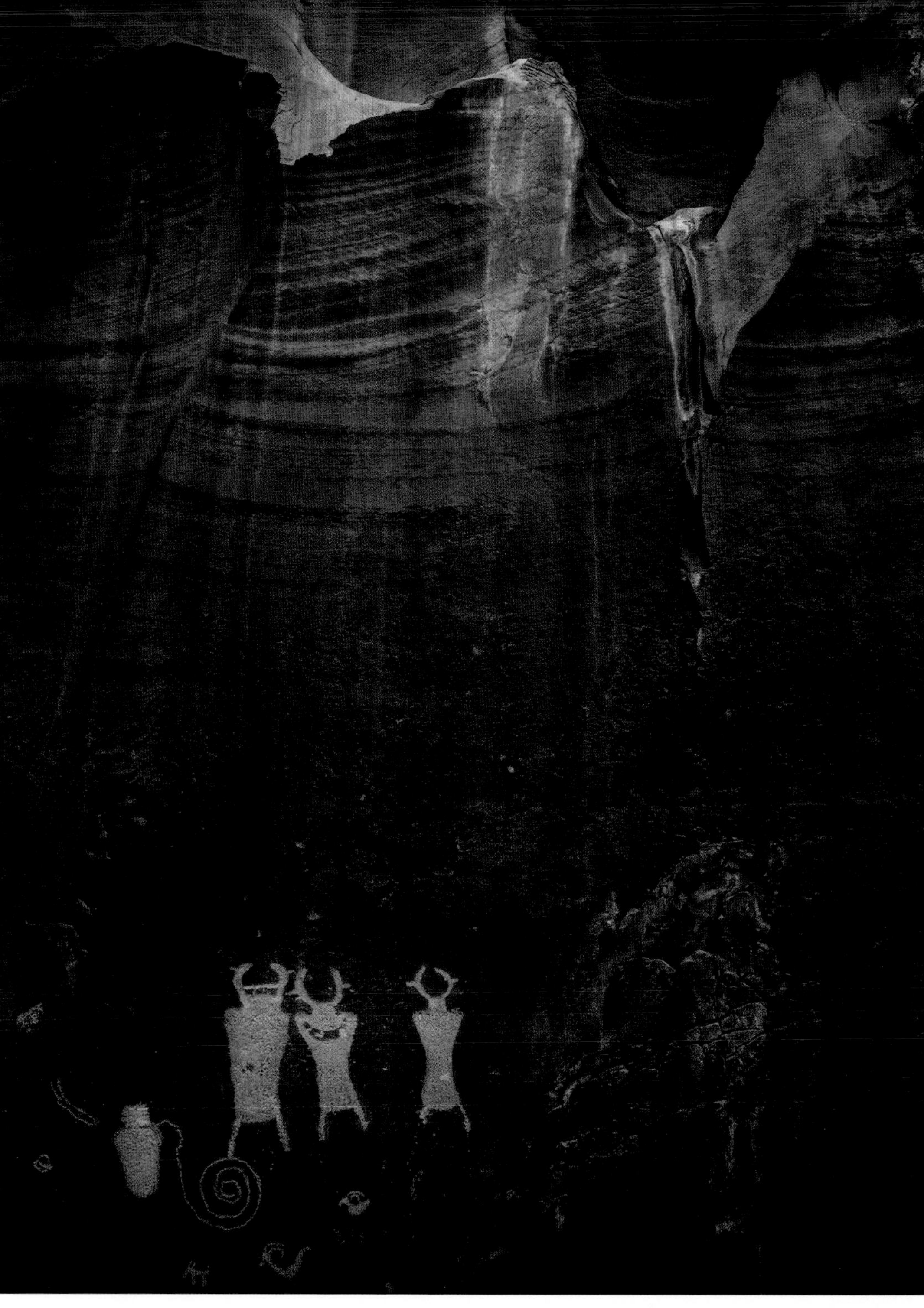

> If the book we are reading doesn't wake us up with a blow on
> the head, what are we reading it for?
>
> —FRANZ KAFKA

Friedrich von Schlegel wrote, "One of two things is usually lacking in the so-called Philosophy of Art: either philosophy or art." Being both artist and philosopher, my goal in writing this book is to offer you some insight into both these areas, including how they may complement each other, and how you may apply them most effectively in the pursuit of meaningful living and artmaking.

For a task of such gravity, simplistic platitudes (such as are commonly found in many self-help books) will not do. My goal is to make you think, to ask you to grapple with hard questions, to nudge you out of your comfort zone, perhaps to make you doubt things you may have so far taken for granted, to urge you to not accept as given common beliefs and attitudes just because they may be popular or seem intuitive, or because influential people advocate them. Rather, my goal is to offer you a baseline of knowledge you may use to examine ideas on your own and to assess their fitness to your own personality, circumstances, and values. Ultimately, I hope to help you find out what Friedrich Nietzsche meant by his admonition: *Become what you are.* What you are is extraordinary—at least in some ways, unlike anyone else.

Both philosophy and art are subjects far broader and deeper than I may cover in a single book, let alone in a book meant to offer practical advice. Albert Einstein suggested that the most important thing a teacher can impart "is not knowledge and understanding per se but a longing for knowledge and understanding, and an appreciation for intellectual values, whether they be artistic, scientific, or moral." He then concluded, "It is the supreme art of the teacher to awaken joy in creative expression and knowledge." This is the high bar I set for myself in writing this book.

I hope you consider this book not as a recipe to guaranteed success, but as a hand-drawn map shared with you by a fellow seeker. I will mark for you the paths and features I found useful in my own travels and warn you against those that led me astray.

As I am about to share with you some of my personal philosophy and encourage you to think about your own, I'd like to first tell you a little about myself, so you know something about the person offering you advice. Although most people likely know me as a photographer, I confess that "photographer" has been for me (at least in part) a good cover story: something through which I can earn a modest income, on my own, without being bound to an office or a city, without having to answer to any social or corporate hierarchy, and without having to suppress my (perhaps overly) individualistic temperament. Having always been a consummate naturalist, an avid learner, and a social misfit, being a photographer allows me to spend my days in places I love, doing things I love, with time left over to pursue my many interests, to study, and to contemplate. Put another way, photography has been most valuable to me not as a career choice or even as a creative choice, but as a means to living what to me is a deeply meaningful life: a naturalist's life, an adventurer's life, an artist's life, a philosopher's life.

Among other lives I've had, I was once a conscripted soldier, a late-night shift worker, an academic, a technologist, a teacher, a corporate manager, an outdoor guide, an author of books, articles, and poems, and a few other things. Being restless by nature, I have tried—and given up on—several careers and lifestyles that failed to satisfy. Despite so many transitions, however, some things in my life remained constant. Since early childhood I have always been an avid naturalist. As an adult, I have been an independent student of science, philosophy, and art. Driven by an overarching goal to make my earthly existence as interesting and meaningful as I can, I have strived to not just broaden and deepen my understanding of these disciplines, but also to apply what I have learned in my own life. Sometimes it has worked spectacularly well, and sometimes it hasn't . . . just as spectacularly.

I've had numerous opportunities to settle down, to live a comfortable urban life, to pursue lucrative and more prestigious career paths, to live by safe and predictable routines. But none of these was sufficient to quell the temptation to keep seeking, learning, experiencing, and discovering new things—about myself and about the world.

These days, I am fortunate to spend more of my time outdoors, in beautiful natural places, than any other person I know (and I know some very outdoorsy people). In fact, I wrote most of this book in various desert and mountain campsites. Now in my sixth decade of life, having done and experienced many things, I am fortunate to be largely free from professional, social, academic, ideological, or other tribal allegiances. I have the privilege of not feeling beholden to any tradition, place, organization, nationality, community, or specialty other than those I choose for myself.

It may seem to an outsider that I have found "success": that my life is entirely blissful and harmonious. Certainly, in some ways, and at some times, it is. But don't

> If the book we are reading doesn't wake us up with a blow on
> the head, what are we reading it for?
>
> —FRANZ KAFKA

Friedrich von Schlegel wrote, "One of two things is usually lacking in the so-called Philosophy of Art: either philosophy or art." Being both artist and philosopher, my goal in writing this book is to offer you some insight into both these areas, including how they may complement each other, and how you may apply them most effectively in the pursuit of meaningful living and artmaking.

For a task of such gravity, simplistic platitudes (such as are commonly found in many self-help books) will not do. My goal is to make you think, to ask you to grapple with hard questions, to nudge you out of your comfort zone, perhaps to make you doubt things you may have so far taken for granted, to urge you to not accept as given common beliefs and attitudes just because they may be popular or seem intuitive, or because influential people advocate them. Rather, my goal is to offer you a baseline of knowledge you may use to examine ideas on your own and to assess their fitness to your own personality, circumstances, and values. Ultimately, I hope to help you find out what Friedrich Nietzsche meant by his admonition: *Become what you are.* What you are is extraordinary—at least in some ways, unlike anyone else.

Both philosophy and art are subjects far broader and deeper than I may cover in a single book, let alone in a book meant to offer practical advice. Albert Einstein suggested that the most important thing a teacher can impart "is not knowledge and understanding per se but a longing for knowledge and understanding, and an appreciation for intellectual values, whether they be artistic, scientific, or moral." He then concluded, "It is the supreme art of the teacher to awaken joy in creative expression and knowledge." This is the high bar I set for myself in writing this book.

I hope you consider this book not as a recipe to guaranteed success, but as a hand-drawn map shared with you by a fellow seeker. I will mark for you the paths and features I found useful in my own travels and warn you against those that led me astray.

What else you may encounter in the great uncharted realms of mind and art, I don't know. Perhaps you may someday discover them yourself and gain a greater understanding than I have, or maybe even find yourself in the fortunate position of feeling you have gained insights that may be useful to others and pay it forward.

I make no promise that the advice I offer here will bring you happiness or riches, certainly not that it would be easy to put into practice. I am confident, however, that I may at least point you in some useful directions and help you progress toward making your life and your art more meaningful in the deepest ways that life and art can be meaningful, which is to say: meaningful to you.

The thesis of this book is this: Meaningful art is an expression—a byproduct—of meaningful living. Meaningful living, in turn, is living according to your own unique personality, values, sensibilities, goals, and circumstances. But art can do more than just express a meaningful life; it can also *make* life more meaningful.

A great deal of dissatisfaction and misery are the results of people attempting (or resigning) to live in ways that don't align with who they are as unique individuals: according to opinions, customs, expectations, or dictates promoted or imposed by others. Hopefully, much such misery may be spared if people put in the effort, however difficult, to find a life that fits them best, and the courage to live it, even if it requires venturing beyond the ordinary. "The individual," wrote Rudyard Kipling, "has always had to struggle to keep from being overwhelmed by the tribe. To be your own man[1] is a hard business. If you try it, you'll be lonely often, and sometimes frightened. But no price is too high to pay for the privilege of owning yourself."

The title of this book refers to this saying by Francis Bacon (the painter, not the philosopher with the same name): "It's all so meaningless, we may as well be extraordinary." As I explain later in the book, Bacon's statement aligns with certain tenets of existential philosophy—namely, that the world is objectively indifferent and meaningless, and that it is up to each of us to make our own lives subjectively meaningful: to find out and to become who we are—to be extraordinary.

---

[1] For much of human history, in most languages, the use of masculine references was considered correct phrasing when making generalized statements. (Alas, in some languages this remains the case even today.) While unfortunate, please consider that it does not imply that an author intended deliberately for their writings to be misogynistic (to wit, women writers in past times used the same forms). While you will not find gendered language in my own writings unless referring to a specific individual, I don't consider it my place to rewrite the words of other authors. Please consider these historical writings as they were intended in their day, and not necessarily as implying prejudice or deliberate bias in their authors.

My art is rooted in a single reflection: why am I not as others are? … my art gives meaning to my life.

—EDVARD MUNCH

Dear reader, I don't know who you are, but I am writing this book for you: you, who may be younger or older than I am; you, whose history and daily life may be similar to my own or different from mine beyond my ability to imagine; you, who may live in my time or in a world I am no longer a part of; you, who may consider becoming an artist or who may already be an artist.

I don't know your name, your gender, or what pronouns you wish to be referred to by (I would use them if I could). I don't know your circumstances or your aspirations. I don't know if we speak the same language, like the same foods, or enjoy the same pastimes. I don't know whether you are an introvert or an extravert, whether you are an optimist or a pessimist, whether you are wealthy or poor, whether you are politically progressive or conservative. I don't know what level of education you have, whether you have studied art, science, or philosophy, or what your spiritual beliefs may be. Alas, there is a lot I don't know about you—a lot that I wish I could use to make this book as useful to you as I can. Still, I'd like to try.

There are some things I *do* know about you: things having less to do with who you are and more to do with what you are. I know that, like me, you are a human being, and as such you are innately creative, curious, and motivated to make the most of the brief time you get be alive, to experience, to feel, to learn, to understand, to engage with the world in the most satisfying and meaningful ways open to you. I know that, as people, you and I share certain traits, perceptions, desires, abilities, and limitations. In short, I know that we are both, as some philosophers have characterized it, *beings in the world*: unique individuals among others, existing in a universe rich with opportunities, ideas, knowledge, and mysteries. As I hope to show you, this is a sufficiently solid foundation to support a personal philosophy of life and to consider the role that art may—if we choose—play in it.

As I am about to share with you some of my personal philosophy and encourage you to think about your own, I'd like to first tell you a little about myself, so you know something about the person offering you advice. Although most people likely know me as a photographer, I confess that "photographer" has been for me (at least in part) a good cover story: something through which I can earn a modest income, on my own, without being bound to an office or a city, without having to answer to any social or corporate hierarchy, and without having to suppress my (perhaps overly) individualistic temperament. Having always been a consummate naturalist, an avid learner, and a social misfit, being a photographer allows me to spend my days in places I love, doing things I love, with time left over to pursue my many interests, to study, and to contemplate. Put another way, photography has been most valuable to me not as a career choice or even as a creative choice, but as a means to living what to me is a deeply meaningful life: a naturalist's life, an adventurer's life, an artist's life, a philosopher's life.

Among other lives I've had, I was once a conscripted soldier, a late-night shift worker, an academic, a technologist, a teacher, a corporate manager, an outdoor guide, an author of books, articles, and poems, and a few other things. Being restless by nature, I have tried—and given up on—several careers and lifestyles that failed to satisfy. Despite so many transitions, however, some things in my life remained constant. Since early childhood I have always been an avid naturalist. As an adult, I have been an independent student of science, philosophy, and art. Driven by an overarching goal to make my earthly existence as interesting and meaningful as I can, I have strived to not just broaden and deepen my understanding of these disciplines, but also to apply what I have learned in my own life. Sometimes it has worked spectacularly well, and sometimes it hasn't . . . just as spectacularly.

I've had numerous opportunities to settle down, to live a comfortable urban life, to pursue lucrative and more prestigious career paths, to live by safe and predictable routines. But none of these was sufficient to quell the temptation to keep seeking, learning, experiencing, and discovering new things—about myself and about the world.

These days, I am fortunate to spend more of my time outdoors, in beautiful natural places, than any other person I know (and I know some very outdoorsy people). In fact, I wrote most of this book in various desert and mountain campsites. Now in my sixth decade of life, having done and experienced many things, I am fortunate to be largely free from professional, social, academic, ideological, or other tribal allegiances. I have the privilege of not feeling beholden to any tradition, place, organization, nationality, community, or specialty other than those I choose for myself.

It may seem to an outsider that I have found "success": that my life is entirely blissful and harmonious. Certainly, in some ways, and at some times, it is. But don't

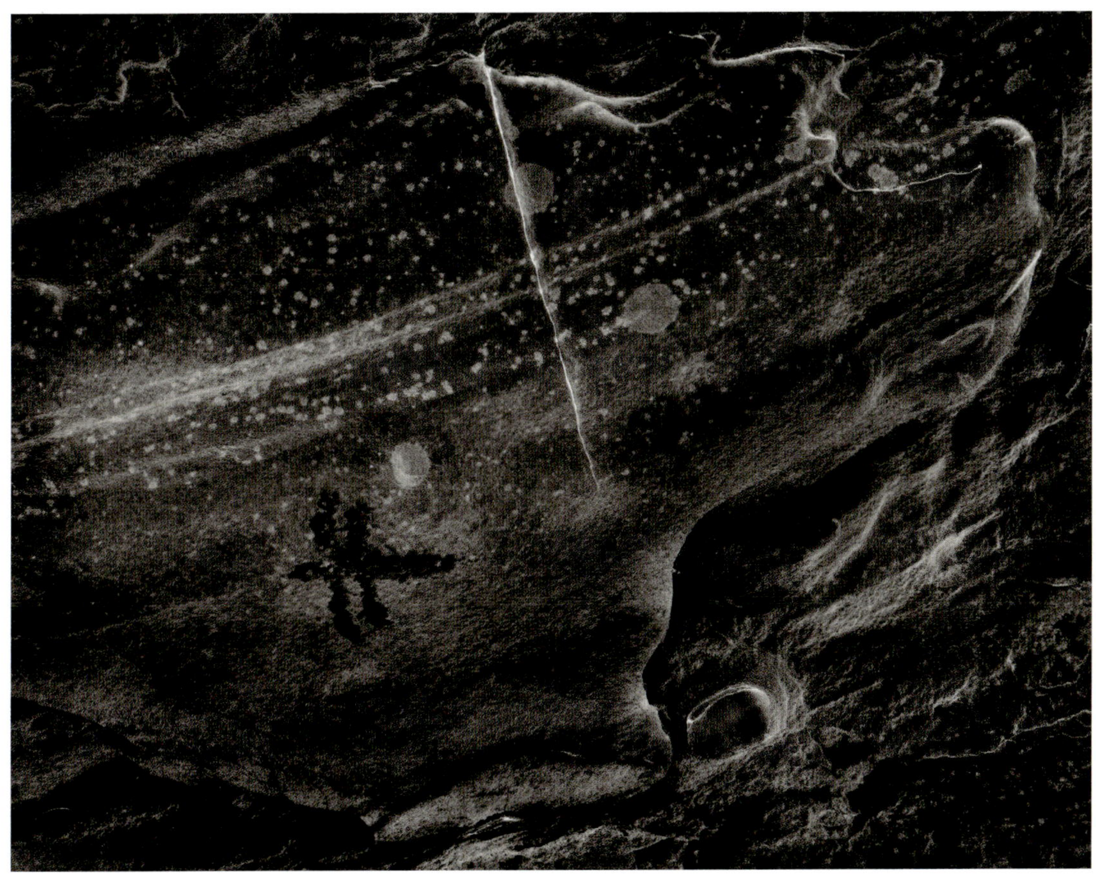

assume that my days are free from difficulties, or that my journey has been easy. Far from it. I will, however, offer you this at the outset: I consider the life I have lived with its many challenges and triumphs, joys and miseries, successes and failures, as my greatest creation—my most important work of art, created for an audience of one. Accordingly, my first and perhaps most important bit of advice to you is this: I urge you to consider your life in this way too.

Guy Tal
Torrey, Utah
May 2023

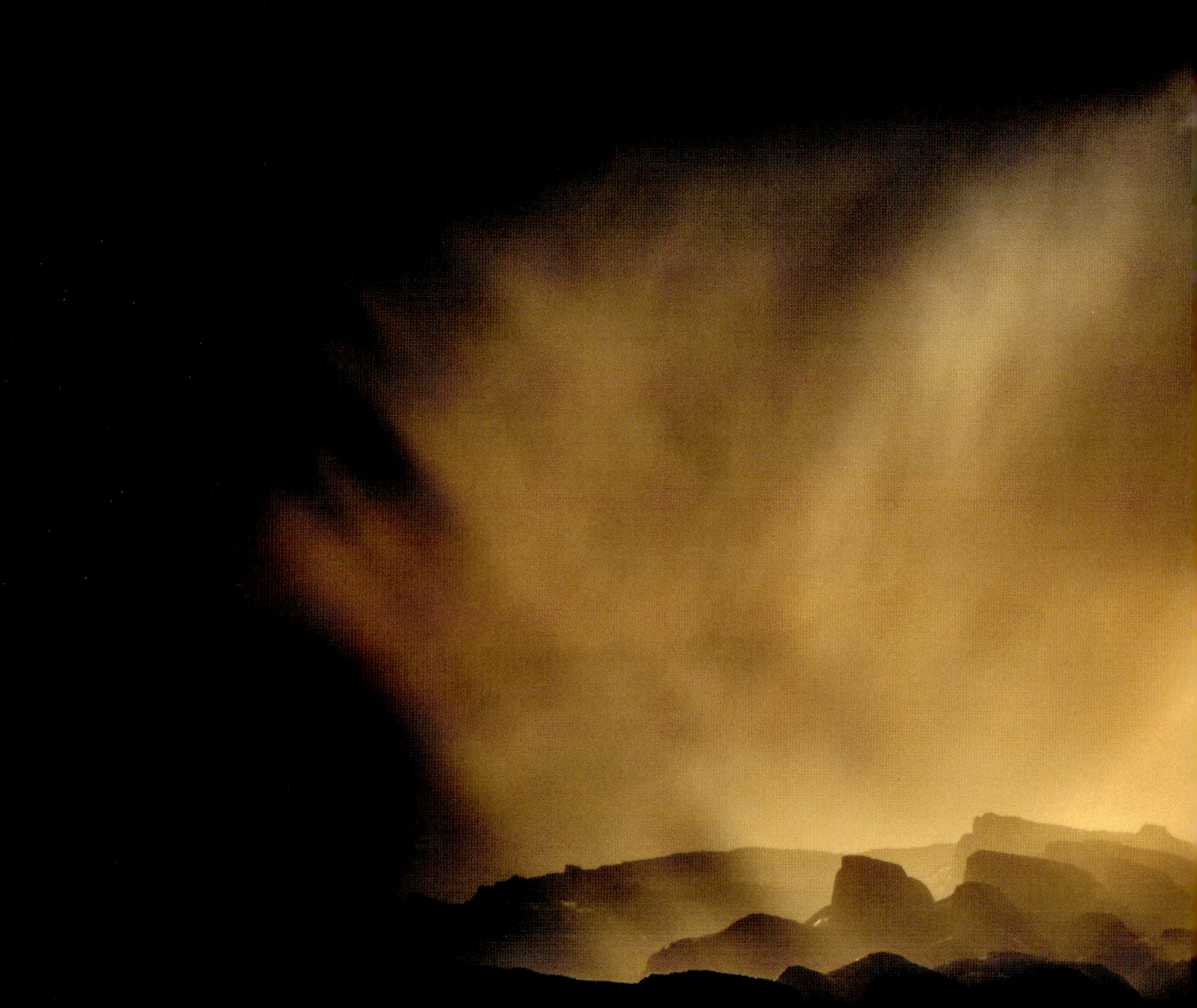

PART 1: FOUNDATIONS

A primary task is thus imposed upon one who undertakes to write upon the philosophy of the fine arts. This task is to restore continuity between the refined and intensified forms of experience that are works of art and the everyday events, doings, and sufferings that are universally recognized to constitute experience.

—JOHN DEWEY

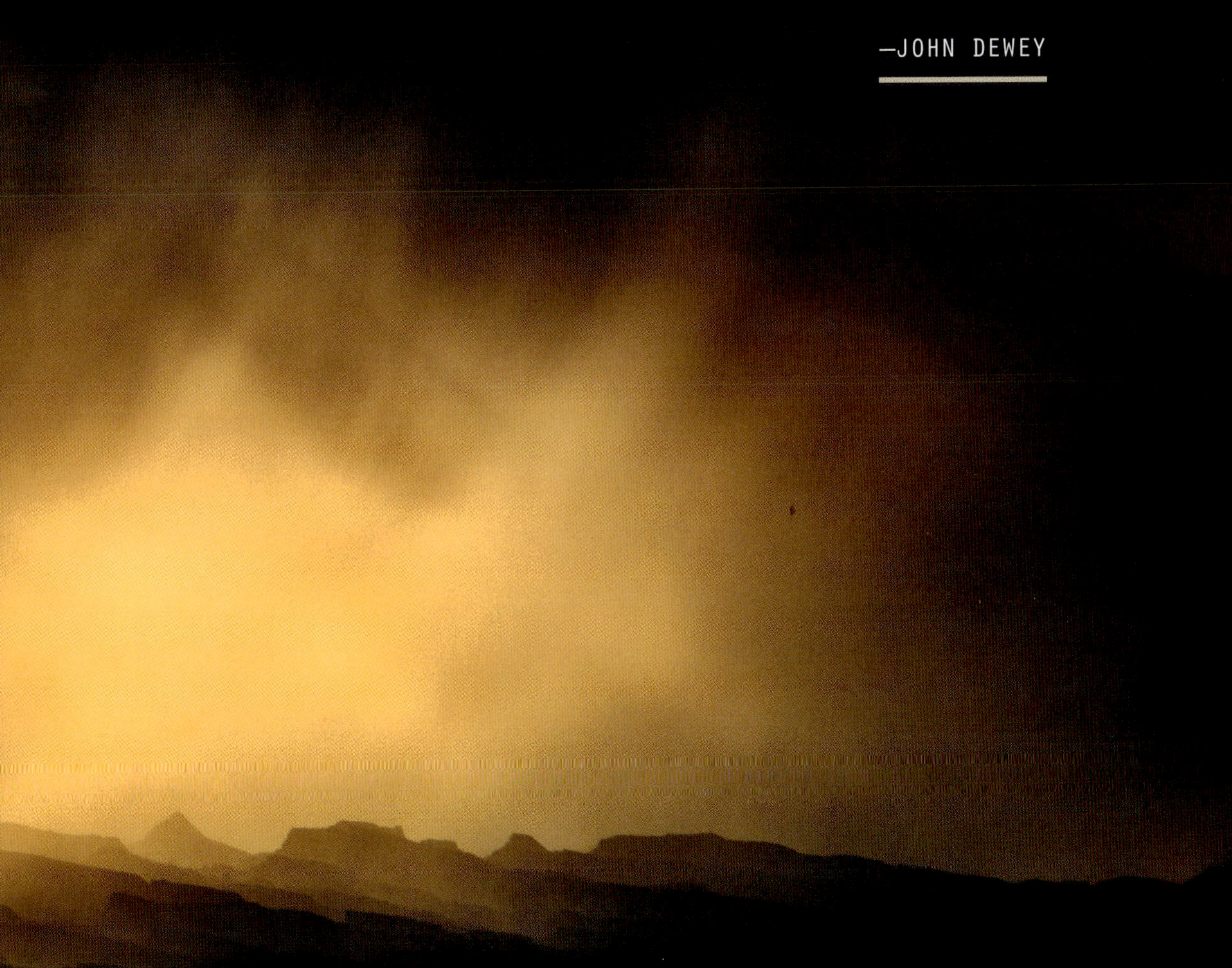

In this part of the book, please bear with me as I review some terms, concepts, and philosophical ideas to establish a baseline of knowledge and reference material for the practical advice I offer in the second part of the book. My choice of subjects in this section is decidedly anecdotal and not intended to be exhaustive, systematic, or (in some cases) even chronological. I just didn't want to assume you are already familiar with them. If you are, feel free to skip ahead or stick around for a refresher.

As I touch on various subjects, I explain how and why I found them useful in my own life and work: how I considered their fitness for my personality and goals, and how they may align with or complement each other. I do so hoping you will see the value of adopting not only the ideas I present, but more so my way of thinking about them—skeptically, critically, seeking correlations with other ideas and knowledge, and striving to find meaning in them that may enrich your life.

Please don't assume that my way is the only way or necessarily the best way for you too. Certainly, to the degree that our personalities and circumstances may be similar, my choices and explanations may convince you to believe and to choose as I have. However, just as certainly, there are also ways in which you and I are not alike, even ways in which you are not like anyone else. I offer my thoughts here hoping to inform you and to clarify for you certain ideas and ways of thinking; not to spare you the effort of, or responsibility for, contemplating and considering seriously the choices available to you, the fitness of certain ideas and attitudes for your own personality and goals, and having to make and accept the consequences of your own decisions.

> I should not like my writing to spare other people the trouble of thinking. But if possible, to stimulate someone to thoughts of his own.
>
> —LUDWIG WITTGENSTEIN

The word *philosophy* derives from a combination of Greek terms translating roughly to "love of wisdom." Throughout history, philosophy has overlapped to varying degrees with subjects now considered as separate disciplines, such as natural sciences, theology, linguistics, and social studies. Today, philosophy is a formalized academic discipline spanning various specialized branches, movements, traditions, and areas of study.

All forms of philosophy have this in common: They are concerned with investigating various aspects of the fundamental nature of the world, attempting to understand, among other things, such foundational topics as the nature of existence (i.e., metaphysics); the nature of knowledge (i.e., epistemology); how to formulate truthful arguments, draw correct inferences, and avoid being misled by fallacies (i.e., logic); how to live and behave properly and morally (i.e., ethics); and what the nature of beauty and the purpose of art are (i.e., aesthetics). As philosopher Iris Murdoch put it, "Philosophy involves seeing the absolute oddity of what is familiar and trying to formulate really probing questions about it."

While many people practice philosophy professionally and/or have dedicated themselves to academic study of various philosophies, philosophers (like artists) exist in all walks of life. Many highly recognized philosophers are or were, by profession or education scientists, writers, artists, politicians, public intellectuals, religious figures, and many other things. This is why the highest degree awarded in most academic fields is PhD—shorthand for the Latin term *philosophiae doctor*: teacher of philosophy.

Some forms of philosophy rely on deep knowledge in specialized areas, and some are rife with esoteric terminology. But there are also many useful aspects of philosophy that are accessible to almost anyone willing to invest time in studying them, formally or independently. Certainly, some philosophical texts are complex and difficult to digest, but others make for relatively easy, enlightening, and enjoyable reading. What I mean to say is that you don't necessarily need to take any class or have a high degree of formal education to begin your journey in philosophy, or even to become a philosopher in the general sense—a lover of wisdom. All it takes is curiosity—a desire to understand— and a willingness to question and seek answers. With even a basic understanding of certain philosophical topics, you may find profoundly useful and practical insights to help guide your life and art in meaningful ways.

Likely, you have heard of (and perhaps even studied or actively practice) some aspects of certain formal philosophical traditions. For example, many people today find such philosophical practices as Stoicism, or the Socratic approach to arguments, or the pursuit of authenticity and individualism promoted by existentialists, useful in their daily lives. I caution you, however, not to become too mired in tribal allegiance to any one school of philosophy or to the entire worldview of any philosopher. If you do so, you may fairly claim to have a philosophy, but you will not be able to claim yourself a philosopher. Consider that even within some well-defined traditions you will find deep disagreements among authors, scholars, promoters, and practitioners.

Too many people who write about philosophy do so as apologists for their favorite personas or "brands." This comes at the risk of degrading philosophy to dogmatic, cult-like thinking. No doubt, some aspects of some philosophical traditions can be immensely useful. But that is also their danger: It's easy to become tempted by anecdotal successes and decide to stop seeking and questioning. This is unfortunate, as no one philosophy, no matter how useful, popular, or seemingly self-evident, has everything figured out. This is especially true in the areas of metaphysics and ethics: what to believe and how to live.

Doubtless, some situations in life are best approached with Stoic or Buddhist equanimity. But, just as doubtless, there are also situations that call for the calculated precision of formal logic, or for Nietzsche's conviction to "love your fate," or for indulgent immersion in beauty for its own sake with Kantian disinterestedness—all terms I explain in due course and all good reasons to not just dabble in one or a handful of aspects of some formal philosophies, but instead to strive to become a "well-rounded" philosopher.

Never assume that other people, even those closest to you, have already figured out the best way to live. Never even assume that there is such a thing as a one-size-fits-all "best way to live." Each of us possesses a unique combination of personality traits, circumstances, and goals. For this reason, what may seem like the best way to live for one person may not necessarily be the best way to live for another.

Recall that philosophy is—in the most literal sense—a love of wisdom, not a recipe for living; and wisdom is a well deep beyond any person's reach (in some ways, likely even beyond the reach of the human species). There are and always will be things beyond your understanding—mysteries to investigate, new information to assimilate, new ways of thinking. Do your best with what you have, and have the courage to revise your thinking and practices as you acquire new knowledge, insights, and experiences.

In this section, I'll give you a taste of what some of humanity's greatest thinkers had to say about life and art (and sometimes specifically about photography). Treat these thoughts as ideas to contemplate. Don't take any of them as gospel, but also don't dismiss them based on gut feeling alone. All are founded in wisdom and knowledge and deserve fair consideration.

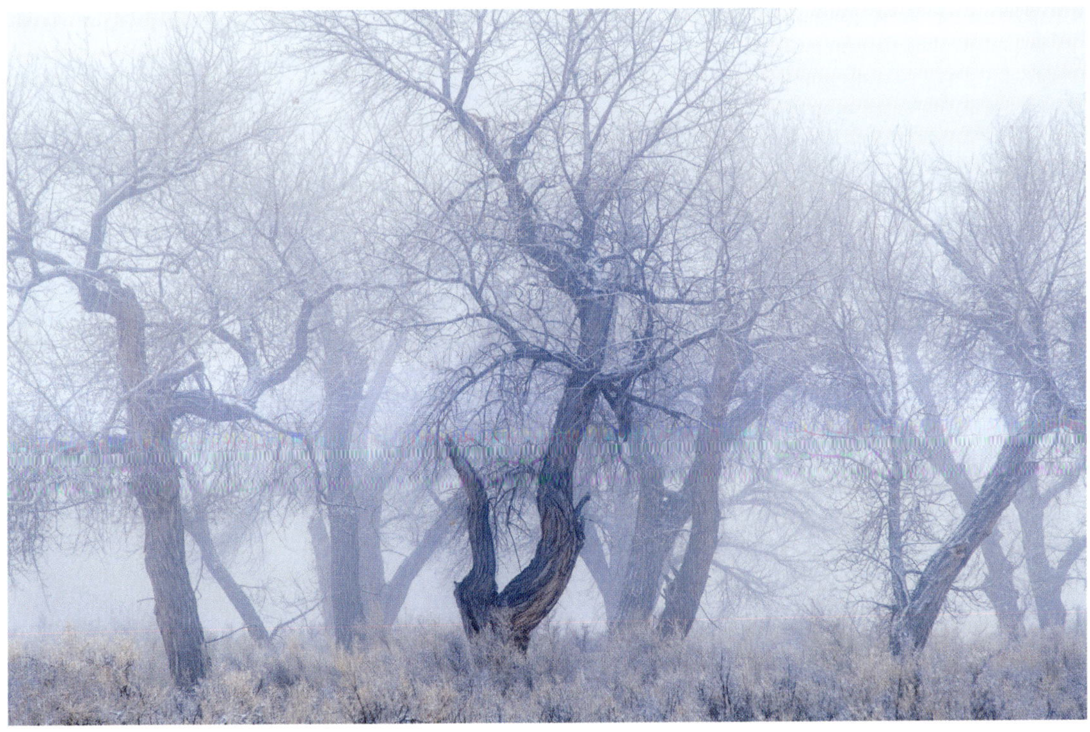

ON HAPPINESS

> The primary reason it is so difficult to achieve happiness centers on the fact that, contrary to the myths mankind has developed to reassure itself, the universe was not created to answer our needs. Frustration is deeply woven into the fabric of life. And whenever some of our needs are temporarily met, we immediately start wishing for more.
>
> —MIHALY CSIKSZENTMIHALYI

In various places in this book I use the word "happiness" in a specific way that may not be intuitive, especially to native English speakers. Happiness can mean many different things, and some languages may have different expressions for types of happiness that may not even be found in other languages. Especially when reading complex and/or translated texts, always keep in mind Ludwig Wittgenstein's admonition: "Language sets everyone the same traps; it is an immense network of easily accessible wrong turnings."

The flavor of happiness most revered by philosophers (as well as by present-day positive psychologists) is known as *eudaemonia*. According to the *Encyclopedia Britannica*, eudaemonia is "the condition of human flourishing or of living well." The same encyclopedia entry also warns, "The conventional English translation of the ancient Greek term, 'happiness,' is unfortunate because eudaemonia ... does not consist of a state of mind or a feeling of pleasure or contentment, as 'happiness' (as it is commonly used) implies."

For clarity, the pursuit of pleasure and contentment is more aptly described as *hedonism*, rather than as eudaemonia. This is important, among other things, to explain an effect known in psychology as "hedonic adaptation," and its closely related concept of "the hedonic treadmill." Both expressions refer to a form of happiness focused entirely on pursuing immediate, short-lived pleasure, as opposed to striving for sustained satisfaction and meaningfulness (the characteristics of eudaemonia). Hedonic pleasure generally involves the relentless pursuit of dopamine spikes, or "hits." Contrary to popular belief, dopamine spikes do not cause happiness directly.

Dopamine is involved in multiple functions of the nervous system, one of which is to produce pleasure indirectly by increasing our motivation to pursue goals and arousing expectations of future rewards. In this way, dopamine "cheats" us by "promising" pleasures that may come from certain activities and choices, and from imagining what it would be like to have the rewards before we have attained them. Ironically, studies in happiness show that the cumulative pleasure we feel from anticipating future rewards are greater than the pleasure we feel when we attain these rewards.

When we attain an expected reward, dopamine dissipates, and so the pleasure we feel is short-lived. That new camera or car or amorous affair we thought would change our world for the better, will soon come to feel ordinary and less exciting. This is the "adaptation" effect referred to in the term "hedonic adaptation"—once we achieve something, we soon adapt to it and start taking it for granted: It becomes less rewarding, leaving us craving the next "hit." This constant seesaw effect of craving something, achieving it, becoming used to it, and craving the next thing is what's known as the "hedonic treadmill." It essentially means we are never satisfied with what we have.

Roman Stoic philosopher Lucius Annaeus Seneca presciently recognized the effect of the hedonic treadmill and advised his friend Lucilius, "Fix a limit which you will not even desire to pass, should you have the power. At last, then, away with all these treacherous goods! They look better to those who hope for them than to those who have attained them."

Another term for the hedonic treadmill comes from philosopher Arthur Schopenhauer, who called it "the will" and described it as "purposeless striving." Unlike Seneca's optimistic outlook that we may choose to fix a limit for ourselves, Schopenhauer recognized that escaping the hedonic treadmill—the will—is not as simple as deciding to stop striving (which, in many cases, we will not be able to stick to, leading to guilt, self-recrimination, and frustration). According to Schopenhauer, the will is the most powerful prevailing force in nature, causing all things to always strive for more: to consume more, to procreate more, to experience more pleasures, etc., all through our lives, without an end goal. No matter how far we go or how much we have,

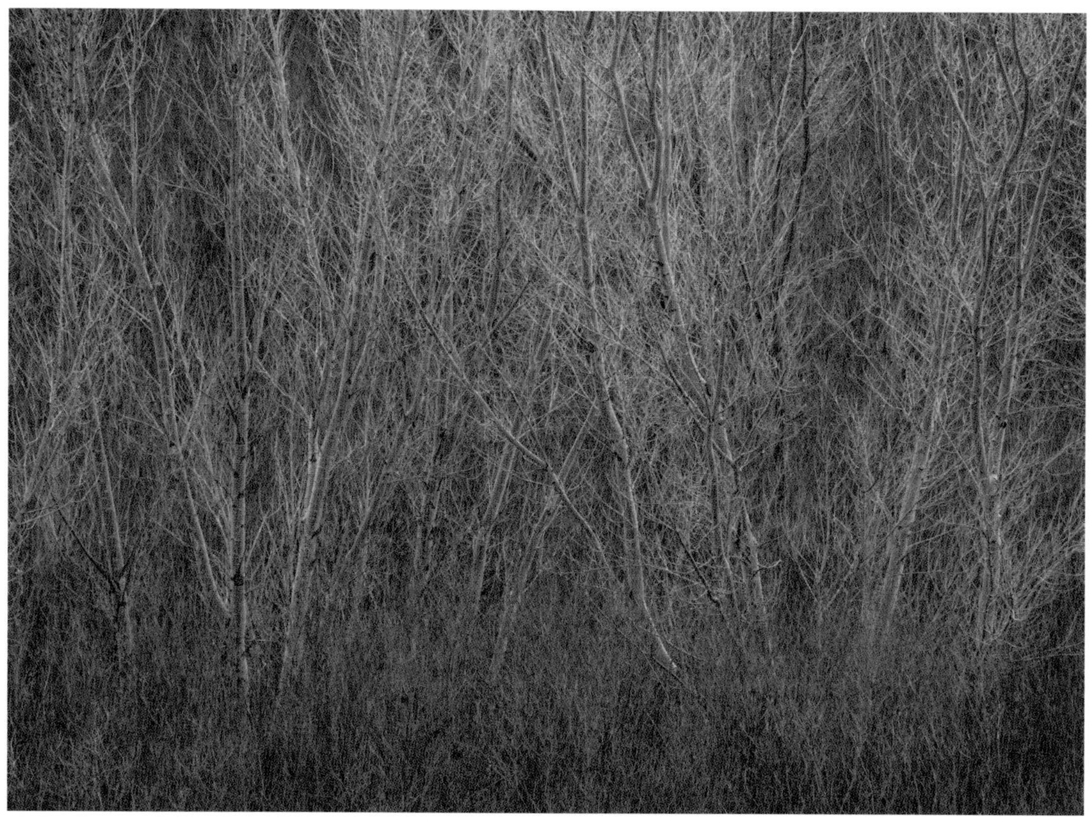

the will always makes us feel dissatisfied and makes us crave more. This effect, according to Schopenhauer, is the source of life's innate misery: the reason we can never achieve lasting happiness, only short respites from boredom and suffering. We can, however, find temporary happiness (i.e., escape the will) in some ways. Schopenhauer specifically identified two ways of doing so: immersing ourselves completely in great art (especially music), and disconnecting ourselves to the degree we can from the daily grind of human affairs (i.e., become ascetics).

In contrast to hedonic or other forms of happiness—which involve heightened, excited states—eudaemonia is more closely associated with the Greek concept of *ataraxia*: a sense of sustained calmness, stability, equanimity, and feeling ourselves unflappable in the face of troubling events and unexpected setbacks. Ataraxia, in turn, is very similar to the even older concepts of *nirvana* or *moksha*, found in ancient Indian

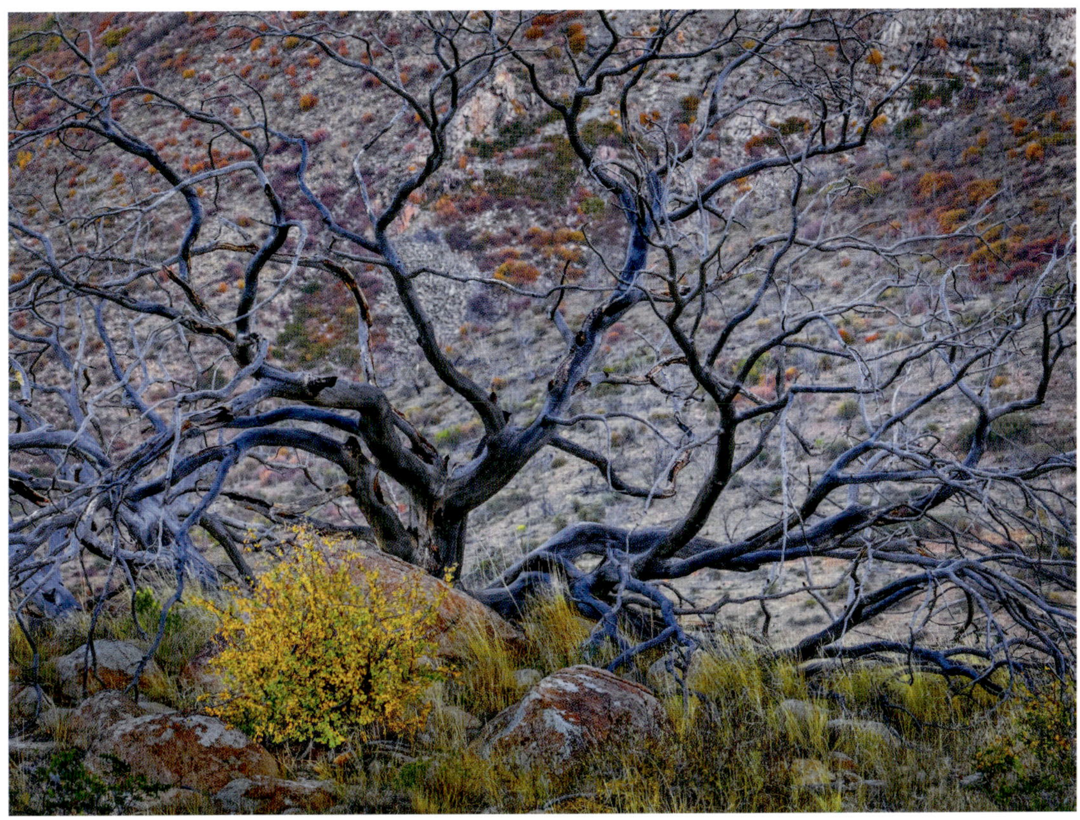

religions (e.g., Buddhism, Hinduism, Jainism, Sikhism). In fact, Schopenhauer formed his idea of the will, and the pleasurable benefits of escaping it, based on his reading of the Upanishads, the ancient Sanskrit texts of Hinduism.

As you read through the rest of this book, please assume that, unless I say or imply otherwise, whenever I use the word "happiness," I am referring to eudaemonia, and not to other forms

ON FREE WILL

> We must believe in free will—we have no choice.
>
> —ISAAC BASHEVIS SINGER

Why do you do what you do? Why do you do it in the way that you do? Scientific research and much philosophical thinking suggests there is a high likelihood you answered one or both these questions intuitively, believing your answers are obvious, unbiased, defensible, and freely chosen, but without taking the time to justify them rationally: to consider their validity relative to other possible answers, their consistency or inconsistency with other beliefs you may hold, or in full consideration of their implications to how you *should* live your life.

If asked or if you felt the need to explain and elaborate your answers further, odds are you will then turn to your rational faculties to construct—after the fact—seemingly plausible explanations in support of your intuitive answers. This may lead to errors in thinking, since we are often not aware of the extent of our ingrained biases and outside influences in driving our intuitions and limit the range of alternatives we may consider. The upshot: What we believe are freely and rationally chosen answers may, in fact, reflect other people's values and beliefs, often without us even being aware of it.

The consensus among scientists who study free will is that what's known as "libertarian free will"—the capacity to form opinions entirely independently of external influences—is not possible. So, the question of free will is, at best, a matter of degree—not *whether* we have complete free will to make our own choices, but *how much* free will we have. On one extreme of the free will debate are people known as *determinists*, who contend that we have no free will at all—that everything is determined by the laws of nature and unconscious processes in our brain. On the other extreme are people known as *compatibilists* who, despite accepting that absolute free will is an illusion, still contend that we have some degree of independent, conscious control over our choices. The reason these two camps exist and that some of the world's smartest people align themselves with one of these positions is that at this time we have no scientifically verifiable explanation for how free will is possible in a world governed by the laws of physics and the biological processes that make life possible. Put another way, we can't point decisively to any gaps in any chain of causation where conscious free will (whatever it is) may insert itself and drive the outcome in one direction rather than another.

Social psychologist Jonathan Haidt set out to understand why, despite ongoing progress in science and rational thinking, people still hold many contradictory and often irrational beliefs and ideologies. In discussing his findings, Haidt used what he termed the "central metaphor" of his writing, which he described thus: "The mind is divided, like a rider on an elephant, and the rider's job is to serve the elephant." The rider in Haidt's metaphor is the rational mind. The elephant is our intuitive, emotional mind (what some philosophers referred to as "the passions"). By this metaphor, the (rational) rider is not in charge; the (emotional) elephant is. The elephant is much bigger and stronger than the rider and is driven by primitive instincts that have been shaped by natural evolution, not by rational reasoning. The rider, being much smaller and weaker than the elephant, can't force the elephant to do anything the elephant doesn't want to do. At best, when the rider and the elephant are at odds, the rider may attempt (often unsuccessfully) to use various tactics to persuade the elephant to change course.

Complicating things further, according to an emerging body of research and philosophical thinking, it may be that neither the rider nor the elephant is capable of making *any* independent choices. Put bluntly, the idea of free will may be an illusion. The most prominent argument for this position at the time of this writing is found in a recently published book titled *Determined*, by Robert Sapolsky. In the book's introduction, Sapolsky wrote, "when people claim that there are causeless causes of your behavior that they call 'free will,' they have (a) failed to recognize or not learned about the determinism lurking beneath the surface and/or (b) erroneously concluded that the rarefied aspects of the universe that do work indeterministically can explain your character, morals, and behavior."[2]

---

[2] In the name of intellectual honesty, I must state here that I have found Sapolsky's arguments both jarring and convincing, and I consider him one of the great thinkers of our time. Still, if he is correct about free will being an illusion, then the premise of this book—that there are things within your control; choices and decisions you are free to make to improve your life and art—may be moot. On the other hand, it also means that I don't really have the choice to not write this book, with this footnote in it.

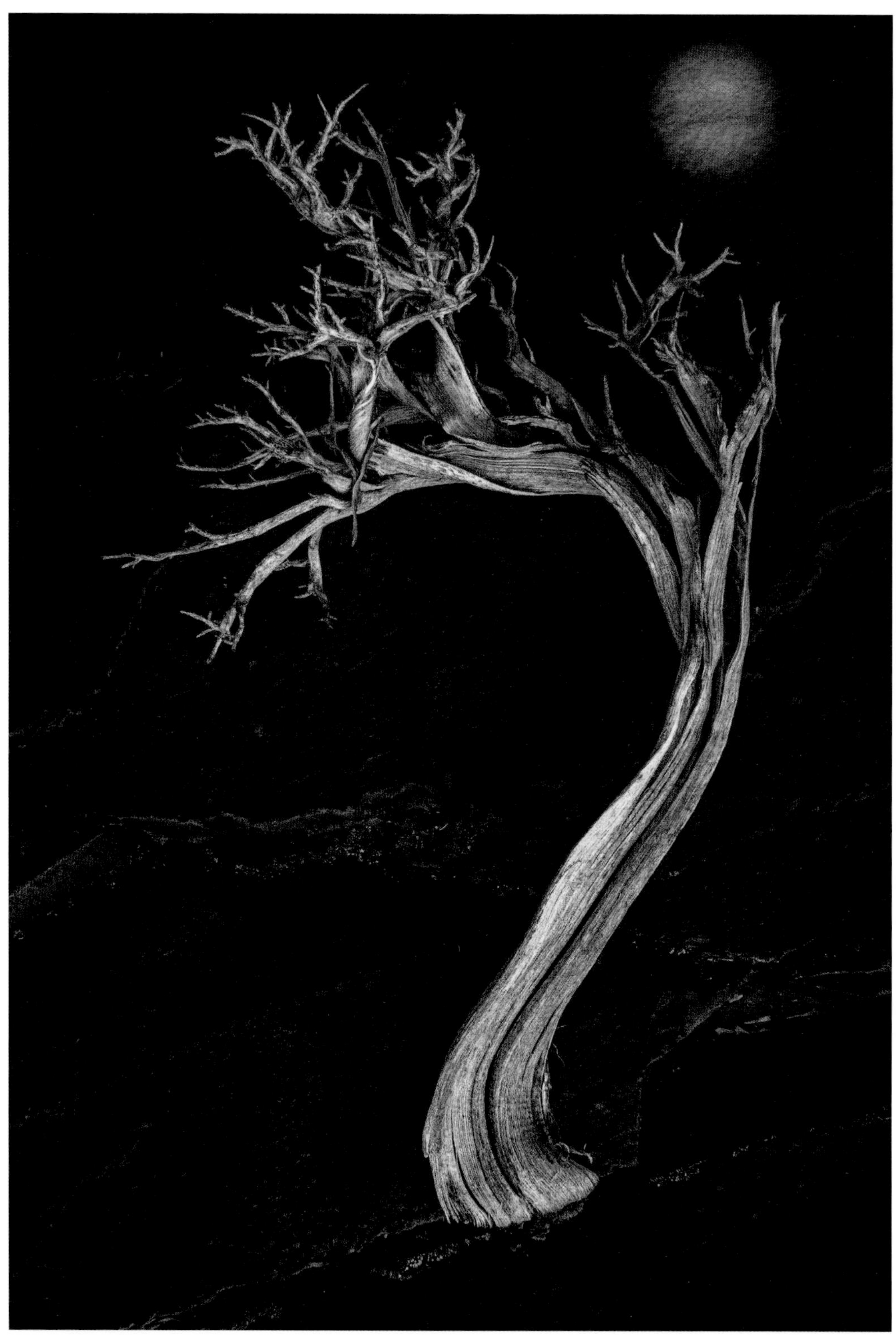

Free will or not, Haidt and Sapolsky have both made room in their writings for mechanisms that may help you adapt your thinking in more rational, rather than emotional, ways. Specifically, both believe in the power of external influences. According to Sapolsky, "we do not freely choose to change; instead, we are changed by the world around us, and one consequence of that is that we are also changed as to what sources of subsequent change we seek." If he is right, then perhaps reading this book may serve as one external influence to steer you down a path to subsequent (hopefully useful) changes, whether you choose them freely or not. Haidt similarly allows for the possibility that "we change our minds on moral issues ... by interacting with other people. We are terrible at seeking evidence that challenges our own beliefs, but other people do us this favor." It is my hope that you consider my advice in this book as such a favor, or at least that I intend it as such.

STOICISM AND THE SHORTNESS OF LIFE

You must either exercise your skill on internal things or on external things; that is you must either maintain the position of a philosopher or that of a common person.

—EPICTETUS

The perfection of moral character consists in this: to spend each day as if it were the last, to be neither agitated nor numb, and not to pretend.

—MARCUS AURELIUS

Stoicism as a formal philosophy evolved in Ancient Greece starting around 300 BCE. It is based largely on Socratic philosophy, although some of its tenets are rooted in or overlap with even older traditions, making it one of the longest-practiced forms of secular personal philosophy still in practice today—a testament to its wisdom, value, and relevance.

Stoic ethics can be summed up as aspiring to live a life of "virtue." Greek Stoics attempted to provide definitions and rational explanations for what virtue is (or should be) and why it is good. Underlying all Stoic ethics is the idea that a virtuous life is a life lived according to the laws of nature. To that end, Stoics developed elaborate theories aiming to study and to explain what the laws of nature are (i.e., physics) and how to interpret these laws rationality (i.e., by use of logic) .[3]

The four fundamental Stoic virtues are *justice* (knowing good from bad), *courage, wisdom,* and *moderation* (self-restraint, or temperance)[4]. In Stoicism, a sage is a theoretical person who embodies these virtues—not just understands them, but also exemplifies living according to them. A true Stoic, therefore, must aspire to live—to believe and to act—as a sage would. Living virtuously, in turn, yields both personal and social rewards. For individuals, the reward for living virtuously is eudaemonia—the flavor of happiness I described earlier in the book. For a society, ancient Stoics also believed that if everyone lived virtuously—according to the laws of nature—the result would be a more harmonious world reflecting an underlying benevolent design[5] (a form of creationism).

In a nutshell, the Stoic proposition is this: If we understand the true nature of the world (i.e., physics) and infer the correct conclusions from this knowledge (by using logic), then we may learn how to guide our beliefs, attitudes, and actions so that we live in the best, though not necessarily the easiest, way we can.

Common practical examples of living Stoically include acknowledging that we can't control the nature of reality nor entirely avoid events that may affect us negatively; we can only control how we feel about and respond to them. The most rational and useful way to respond to life's challenges is to accept and adapt to them with equanimity, no matter how painful or upsetting they may be. A great summary of this attitude is reflected in the famous Serenity Prayer, in which a person asks for "the serenity for accept the things I cannot change, the courage to change the things I can, and the wisdom to know the difference."

Accordingly, true Stoics believe that you should never permit yourself to love another person, thing, or activity so much that losing it will cause you deep and lasting grief. This is where I take issue with Stoicism (and similar tenets in Buddhism and other traditions). I believe life becomes richer, deeper, more rewarding, and more meaningful when it involves such things as passionate love, great compassion, the thrill

---

[3] Alas, many practitioners of Stoicism today simply accept as given the ethics of virtue as set by the philosophy's ancient forebears and ignore the underlying rationale: Ethics must ensue from scientific study interpreted by logic. As our understanding of both science and logic is far deeper and broader today than it was in ancient times, it should ostensibly follow that our ideas of virtue must also be examined (and, where necessary, revised) according to this new knowledge, but you will rarely find this attitude among self-described Stoics.

[4] For better or worse, Stoic thinkers naively assumed that all people are rational by nature and generally agree on what these terms mean. Later philosophers, as well as scientists in various disciplines, have since shown that neither is, in fact, the case. Human beings are in some ways innately irrational, and often disagree on what constitutes right or wrong.

[5] The idea that certain things exist in certain forms for the purpose of bringing about a better future is known in philosophy as *teleology*. Most present-day philosophers dismiss all forms of teleology.

of certain risky activities, feeling awed by intense beauty, and caring deeply about some things, even knowing that they are by nature ephemeral and that their loss may end in grief and a lasting sense of loss. I suspect that even among those who consider themselves Stoics, many would still agree with Alfred Tennyson that "'Tis better to have loved and lost / Than never to have loved at all." Or, as Rebecca Solnit put it beautifully, "when everything else is gone, you can be rich in loss."

While Stoic philosophers generally had little to say about art, there is one important aspect of Stoicism that artists may benefit greatly from: the idea of pursuing excellence for its own sake—for intrinsic (inner, eudaemonic) rewards rather than extrinsic ones (i.e., rewards bestowed by or dependent on others). Seneca presciently even described the effect that many years later would come to be known as *flow*, and its relation to artistic activities. He wrote, "When one is busy and absorbed in one's work, the very absorption affords great delight; but when one has withdrawn one's hand from the completed masterpiece, the pleasure is not so keen. Now it is the fruit of his art that he enjoys; it was the art itself that he enjoyed while he was painting."

Since the fear of death is one of the greatest hurdles to any form of happiness, several Stoic philosophers have grappled with the idea of mortality. Like all external events, being something imposed on us and not something we can choose to avoid, death to a Stoic is not inherently good or bad but something we must accept and make peace with. Unlike other external events, which may catch us by surprise and force us to decide our response to them only after they happen, death is unavoidable, so we may decide our response to it (rather, to the idea of it) at any time by accepting and preparing for it. More than that, by acknowledging the inevitability of death, we may find the courage to live more meaningfully, courageously, and urgently. In his essay "On the Shortness of Life," Seneca wrote:

> *It is not that we have a short time to live, but that we waste a lot of it. ... Putting things off is the biggest waste of life: it snatches away each day as it comes, and denies us the present by promising the future. The greatest obstacle to living is expectancy, which hangs upon tomorrow and loses today. You are arranging what lies in Fortune's control, and abandoning what lies in yours. What are you looking at? To what goal are you straining? The whole future lies in uncertainty: live immediately.*

EXISTENTIALISM, INDIVIDUALITY, AND FREEDOM

Anybody can prove the world's pointless. But so what?
You're in it.

—CHARLES BOWDEN

Perhaps the most dominant philosophical tradition I draw on in my advice later in this book is broadly known as existentialism, or "existential philosophy[6]." Psychiatrist and philosopher Karl Jaspers considered Søren Kierkegaard and Friedrich Nietzsche as the fathers of existentialism, although some tenets of the philosophy date back much further (e.g., to Socrates).

One might expect that the philosophy of Kierkegaard (a devout Christian) and the philosophy of Nietzsche (famous for asserting that God is dead) will have little in common. In fact, these philosophers shared important notions about how we should live—ideas founded in individualism, freedom of and responsibility for deciding your own values and making your own choices, and the idea of living authentically.

According to the *Stanford Encyclopedia of Philosophy*, "An authentic life is one that is *willing to break with tradition and social convention and courageously affirm the freedom and contingency of our condition*. It is generally understood to refer to *a life*

---

[6] Although the terms "existentialism" and "existential philosophy" are sometimes used interchangeably, there is a subtle distinction between them. Some prominent existential thinkers, despite sharing some core tenets of their philosophy with those who openly referred to themselves as existentialists, nonetheless rejected the term because they did not want to associate themselves with controversial political views expressed by some existentialists (perhaps most notably, by Jean-Paul Sartre). In fact, other than Sartre, only one other philosopher openly assumed the label "existentialist"—his partner Simone de Beauvoir, who also did not share some of Sartre's political views.

lived with a sense of urgency and commitment based on the meaning-giving projects that matter to each of us *as individuals.*" (Italics mine)

An authentic life is a life that expresses your own freely chosen values. An inauthentic life (sometimes referred to as living in "bad faith"), in contrast, is a life lived by the dictates or expectations of other people, pursuing hedonic pleasures without giving serious consideration to ethical values, or pretending to be someone you are not. To clarify, authenticity is not a binary distinction. No person is purely authentic or inauthentic. Each of us falls somewhere between these extremes. Our goal should be to strive to live as authentically as we can, but to never assume that we have achieved authenticity and stop there. To live authentically means to constantly question our beliefs, values, and actions; to constantly strive to learn as much as we can about the world and about ourselves; and to constantly adapt our values and lifestyles as we acquire new knowledge and understanding. To "be extraordinary," in the sense that I use the phrase in the title of this book, refers to living authentically—striving constantly to become and to live, to the extent you can, as an individual: as your unique self, according to your freely decided values.

Although existential thinkers differ on many topics, one thing that unites all of them is their belief in the importance of individualism: being yourself, taking responsibility for the (burdensome, anxiety-inducing) freedom given to you to make, to live by—and sometimes to suffer the dire consequences of—your own choices. In this sense, existentialism is sometimes referred to as "the philosophy of no excuses." In every choice you make, you are either being authentic (i.e., acting in "good faith," according to your own values) or you are being inauthentic (i.e., acting in "bad faith," making excuses to avoid inconvenience, to ignore material or ethical implications of your choices, or to fall in line with other people's values or expectations just to avoid conflict or isolation).[7]

In existential writing, as philosopher Walter Kaufmann put it, "Individuality is not retouched, idealized, or holy; it is wretched and revolting, and yet, for all its misery, the highest good." Perhaps the best-known expression of this sentiment is this famous quip by Sartre: "Man is condemned to be free. Condemned, because he did not create himself, yet is nevertheless at liberty, and from the moment that he is thrown into the world he is responsible for everything else he does."

Sartre's life partner, Simone de Beauvoir, described existentialism as "a philosophy of ambiguity." The ambiguity, according to her, is this: Each of us is in some ways an object and in other ways a subject. As objects, we are each limited by things beyond

---

[7] Kierkegaard used the terms "aesthetic" and "ethical" to denote, respectively, bad faith and good faith—terms that were coined much later by Sartre. I explain Kierkegaard's use of these terms later in the book (see page 131).

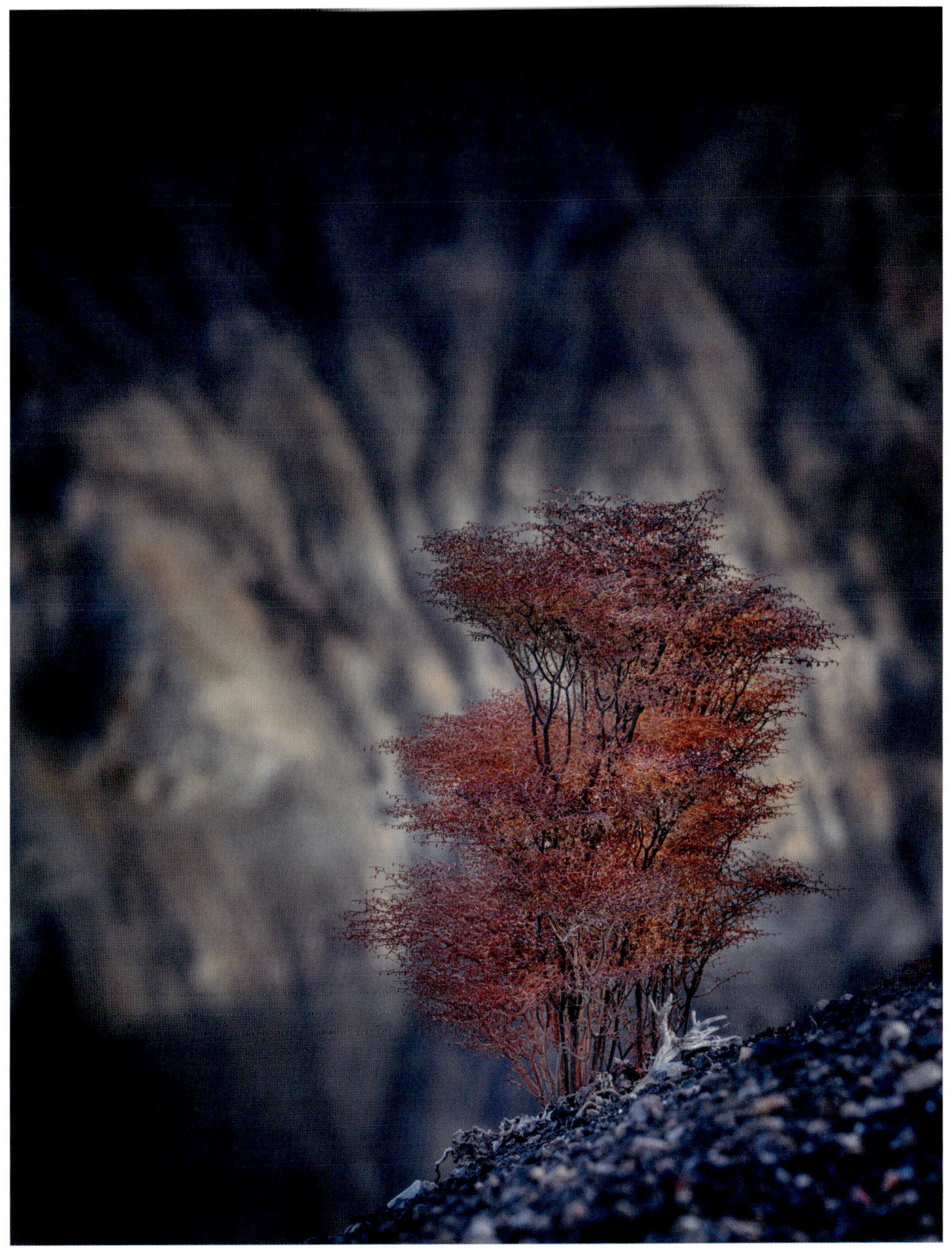

our control (described in some existential writings as our *facticity*): the laws of nature; the laws and traditions of the society we live in; our need for nourishment, shelter, and safety; opportunities that may or may not be open to us. As subjects, on the other hand, we are free to make our own choices. Asserting our subjective choices rather than kowtowing to what is easy or expected of us is often referred to as *transcendence*, in the sense that we must strive to transcend our objective circumstances (facticity) in order to (as Nietzsche put it) become what we (subjectively) are.

To an existentialist, the objective world is inherently meaningless, or as Albert Camus referred to it, absurd. The absurdity is this: Many people intuitively hope to find objective meaning in a meaningless world and end up becoming discouraged and disappointed when they can't find it. Instead of looking in vain for objective meaning, it is up to each of us to make our own worlds subjectively meaningful. Meaning in life is not something we can hope to find in the world, nor is it something to be given or imposed on us by others; it is something we must create for ourselves.

It is wrong to think that existentialists believe everything is meaningless (i.e., that existentialism is synonymous with nihilism). In fact, the world is full of meanings: meanings created individually by each person according to their own understanding of what it means to live authentically. Put another way, meaning is something individuals must make for themselves to transcend nihilism.

Existential thinkers had a lot to say about art and about the roles that art, if pursued as expression of individualism and authenticity, may serve in elevating life and in making life meaningful. I will mention some of these ideas later in the book, where relevant.

ON ART

Any system of aesthetics which pretends to be based on some objective truth is so palpably ridiculous as not to be worth discussing.

—CLIVE BELL

The majority of photographs are representations of the external events in the world about us; what emotional response is evoked arises from the subject itself. But art, I believe, is most concerned with the internal event; the incredible spiritual and emotional insight and enlightenment generated within us, the deeper penetration of meaning and the ability to communicate to others what we experience and what we create.

—ANSEL ADAMS

Art seems to us today a quintessential part of human life, but this was not always the case. The oldest paintings we know of, such as those adorning the walls of the Cave of Altamira in Spain, date back around 40,000 years, which is also the estimated age of the oldest known figurines, such as the *Venus of Hohle Fels*, discovered in southwestern Germany. Bits of rock decorated in abstract patterns found at the Blombos Cave

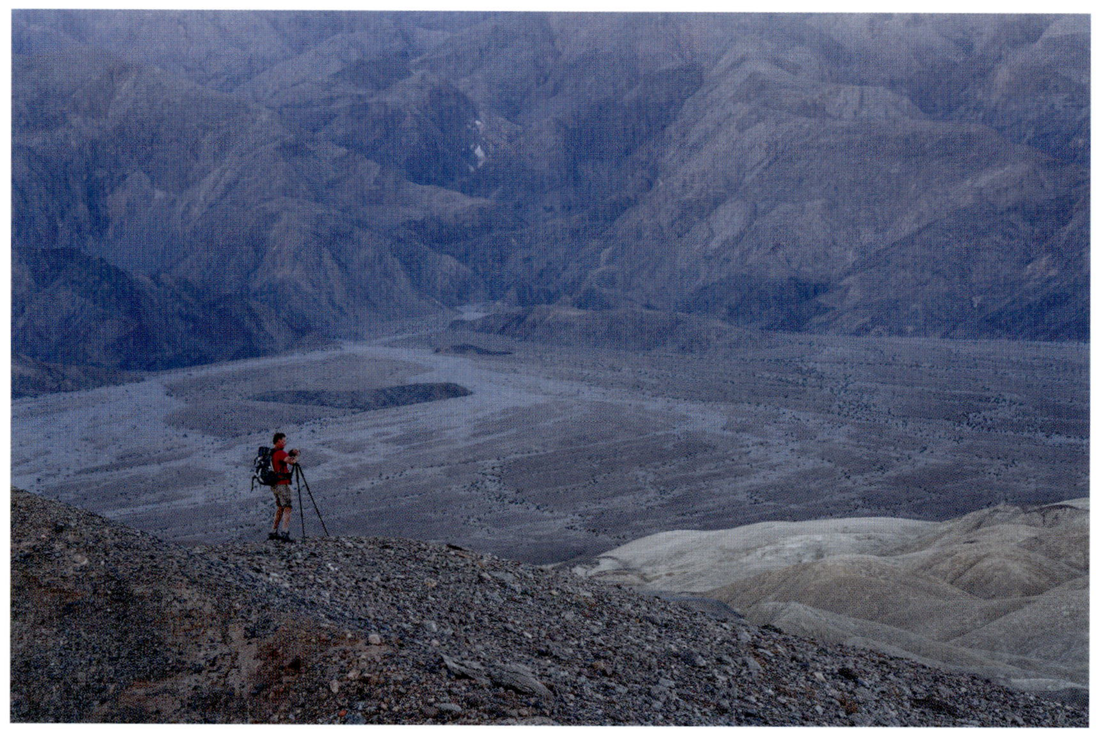

in South Africa, believed to have been some of the earliest artworks, are about 75,000 years old. To put these timespans in context, consider that our species—*Homo sapiens*—has been in existence for about 300,000 years. The conclusion: For most of the time humans of our kind have existed, they did not make art.

The most advanced manufactured objects for much of the time humans have existed were stone tools created for practical, rather than aesthetic, purposes. Conceiving and manufacturing these tools required creativity—the capacity to imagine and to innovate. We can therefore say that while artmaking may not be a quintessential human trait, creativity is.

This leads to a further conclusion: Art is not something humans create intuitively and inevitably; it is something humans have discovered, realized the benefits of, and chose to continue to evolve. This evolutionary process is far from done. Recent history is marked by a constant flux of new methods, modes, and ways of thinking about art. Therefore, to remain stuck in any tradition or philosophy of art is almost certain to result in denying ourselves the benefits of creativity, of making new discoveries and evolving new ways of thinking about of art and artmaking that may transcend and improve upon what we already know and think today. As photographer Al Weber put it, "The sneakiest of obstacles may be Tradition ... In this world, that is ever changing at a faster and faster pace, one must constantly be alert regarding traditional practices."

Art did not come to exist until ancient humans gained sufficient control of their environments and evolved ways of securing adequate food, water, shelter, and safety, so they could have leisure time to create things for sheer pleasure and meaning, and not out of existential necessity. Not having to spend all their resources on bare survival, our ancestors gained more time to think about, experiment with, and evolve new technologies, and to seek ways of improving the quality of their lives not only in material ways, but also by evolving more complex and effective ways of communication, more sophisticated cultures, more advanced sciences, and more sources of aesthetic pleasure—beauty for beauty's sake. Although we don't know for certain how or why, one or more of these leisure-born activities led to the birth of art.

Art can therefore be considered in one sense as an expression of freedom: more freedom (from worrying about existential necessities), more art. Put another way, the expression "necessity is the mother of invention" is patently false when it comes to art. Necessity makes people stick to what is safe and tried-and-true; they avoid taking risks or "wasting" resources on nonessential activities. Art can only exist when people have the freedom to try new, unproven things and the safety to be able to recover from failure. Art would not have existed if our ancestors were too busy tending to their material needs to invest time and energy in nonessential activities, such as painting, sculpting, theater, or creative writing.

Historically, advancements in art correlated with times of freedom from oppression, coercion, dogma, and poverty. For example, art blossomed in Ancient Greece with the rise of democracy, and during the Renaissance, alongside the decline of religious tyranny. The opposite is also true: Art stagnates and becomes more utilitarian in less-free times. For example, we see very little progress or diversity in the arts during the thousand-year period known as the Middle Ages (or, colloquially, as the "Dark Ages") following the fall of the Roman Empire, which was marked by religious oppression, widespread poverty, and deadly epidemics.

Fast forward to today: After a long period of flourishing in the arts, it is concerning to see some old trends repeating. Art institutions—galleries, museums, academies, and other organizations that collectively make up the so-called "art world"—have come to dominate and, in many venues, exert strict control over what is accepted as art. In addition, the rise of internet-based communities and social media is now fostering cultures marked by conformity and concentrations of influence in the hands of a few individuals with large followings, as well as widespread imitation and derivation as artists become driven by or financially dependent on popularity (which, by necessity, is correlated with appealing to low common denominators) and corporate sponsorships, rather than by individuals' desire to produce creative and personally expressive work.

Troubling studies show a measurable decline in creativity in recent years in multiple countries, age groups, and professions. Art again seems to be less free—less diverse, less innovative, and less accessible than it was during the modern era in art (estimated to have ended around the mid-1900s), which was marked by such vibrant movements as impressionism, postimpressionism, expressionism, cubism, fauvism, and surrealism.

Photography, alas, seems to be among the most stagnant and dogmatic among artistic media today, despite great advancements in photographic technology. Most prominently, we see today many photographers willingly adhering—unquestioningly and sometimes with quasi-religious fervor—to the tenets of realism, photojournalism, and "straight photography" established in the previous century, even when using photography as a medium for artistic creation, where adherence to strict rules and feeling ethically bound to a narrow range of imposed styles can fairly be considered a handicap rather than a necessity (recall the historic correlation between art and freedom).

As a result, most photography presented today as "fine art" consists largely of repetitive, derivative, even plagiarized works aiming no higher than to copy former masters or their styles, to appeal to popular low common denominators, to portray familiar subjects, or to comply with the prevailing tastes and strict guidelines imposed by camera clubs, online communities, corporate entities, and contest organizers.

Art as an expression of freedom is patently incompatible with tyranny, dogma (too-strict adherence to former traditions), and competition for popularity. Likewise, the value of art as an expression of freedom must never be measured strictly in terms of fashionableness, profitability, compliance with common aesthetic canons, or the opinion of any judge or jury. "Art at its most significant," wrote Marshall McLuhan, "is a distant early warning system that can always be relied on to tell the old culture what is beginning to happen." If this is true, consider the warning given to us by much present-day artistic photography: We are sacrificing creativity for conformity, inner emotional rewards for vanity and economic concerns; we sanction and accept obvious plagiarism and treat imitations on equal footing with novel, original work. It's important to remember, however, that even if "the old culture" in the greater sense may not be heeding these warnings, as individual artists we are free to do so, and it would behoove us to.

In this section, I hope to give you a deeper understanding than most laypeople may have of what art means today (which is different, at least in some ways, from what art has meant in other times). My goal in doing so is to help you consider what kind of artist you may wish to be and what kind of art you may wish to create. Among other things, I hope to convince you that there is more than one way to think about art— what it is, why it is important, and the roles it may play in your life. This, in turn, means that to know what kind of art is likely to prove most satisfying and meaningful to you, you must consider for yourself a variety of opinions, ideas, and definitions, and choose the one that best fits who you are, not necessarily the one that is most popular, easiest, or even most financially profitable.

WHAT IS ART?

At first only mimesis[8] was art, then several things were art but each tried to extinguish its competitors, and then, finally, it became apparent that there were no stylistic or philosophical constraints. There is no special way works of art have to be. And that is the present and, I should say, the final moment in the master narrative. It is the end of the story.

—ARTHUR DANTO

After reviewing the evolution of various definitions of art, philosopher Arthur Danto realized with dismay that in recent times we seem to have arrived at a point where, as he put it in his book *After the End of Art*, "as far as appearances were concerned, anything could be a work of art." Because of that, Danto realized, it is impossible to define what makes something art solely based on its content or any other physical characteristic. So, where does that leave us? What other way is there to define art if not by its physical, observable characteristics?

Danto suggested, "if you were going to find out what art was, you had to turn from sense experience to thought. You had, in brief, to turn to philosophy." His philosophical investigation led him to conclude that the one definition of art that holds true for every work presented or considered as art, regardless of content or style or any other feature, is this: "artworks are embodied meanings."

---

[8] Mimesis is defined as, "the attempt to imitate or reproduce reality" (Merriam-Webster). The word comes from the same Greek origin as the words mimicry and mime.

By Danto's definition, instead of asking about any object, "is it art?" (which may, at best, lead us to ambiguous answers due to a multitude of different and sometimes incompatible definitions), we should instead ask more useful questions like, "what is the meaning embodied in this work?" Or, "is this meaning important? enjoyable? profound? dull? obscure? ambiguous? obvious? interesting? powerful? creative? expressive? absent?"

Many years before Danto, Leo Tolstoy had similar thoughts about the definition of art. He wrote:

> *It is necessary for a society in which works of art arise and are supported, to find out whether all that professes to be art is really art; whether (as is presupposed in our society) all that which is art is good; and whether it is important and worth those sacrifices which it necessitates. It is still more necessary for every conscientious artist to know this, that he may be sure that all he does has a valid meaning; that it is not merely an infatuation of the small circle of people among whom he lives which excites in him the false assurance that he is doing a good work.*

Edgar Allan Poe ventured his own definition. He wrote, "Were I called on to define, very briefly, the term 'Art,' I should call it 'the reproduction of what the Senses perceive in Nature through the veil of the soul.' The mere imitation, however accurate, of what is in Nature, entitles no man to the sacred name of 'Artist.'"

Poe's definition may rattle some who consider themselves photographic artists but choose to restrict themselves to strict realism. But consider that no lesser a photographer than Ansel Adams expressed a similar attitude to Poe's. He wrote:

> *It is not so much the intensification of the outer world, but a clarification of the inner world of the spectator; the photographer, instead of being just an informer, becomes a catalyst of consummate power. Here lies, I believe, a suggestion for a prime definition of art and especially of the art of photography.*

Look up the word "art" in any present-day dictionary or other formal reference, and you will likely find several entries—some distinctive, some overlapping with other definitions, some literal, some metaphorical. This suggests that not all art is art by the same definition, and therefore not all artists are artists by the same definition. Some formal definitions of art may be summed up as "anything can be art if someone says it is art"; some as, "art is synonymous with beauty"; and others as, "art is anything that requires uncommon skill to produce," or "art is whatever influential critics and institutions (a.k.a. 'the art-world') say is art." So, before calling yourself an artist and your work art, it is important that you choose a definition for what these terms mean *to you*. In practical terms, since not all definitions are equally demanding or venerable, your choice of definition will also answer this question: How high do I set the bar for myself?

I recall visiting a popular sandwich restaurant several years ago. The employee who took my order wore a tag identifying him as a "sandwich artist." It is true that among the many proposed definitions of art there is likely one by which making sandwiches according to standard, prescribed recipes may legitimately be considered an art. Likely, however, it is not the same definition by which Michelangelo's *Pietá*, or Picasso's

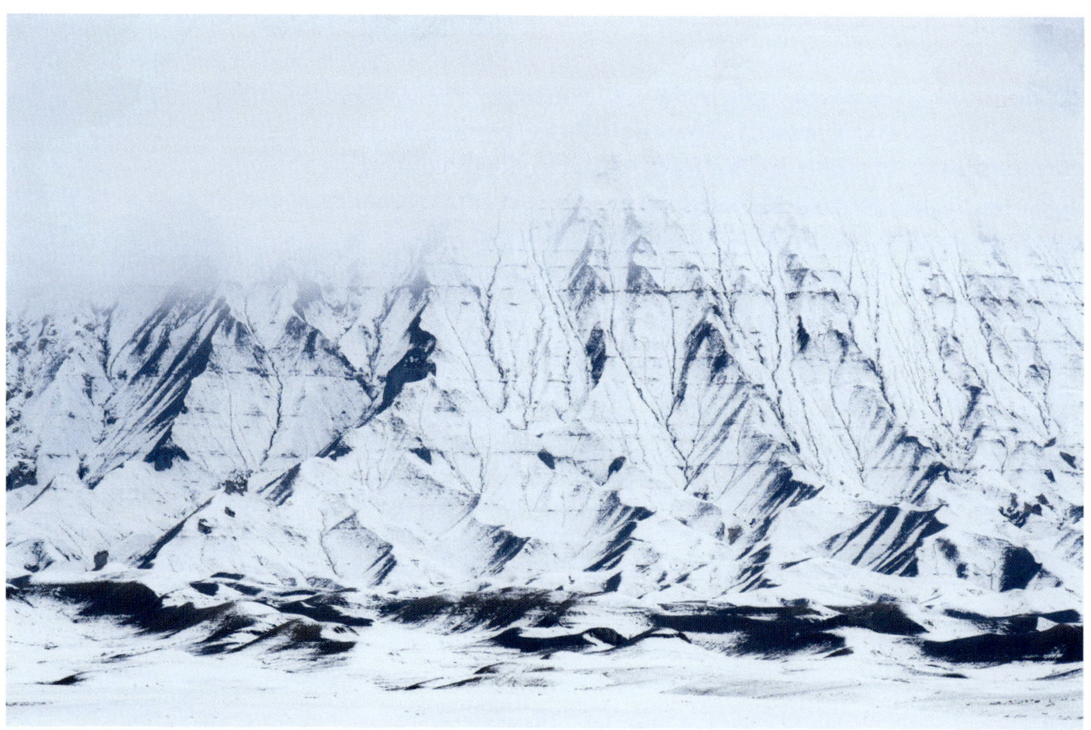

Les Demoiselles d'Avignon, or Dorothea Lange's *Migrant Mother*, or Frédéric Chopin's *Prelude, Op. 28, No. 4* are considered art.

Of course, you may refer to yourself as an artist in the same sense that a sandwich restaurant employee is an artist, by which I mean one who applies practiced skill, perhaps even great talent, toward following a recipe or adhering to a template conceived by someone else, aiming to produce works designed to appeal to a common (perhaps even profitable) taste—to the deliberate exclusion of things like personal expression, imagination, experimentation, and creativity, which always involve the risk of other people not liking or understanding your work. Also, consider that by this definition you cannot claim yourself to be an *authentic* artist in the philosophical sense of choosing freely to create, and how to create, your work according to your own values and sensibilities, free (to the extent possible) of external constraints and other people's tastes and expectations.

Some scholars suggested that given the variety of opinions on the matter, it is pointless to focus on definitions of art. Instead, we should consider art as things (whatever they turn out to be) produced by persons who are artists. For example, historian E. H. Gombrich wrote, "There really is no such thing as Art. There are only artists." Photographer Edward Steichen would have agreed. He wrote, "The thing that makes any medium an art is the artist who makes the picture." Tooting my own horn, I have made this same point in my book *More Than a Rock*, where I defined art simply as "a product of artists." Put simply: Art is not a quality inherent in any object nor something that can be decided by other people; it is a quality conferred by the mindset of the individual person who created this object.

By what definition, then, do I consider *myself* an artist? The kind of art I aspire to make—the bar I set for myself—is the kind of art defined in the *Oxford Dictionary* as, "the expression or application of human creative skill and imagination." Similar definitions can be found in other sources, too. For example, "the conscious use of skill and creative imagination especially in the production of aesthetic objects" (*Merriam-Webster*), and "a visual object or experience consciously created through an expression of skill or imagination" (*Encyclopedia Britannica*).

Consider the commonalities among the definitions I listed: expression, creativity, skill, imagination, human consciousness. Note that these are, at least to a considerable extent, incompatible with (perhaps even antithetical to) mimetic, objective representation. They are also incompatible with artifacts that are entirely machine-made, such as are commonly produced by computerized artificial intelligence (AI) without involving creative choices made by a human artist. The implication is this: As an artist aspiring to make art by this definition, I consider it my job to *create* things—to bring new things into existence using my own (human) skills and imagination; not to simply document what is already in the world, not to copy or imitate the creations of others, and not by employing AI or other technologies to create things on my behalf (although they may certainly be helpful in automating some noncreative aspects of my work).

The definition I choose to aspire to in my own art is also in accordance with the etymology (historical origins) of the very word "art," which derives from the Latin *ars*, meaning "skill" or "craft"—something produced by human beings, as opposed to something occurring naturally or randomly. Thus, in the simplest sense, an artist by my preferred definition is a person possessing the skill and desire to manufacture things that express subjective meanings—not to simply record things or to instruct machines to create things.

WHY MAKE ART?

The poet is, etymologically, the maker. Like all makers, he requires a stock of raw materials—in his case, experience. Now experience is not a matter of having actually swum the Hellespont, or danced with the dervishes, or slept in a doss-house. It is a matter of sensibility and intuition, of seeing and hearing the significant things, of paying attention at the right moments, of understanding and co-ordinating. Experience is not what happens to a man; it is what a man does with what happens to him.

—ALDOUS HUXLEY

The intense feeling, ecstatic or terrible … is something which every person of sensibility has known; it is doubtless a study to pathologists. It often occurs in adolescence: the ordinary person puts these feelings to sleep, or trims down his feeling to fit the business world; the artist keeps it alive by his ability to intensify the world to his emotions.

—T. S. ELIOT

In the previous section, I mentioned Arthur Danto's definition of art as "embodied meaning." In coining this definition, Danto's goal was to suggest that art critics should focus on *meaning* in art, rather than on *content* (what the art portrays) or *form* (how it is portrayed). To do so, a critic must possess certain qualifications to be able to recognize and evaluate an artwork's "meaningfulness" on behalf of the public. But what about art's value to the artists who make it?

While no one doubts that artworks may be enjoyable and/or meaningful to behold, why would anyone go to the effort of making (not just beholding) art? Danto offered a possible, if a bit ambiguous, answer to this question in his later book *What Art Is*. He wrote, "I have decided to enrich my earlier definition of art—embodied meaning— with another condition that *captures the skill of the artist* ... I will define art as 'wakeful dreams.' ... My sense is that everyone, everywhere, dreams. Usually this requires that we sleep. But wakeful dreams *require of us that we be awake*." (Italics mine)

Danto's realization echoes a sentiment expressed more than a century before him by Nietzsche in his book *The Birth of Tragedy*. In his famously dramatic style, refer- ring to the experiences of both artists and beholders of art, Nietzsche proclaimed, "the aesthetically sensitive man stands in the same relation to the reality of dreams as the philosopher does to the reality of existence; he is a close and willing observer, for *these images afford him an interpretation of life*[9], *and by reflecting on these processes he trains himself for life*." (Italics mine)

Making art may yield many kinds of rewards. Some of these rewards are extrinsic (e.g., income, fame, social interaction) and some are intrinsic (e.g., deepening of emo- tional engagement, contentment, pride, relief from anxiety or other undesired feelings). Many artists pursue explicitly one or more of these rewards, but some artists have been known to practice their art even when doing so caused them the opposite of some of these rewards: financial hardship, social isolation, anxiety, infamy. Why? One answer is the experience of flow—the state of mind characterized by psychologist Mihaly Csikszentmihalyi as "optimal experience." Flow arises from intense, prolonged invest- ment of attention in a skilled activity to such a degree that no attention is left over for other preoccupations, such as ruminations, anxiety, or discomfort.

When in a state of flow, people lose track of time and pay no attention to any- thing—including worries, regrets, and even pain—beyond their immediate experience. No matter what challenges and difficulties may plague you, time spent in a state of flow will liberate you from these for as long as you can sustain it. In time, it will also train you to become more resilient and calmer in the face of adversities, knowing you can always find peace within yourself while engaged in certain activities that may reward

---

[9] Note that Nietzsche referred to an interpretation of life—a personal, subjective interpretation—not a universal, objective depiction.

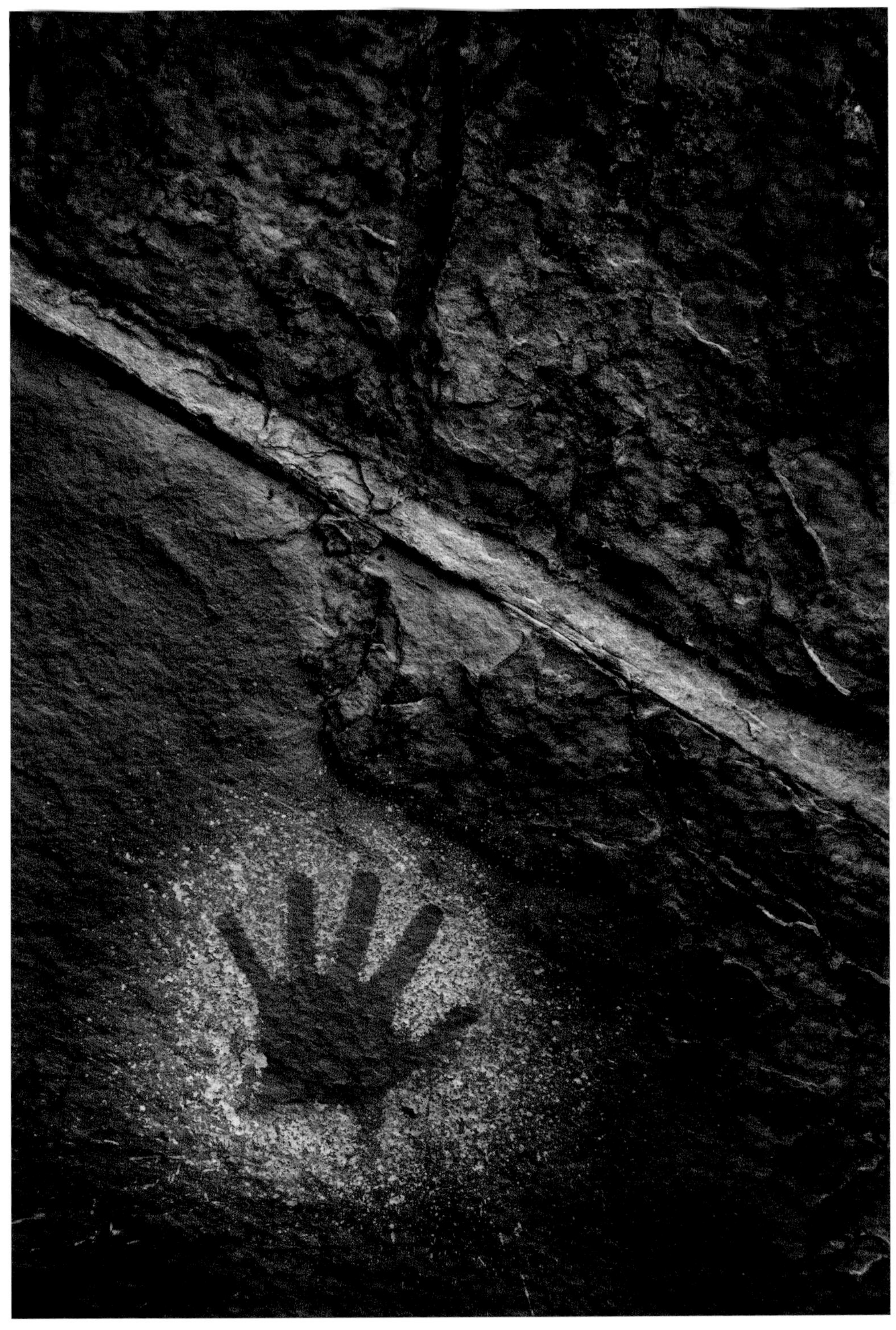

you with flow. Artmaking, which demands investment of skilled work and focused attention for prolonged periods, is one such activity. As Paul Gauguin, who suffered much in his life, described it:

> *In art, these sacrifices have to be made, stage by stage—groping efforts, half-formed thoughts lacking direct and definitive expression. Bah! for a minute you touch the sky and then it slips away afterward; yet this glimpse of a dream is something more powerful than any matter.*

In his book *Flow: The Psychology of Optimal Experience*, Csikszentmihalyi wrote, "Contrary to what we usually believe ... the best moments in our lives, are not the passive, receptive, relaxing times—although such experiences can also be enjoyable, *if we have worked hard to attain them.* The best moments usually occur when a person's body or mind is stretched to its limits in a voluntary effort to accomplish something *difficult and worthwhile.*" (Italics mine) This qualification—difficult and worthwhile—explains why so many artists who limit their work to short-lived and undemanding activities fail to experience flow in their work, and settle instead, often without realizing it, for lesser rewards, such as popularity and awards.

In art, the most "difficult and worthwhile" aspects are generally not overcoming technical challenges or achieving aesthetic appeal, both of which may be learned and mastered by practice to a point where they become intuitive. Rather, the most difficult and worthwhile goals in art are creativity and self-expression, which demand a high degree of cognitive effort and emotional investment every time. In fact, the longer you practice art, the harder you will have to push yourself to remain creative and expressive, rather than repeat what you've already done.

Coming up with creative ways to channel your own thoughts and feelings into your artworks, is difficult, potentially unproductive, and fraught with risk of failure. This is exactly why flow in art is most likely to occur when your process involves investing prolonged time and conscious effort (rather than following predictable recipes or relying on labor-saving shortcuts), aiming to express your deepest thoughts and feelings in novel and personally meaningful ways.

The inner rewards of living and working with the goal of creative self-expression are difficult, not only to accomplish but also to describe to people who have not experienced them firsthand. But many who have experienced them have also testified to their great power, if only to the artist alone. As Nietzsche put it:

The artistic genius wants to give pleasure, but if he stands on a very high level there can easily be a lack of others to enjoy it; he offers food but no one wants it. This sometimes bestows upon him a moving and ludicrous pathos; for fundamentally he has no right to compel people to enjoy themselves. He sounds his pipe but no one wants to dance: can that be tragic?—Perhaps it can. After all, he has, as a compensation for this privation, more enjoyment in creating than other people have in any other species of activity.

Art is the application of knowledge for certain ends. But art is raised to Fine Art when man so applies this knowledge that he affects the emotions through the senses, and so produces aesthetic pleasure in us; and the man so raising an art into a fine art is an artist.

—PETER HENRY EMERSON

Our need for beauty is not something that we could lack and still be fulfilled as people. It is a need arising from our metaphysical condition, as free individuals, seeking our place in a shared and public world. We can wander through this world, alienated, resentful, full of suspicion and distrust. Or we can find our home here, coming to rest in harmony with others and with ourselves. The experience of beauty guides us along this second path: it tells us that we are at home in the world, that the world is already ordered in our perceptions as a place fit for the lives of beings like us.

—ROGER SCRUTON

Victorian novelist Margaret Wolfe Hungerford coined the phrase "beauty is in the eye of the beholder," suggesting that aesthetic judgment is a subjective matter. Note that

she did not say that *art* is in the eye of the beholder. While there is no doubt that art
and beauty often go hand in hand, they are not the same thing, nor is one necessarily
dependent on the other. Many forms of beauty occur in the world without any involvement or intention of a human creator (i.e., artist), whereas some forms of art (i.e.,
products made consciously and skillfully by human beings[10]) may not necessarily or
universally be considered beautiful.

The term "fine art" refers to art made primarily (or only) with the goal of rewarding viewers with aesthetic pleasure (i.e., to be beautiful). While imparting beauty is perhaps the most common purpose for art, it is not the only purpose that art may serve.
Thus, the qualification "fine" is not a reference to the excellence or value of a work
of art, rather only to its intended purpose. A work of fine art is not necessarily better,
more creative, more expressive, more important, or more meaningful than "non-fine"
art. These qualities must be evaluated on a case-by-case basis and according to the artwork's intended purpose, be it aesthetic beauty, social commentary, arousing emotions
or intellectual contemplation, defiance of norms, or anything else.

What is beauty? Oddly, there are very few things we know of that are universally
considered as beautiful—that are guaranteed to give aesthetic pleasure to any beholder.
One example of a quality considered universally pleasing is symmetry in a human face.
Of course, this is of little help to an artist who does not render faces. By and large, our
assessment of beauty beyond such anecdotal preferences is not innate or universal. It
comes in large part from the culture and society we live in. For example, some styles
of music that are loved by one culture may seem cacophonous or even offensive to
another. Likewise, prodigious use of bold colors may be considered beautiful in some
cultures but kitschy in others. Some photographers wax poetic about the beautiful
tonality of silver gelatin prints, while others consider all monochromatic photography
as boring. "Beauty," wrote David Hume in 1757, "is no quality in things themselves: It
exists merely in the mind which contemplates them; and each mind perceives a different beauty." He was correct.

One implication of the subjective nature of beauty is that Hungerford was right:
Beauty *is* for the most part in the eye of the beholder, a matter of subjective judgment.
Another implication is that each of us may, if we choose, broaden our ability to experience aesthetic pleasure by opening ourselves up to forms of beauty beyond just those
that are intuitive to us, or that are sanctioned by or common in our environment. This
extends beyond beauty in art. For example, some mathematical theorems may be considered beautiful by those who understand them, as are some food flavors one may not

---

[10] The recent trend to label some creations made by AI as art are disconcerting. Some institutions refuse to allow such works to be
copyrighted, and the legal question of authorship in these works is still undecided at the time of writing this book.

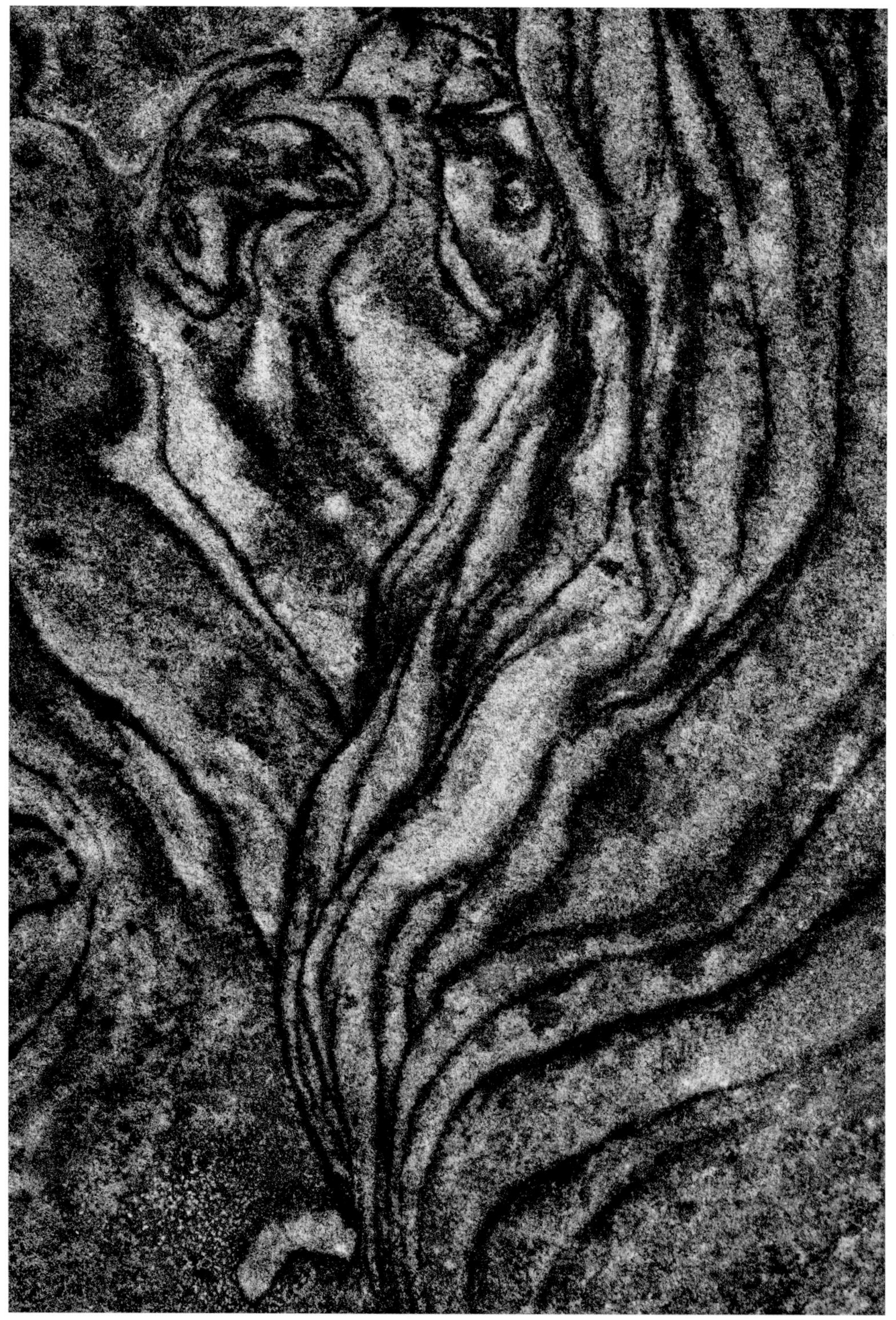

be familiar with but learn to appreciate and enjoy. Aldous Huxley described this effect in his book *Ends and Means*. He wrote:

> *First Shakespeare sonnets seem meaningless; first Bach fugues, a bore; first differential equations, sheer torture. But training changes the nature of our spiritual experiences. In due course, contact with an obscurely beautiful poem, an elaborate piece of counterpoint or of mathematical reasoning, causes us to feel direct intuitions of beauty and significance.*

There is no disputing the elevating effect that beauty (whatever you consider it to be) adds to our experiences. The same is true of the effect of gratitude we as creators may receive from others if we introduce beauty into their lives.

Just like beauty is often aligned with but not synonymous with art, beauty is also often aligned with but not synonymous with meaning. Meaning is often neglected as a criterion in our evaluation of art, which is a shame. Meaning, whether associated with beauty or not, may enrich our experience of art every bit as much as aesthetic appeal alone, and often more so. Meaning without beauty may still leave lasting, memorable impressions, whereas beauty without meaning is likely to leave only fleeting ones. Beauty alone is generally experienced passively, whereas meaning engages our minds actively, leading us to contemplation, powerful emotions, and perhaps even revelations.

Recall Danto's definition of art as "embodied *meaning*," not necessarily as something that possesses *beauty*. Nobel Prize laureate Hermann Hesse warned of the numbing effects of beauty without meaning. Being a poet, he wrote about poetry, but his words apply just as well to any form of artistic expression. He wrote:

> *Because "beautiful" poems make the poet beloved, a great quantity of poems come into the world that attempt nothing except to be beautiful, that pay no heed to the original primitive, holy, innocent function of poetry. These poems from the very start are made for others, for hearers, for readers. They are no longer dreams or dance steps or outcries of the soul, reactions to experience, stammered wish-images or magic formulas, gestures of a wise man or grimaces of a madman—they are simply planned productions, fabrications, pralines for the public. They have been made for distribution and sale and they serve to amuse or inspire or distract their buyers.*

Placing meaning in relation to beauty, I propose that the noblest role for beauty in art is not as a singular goal but as a vehicle for conveying or amplifying meaning. In pursuing my work as a photographer, I am fortunate to witness great natural beauty often, but I am never satisfied with just "capturing" or making a record of beauty. Beauty to me is a starting point. My job as an expressive artist is to add meaning to found aesthetics. Making beautiful art, especially in photography, is not very difficult. In some cases, it can even be reduced entirely to simple mechanics, following recipes and directions, or imitating other people's work. Deep meaning, on the other hand, comes from deep experiences. Your audience will not always be able to tell whether the experience of making your work was meaningful, but you will.

I would be remiss if I did not also point out that some profoundly meaningful experiences may not necessarily be rooted in beauty. Indeed, in some cases, beauty may distract from deeper meaning. In other cases, meaning may even be rooted in the *absence* of beauty. As T. S. Eliot put it, "The contemplation of the horrid or sordid or disgusting, by an artist, is the necessary and negative aspect of the impulse toward the pursuit of beauty."

Eugène Delacroix noted to himself in his journal, "Nourish yourself with grand and austere ideas of beauty that feed the soul." I agree with him wholeheartedly: Don't ever give up the pursuit of beauty. Seek to find it not only in art, but also in ideas and experiences. This is a good reason to educate yourself in art, science, and philosophy, and to pursue meaningful activities, so you may learn to appreciate and take pleasure in more forms of beauty than just those that seem obvious and intuitive to you. Your life will be better for it.

However, in those cases where beauty and meaning may be at odds, my advice to you is this: Choose meaning.

> So it is with every true work of art: each is susceptible of
> infinite interpretation, as though there were an infinity of
> intentions within it, yet we cannot at all tell whether this infinity
> lay in the artist himself or whether it resides solely in the art-
> work. On the other hand, in a product that merely simulates
> the character of a work of art, intention and rule lie on the
> surface and appear so limited and bounded that the product
> is nothing other than a faithful impression of the conscious
> activity of the artist and is altogether merely an object for
> reflection, but not for intuition.
>
> —FRIEDRICH WILHELM JOSEPH VON SCHELLING

Oscar Wilde wrote, "The work of art is to dominate the spectator: the spectator is not to dominate the work of art. The spectator is to be receptive. He is to be the violin on which the master is to play." Similarly, Edward Weston expressed what may seem obvious to many of us who consider ourselves as fine art photographers when he wrote, "In common with other artists the photographer wants his finished print to convey to others *his own response* to his subject." (Italics mine)

For many of us, self-expression—the desire to imbue our creations with specific meanings of our own making—is at the core of what we do. We relish seeking personal, creative ways to convey in our work certain feelings and moods—to learn, discover, and apply the language of visual expression: the use of colors, tones, lines, shapes, and other visual cues composed such that their effect is, in the words of Minor

White, to "direct the viewer into a *specific and known* feeling, state or place within himself." (Italics mine) We aim to prompt in our viewers feelings that are, to use Alfred Stieglitz's term, *equivalent* with our own. Often, when we solicit critique of our work, we ask of our viewers specifically to assess whether we have succeeded in conveying our intended meaning. But do we really get to decide what meaning viewers will ultimately make of our creations? Is it even realistic to expect that we can control this meaning with any degree of specificity? And if we can, should we? Why impose on our viewers a meaning (which may not necessarily be as inspiring or relevant to them as it may be to us), rather than allow them to form their own?

In 1967, philosopher and semiotician Roland Barthes argued that interpretation of texts (and by extension, of any creative product) should not be, in his words, "tyrannically centered on the author." In an article titled "The Death of the Author," Barthes claimed that, as viewers or spectators, we should avoid trying to decipher the meaning of works based strictly on what we presume the intent of the author was (which may be relevant in a historical sense but may not necessarily be useful or important to any given reader or spectator).

For most of my years as a "serious" fine art photographer, I considered Stieglitz's *equivalence* (between the experience of the photographer and that of the viewer) as the highest aim for photographic art. I found Barthes's idea of ignoring the artist's meaning and leaving it to viewers to decide meaning for themselves a hard pill to swallow. I have changed my mind. I now believe Barthes was correct.

One reason for my change of heart is this: I realized that the meanings I experience most intuitively and profoundly arise from who I am and ensue from events, circumstances, personality traits, moods, and many other subjective factors that make me, me. It would be naïve of me to expect that the same stimuli—views, sensations, feelings— that inspire a given meaning in my own mind will necessarily have the same effect on another person. Perhaps this person may even derive greater value and enjoyment from interpreting my work in his or her own way.

The author, according to Barthes, is just a linguistic reference to a role a person plays at the time of creating a work, not to that person as a complete human being with a history, traits, and experiences that extend far beyond the role of creating a given work. The author comes into being at the time of creation and is no longer relevant once the work is done. From that point on, the work—whether a text, an image, or anything else—is given to others to make their own meaning from. In Barthes's words, "the birth of the reader must be ransomed by the death of the Author."

This idea may seem in conflict with the importance of striving to be personally expressive in your art, but in fact it is not. It merely separates the value (to the artist)

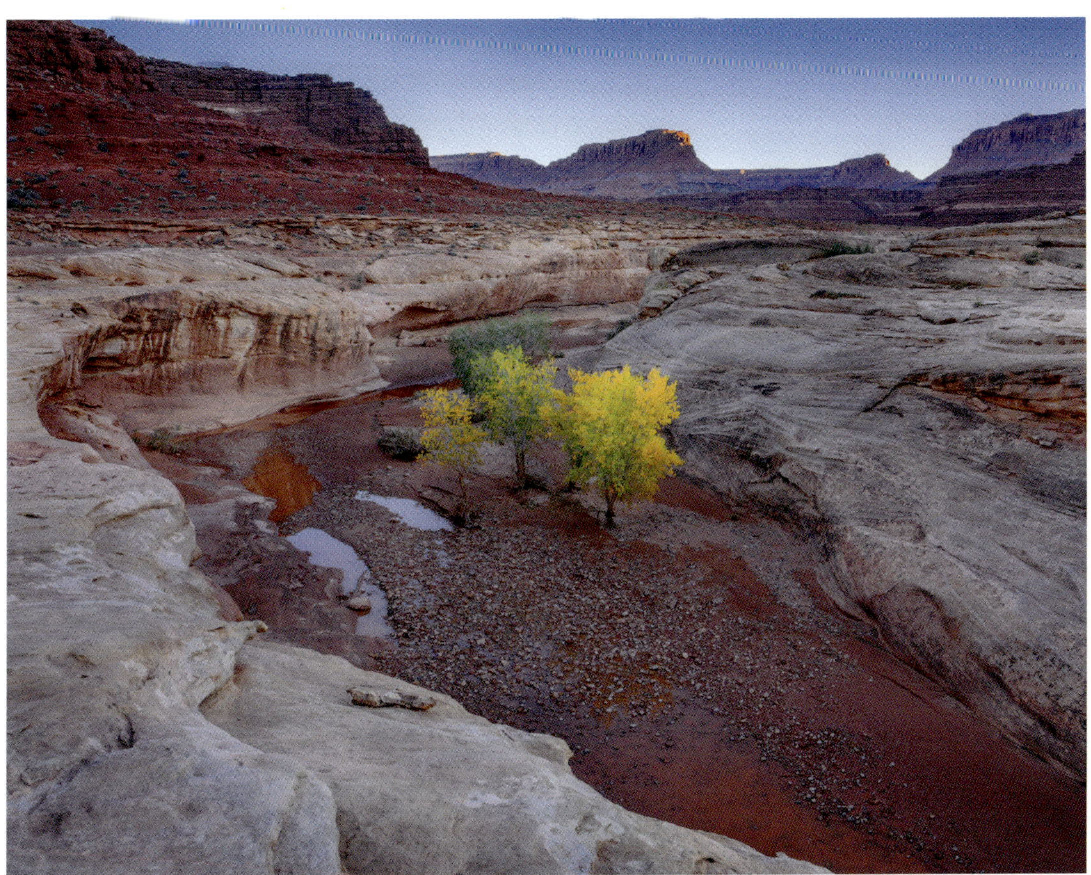

of striving to express meaning from the value (to the viewer) of striving to *find* meaning in the finished work. Both forms of value may be powerful and rewarding regardless of whether they end up referring to the same meaning. In fact, by decoupling the two forms of meaning, we allow ourselves (being that we are sometimes the authors and sometimes the viewers of an artwork) to make the most of, and to personalize, both forms of meaning, rather than allow one of them to be dictated to us by someone else.

Ansel Adams described this sentiment well when he commented about his own approach to Stieglitz's equivalence. "I'm a total believer in the concept of the equivalent," Adams wrote, "I present the photograph as an equivalent of my response to this world which I wish to share with the spectator. *But, I might add, only if it means anything to him. I hope it will mean something to him, but not necessarily just what it means to me.*" (Italics mine)

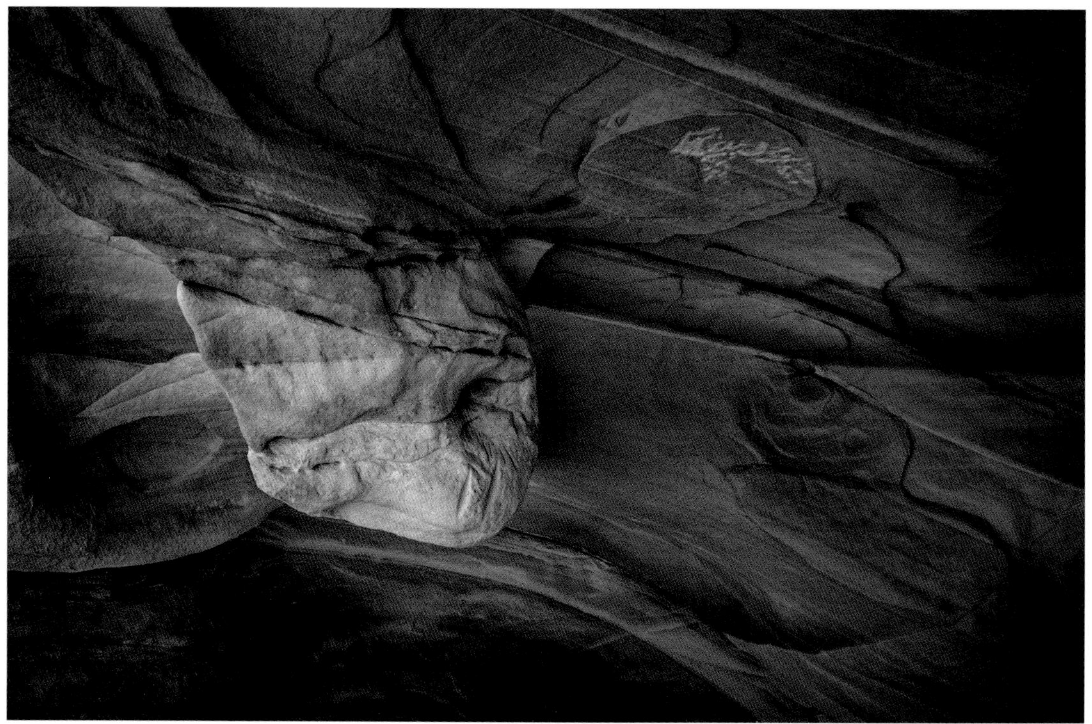

What finally convinced me of the truth of Barthes's argument was an experience I had several years ago listening to a piece of music on headphones while hiking in a favorite desert canyon. My mind wandered and the music consumed me. After a while, the notes began to weave with other sensations: align with shapes and patterns in the rocks and plant life, accent lines and colors, even combine with the scents in the air and the feeling of the breeze on my skin to produce a rich multisensory experience. As it happened, the music was an overture written by Felix Mendelssohn, titled *The Hebrides*.

I have never been to the Hebrides islands—a landscape I know to be vastly different from the desert I was in, which I love and know intimately. I realized that the fact that Mendelssohn's music was inspired by his visit to the islands was entirely irrelevant to my own experience. Likewise, I often revel in the beauty of artworks like Wolfgang Amadeus Mozart's *Requiem* or Rembrandt van Rijn's *Christ in the Storm on the Sea of Galilee*, despite not having any strong feelings for the religious references that inspired these creations. These references and connotations no doubt influenced the artists' own experiences as they created the works. And I, in turn, benefit greatly from the fact that these artists were so deeply inspired as to produce such magnificent creations. However, being a different person, in a different time, with different beliefs from those of the artists, the meaning and joy I experience is of a different nature than theirs. And why wouldn't it be?

Pablo Picasso asked, "How can you expect a beholder to experience my picture as I experienced it?" "A picture," he wrote, "comes to me a long time beforehand; who knows how long a time beforehand, I sensed, saw, and painted it and yet the next day even I do not understand what I have done. How can anyone penetrate my dreams, my instincts, my desires, my thought, which have taken a long time to fashion themselves and come to the surface, above all to grasp what I put there, perhaps involuntary."

Similarly, Arnold Schoenberg—articulating the idea later dubbed by E. H. Gombrich "the beholder's share"—wrote, "An artistic impression is substantially the resultant of two components. One what the work of art gives the onlooker—the other, what he is capable of giving to the work of art." In contrast to Wilde's idea that an artist should "dominate" the viewer, Schoenberg proposed instead that the experience of meaning-making in art is a collaboration between artist and viewer, each bringing their own share.

It seems that equivalence in the sense that Stieglitz had intended—a perfect parity between the feelings of the artist and the feelings of viewer—is only possible when the artist and viewer are the same person (as in, when an artist looks at their own finished work and experiences the same feelings he or she had at the time of creation). This may seem anathema to some, but I think it is still a high and worthwhile bar for an artist to aspire to. Likewise, I think it is a high and worthwhile bar for viewers to strive to find the deepest and most elevated meaning they can find in a work of art according to their own personality, experiences, and sensibilities, regardless of whether it ends up being the same meaning the artist had intended.

Art has no right to exist if, content to reproduce reality, it
uselessly duplicates it. Its mission is to conjure up imaginary
worlds. That can be done only if the artist repudiates reality
and by this act places himself above it. Being an artist means
ceasing to take seriously that very serious person we are
when we are not an artist.

—JOSÉ ORTEGA Y GASSET

In his 1890 book *The Gentle Art of Making Enemies*, painter James McNeill Whistler
wrote sarcastically, "If the man who paints only the tree, or flower, or other surface
he sees before him were an artist, the king of artists would be the photographer. It is
for the artist to do something beyond this." Setting aside the unfortunate fact that
Whistler, like many other critics of photography as a medium for art, assumed incor-
rectly that photography is limited by its nature to just mimetic representation, it may
surprise you to learn that as a photographic artist I agree completely with his final
point: It *is* for the artist to do something beyond just direct representation of reality
(i.e., rendering objects as a random person would see them).

Philosophers of art often use the term "imitation" to refer to mimetic reproduction
of realistic appearances (not to be confused with imitation in the sense of plagiarizing
other people's work). For many years, leading up to impressionist art in the nineteenth
century (signaling the beginning of what is now known as the modern era in art), imitation was practically synonymous with art. During that period, the skill to reproduce

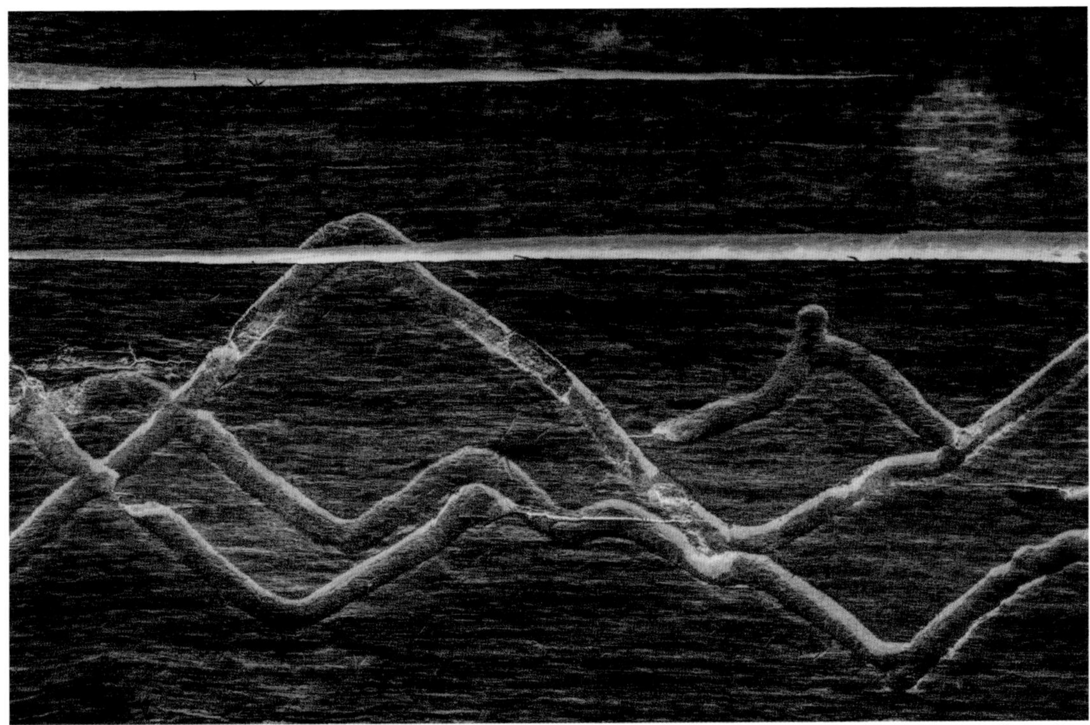

accurate, realistic appearances was considered the measure of being a good artist. But art has come a long way since then. As Tolstoy explained:

> *Little can imitation, realism, serve, as many people think, as a measure of the quality of art. Imitation cannot be such a measure; for the chief characteristic of art is the infection of others with the feelings the artist has experienced, and infection with a feeling is not only not identical with description of the accessories of what is transmitted, but is usually hindered by superfluous details....To value a work of art by the degree of its realism, by the accuracy of the details reproduced, is as strange as to judge of the nutritive quality of food by its external appearance. When we appraise a work according to its realism, we only show that we are talking, not of a work of art, but of its counterfeit.*

It's worth pointing out that part of the reason impressionists and later modern artists chose to depart from precise realism was the invention of photography, portending an era where realistic reproduction could be accomplished by technology and required no great human skill. Artists realized that if art was to remain viable and important as a distinctive and venerable human activity, it had to, as Whistler put it, "do something beyond this."[11]

However, the idea that realistic depiction may be at odds with some of the loftier goals of art is much older than impressionism. Plato famously excluded mimetic artists from his ideal Republic because, according to his *theory of forms*, reality as we perceive it is not "real reality," which exists in realms beyond the reach of human beings. Mimetic art, according to Plato, merely mimics our innately flawed perceptions of reality and may reinforce common errors about the true nature of things (i.e., their ideal forms). In Plato's words:

> *For there is no light of justice or temperance or any of the higher ideas which are precious to souls in the earthly copies of them: they are seen through a glass dimly; and there are few who, going to the images, behold in them the realities, and these only with difficulty.*

Immanuel Kant likewise suggested that when we behold a work of art, we must go out of our way to experience it with "disinterest"—to deliberately exclude from our consideration any interest in whether the objects depicted in the artwork even exist outside of it. Instead, we must learn to appreciate a work of art as a purely self-contained aesthetic experience. Natural appearances, to Kant, should be prized for their sheer beauty, not for any relation they may have to real objects. In his 1790 book *Critique of Judgment*, he wrote:

> *In a product of beautiful art, we must become conscious that it is art and not nature; but yet the purposiveness in its form must seem to be as free from all constraint of arbitrary rules as if it were a product of mere nature.*

As artists in other media spent much of the last century and a half charting new paths to artistic expression beyond realistic depiction (i.e., beyond mimesis, or

---

[11] As I write this book, we artists are facing a similar conundrum with the advent of generative AI, capable of producing photorealistic images without relying on human skill. I therefore believe it is as important now to defend art strictly as products of *human* skill and imagination, rather than as mere mimesis of realistic objects.

imitation), photographers for the most part remained stuck in realism, mired in conservative dogmatism (such as rules of objective reportage applied even to images not intended as photojournalism), in anachronistic traditions (such as "straight photography"), in outmoded fashions (such as "decisive moments"), and in outworn compositional styles (such as the wide-angle near-far landscape). This failure to keep up with stylistic and philosophical advances in art, we must concede, was abetted to a large degree by photographers' obsessive preoccupation with technology and by unnecessary conflation of artistic aesthetics with journalistic ethics.

Where other artistic media evolved to embrace artists' right to creative freedom, to accept and to value a diversity of philosophies, styles, and purposes for artworks, and even opencd themselves to unions and collaborations with other media, photography's unfortunate coupling of ethics with the false assumption that "a camera can't lie" gave rise to a quasi-religious belief system in which there is but one true and noble path: the path of realistic depiction.

By the dicta of this belief system, departure from realistic appearances (or, among the staunchest purists, any postexposure manipulations not sanctioned by the beatified saints and hallowed scriptures of the medium's short and recent past) amounts to sacrilege, depravity, blasphemy: moral transgressions punishable by public shaming and unceremonious excommunication from the pious community of "real photographers."

In most artistic media today, fidelity to realistic appearances is no longer considered necessary or even relevant. In some genres of art, it may even be seen as a detriment and as a distraction from the purpose of some artworks. Following impressionist artists' realization that art may express meanings and moods merely by use of realistic colors, shapes, lines, and patterns without having to maintain strict fidelity to details, postimpressionists took things even further, showing that art may express feelings even without sticking to realistic colors or shapes at all. As Gauguin put it:

> *I borrow some subject or other from life or from nature, and, using
> it as a pretext, I arrange lines and colors so as to obtain symphonies,
> harmonies that do not represent a thing that is real, in the vulgar sense
> of the word, and do not directly express any idea, but are supposed to
> make you think the way music is supposed to make you think, unaided
> by ideas or images, simply through the mysterious affinities that exist
> between our brains and such arrangements of colors and lines.*

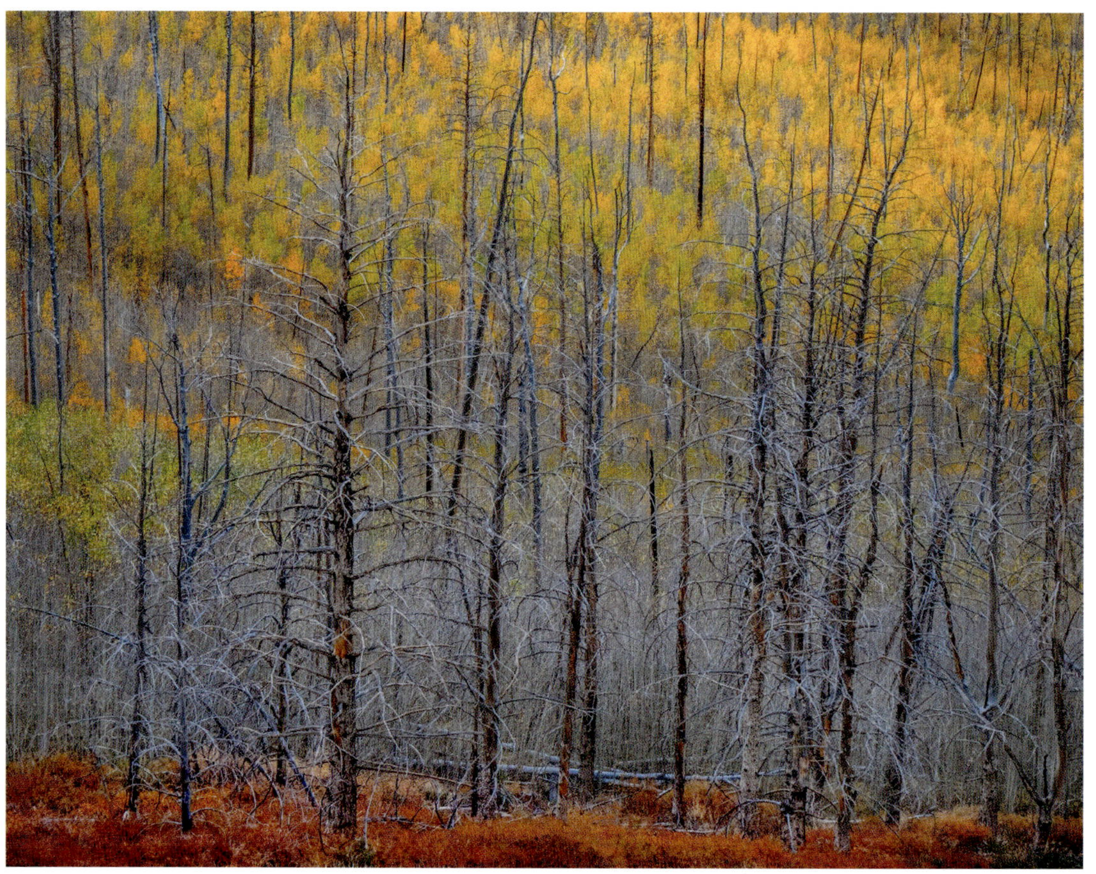

In today's art, realism and even aesthetic beauty, which were once the primary goal of art, are no longer considered necessary. Much art considered "postmodern" is not concerned with any kind of representation or aesthetics. Instead, such works as Marcel Duchamp's *Fountain* (a store-bought urinal, signed and entered into an exhibition) or composer John Cage's composition titled *4′33″* (in which a musician sits quietly without playing any instrument for 4 minutes and 33 seconds) seek to prompt viewers to ask such questions as, "why is this considered art?" or "what is the role of art?" or "why is art important?"

Philosophers such as Schopenhauer and Nietzsche explicitly considered art as a way of escaping reality. Reality, according to these philosophers, can be meaningless, boring, and full of suffering. Art allows us temporary respites from the wretchedness of reality. As Nietzsche put it, "Art is with us in order that we may not perish through truth."

Expressing the sentiment of the role of art in the modern age, Picasso said, "We all know that Art is not truth. Art is a lie that makes us realize truth, at least the truth that is given us to understand. The artist must know the manner whereby to convince others of the truthfulness of his lies."

The point is not that we should avoid realism in art completely, but that realistic depiction alone, no matter how beautiful or skillfully rendered, is not the measure of art or of artistic merit. When realism contributes to the meaning or message an artist wishes to communicate, it may be a powerful and important aspect of art. But for some kinds of meanings (which may also be expressed legitimately in art), realism may be a distraction or at best an unnecessary imposition. This is true regardless of the artist's choice of medium.

The photographs that excite me are photographs that
say something in a new manner; not for the sake of being
different, but ones that are different because the individual
is different and the individual expresses himself. I realize
that we all do express ourselves, but those who express
that which is always being done are those whose thinking is
almost in every way in accord with everyone else. Expression
on this basis has become dull to those who wish to think
for themselves. I wish more people felt that photography
was an adventure the same as life itself and felt that their
individual feelings were worth expressing. To me, that makes
photography more exciting.

—HARRY CALLAHAN

Historically—and in some places, to this day—photographic art did not garner the same respect, nor was it considered as valid or as "real" art, as painting or music. Photographer Paul Strand praised his mentor and friend Alfred Stieglitz for displaying photographs in his gallery—291[12]— alongside post-impressionist and cubist artworks, which were considered controversial at the time. Strand recalled, "The acknowledgment of the validity of photography as a new material, as a new way of seeing life through a machine, was questioned and fundamentally denied. Well, here were these pictures by the Cubists, which were also looked upon as the work of idiots. I used to

---

[12] In reference to the gallery's address on 291 Fifth Avenue in New York

hear people at '291' say that some of these painters should be in a lunatic asylum, they should be punished, they shouldn't be allowed to do these things!"

Stieglitz himself stated that he didn't care much about what other people considered as art. "It is not art in the professionalized sense about which I care," he wrote, "but that which is created sacredly, as a result of a deep inner experience, with all of oneself, and that becomes 'art' in time."

Photographs may be divided into two categories, documentary or creative, based on their intended use. Documentary, or representational, photographs are those intended primarily to relay faithfully the appearance of things in the world. Creative photographs, on the other hand, are intended primarily to impart an aesthetic experience to viewers. I use the qualification "primarily" to acknowledge that some photographs may be both representational and creative, but one must take precedence over the other in terms of the photographer's intent, which must also inform the judgment of viewers.

While any object created skillfully or possessing aesthetic appeal may be considered as art by some definition of the term, not all such objects are art according to the narrower and more demanding definition I chose for my own work (which, to remind you, is this: Art is "the expression or application of human creative skill and imagination"). According to this definition, artistic photography falls squarely and exclusively within the "creative" category.

A creative, artistic photograph may still be representational, but we should never assume that anything presented as art—regardless of medium—is intended as a realistic representation. Therefore, the value and artistic merit of such a photograph should not be associated with any consideration of the accuracy of its representation of any real objects. Put another way, to be experienced as intended, artistic photographs should be considered and evaluated as any other works of art: not as "pictures of" things, but with the attitude described by Kant as "disinterestedness"—as standalone objects, not as copies or depictions of other objects.

To evaluate an artistic photograph by its fidelity to realistic appearances (i.e., as if intended to serve a documentary purpose) may also lead to misconceptions and disappointment. A viewer who chooses to believe that all photographs must never depart from realistic depictions is almost certain to be distracted from, or miss entirely, such aspects of a creative, artistic photograph as expression, symbolism, metaphorical meaning, intellectual challenge, and mood. Alas, such failure to distinguish, based on intent, between art and documentation in photography is often self-inflicted, enforced and perpetuated by certain photographic organizations and influential purists, and sometimes blamed on artists even if they communicate their intent clearly. Alas,

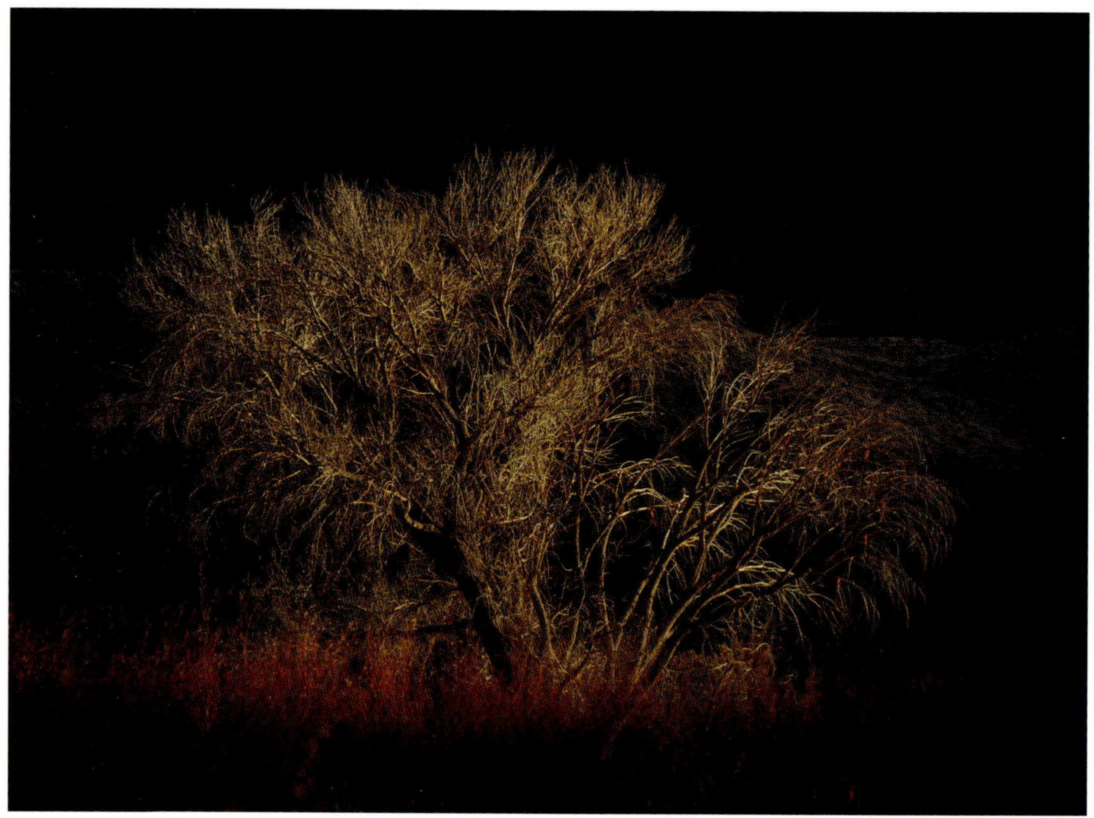

sometimes, as Rabindranath Tagore wrote, "We read the world wrong and say that it deceives us."

You may fairly wonder why I chose photography as my medium, given the definition of art I chose to aspire to in my own work and the pervasive prejudice among many viewers of photography about the role and necessity of strict realism in photographic work. After all, photography is ostensibly a medium designed specifically to facilitate objective, mimetic representations, rather than subjective, creative expressions. Also, photography relies to a high degree on technology to do much of the "heavy lifting," and thus generally requires less human skill than many other art media. The short answer is this: I did not. I was already an experienced (mimetic) photographer long before I realized I wanted to become an artist and thought seriously about the kind of art I wished to make.

But there is more to my decision to stick with photography than just that I was already good at it. The more I learned about art, the more I have also come to realize that the medium of photography, despite its ostensible documentary purpose and reliance on technological automation, does not in fact limit me to objective, realistic, mimetic depiction. Despite so much prejudice and pretense to the contrary, photography allows those of us who practice it as art a great deal of freedom to employ and evolve our creative and expressive skills—to make novel, nonobvious artwork that is far and beyond mere records of realistic appearances.

While it may have been easier for me to train as a painter or sculptor, and thus spare myself having to work in a medium hobbled (in some venues) by prejudice, I also realized that photography enables for me some modes of work that other media cannot—modes that have become crucial to the kind of art I now make. I am referring to the ability to create artwork as a part of—and at the height of—an inspiring experience. As Edward Weston put it, "I take advantage of chance—which in reality is not chance—but being ready, attuned to one's surroundings—and grasp my opportunity in a way which no other medium can equal in spontaneity, while the impulse is fresh, the excitement strong."

Being a consummate naturalist and recluse, the times I feel most inspired almost always coincide with solitary experiences in remote natural settings. I have found that creativity for me is correlated with such states of mind as awe, intense sensory stimulation, and a sense of feeling myself free and detached from the presence of other people and from preoccupation with the affairs of the human world. In such times, it would be challenging, awkward, time-consuming, or outright impossible for me to set up a stretched canvas on an easel, to chip away at a slab of rock, or to sit comfortably at a piano keyboard. But I can still make photographs. I can also write. That is why my creative tools are a camera and a notepad (these days, a note app on my mobile phone).

If I could accomplish the same synchronicity of inspiration and creative energy in a studio or in other settings, perhaps I would have chosen a different medium for my work. Perhaps I would have even considered my products in other media as more elevated and as having greater expressive powers than photographs. But if I must choose between the experiences that make my life worth living and my art worth making, and art that may be considered by others as more important or venerable, the choice for me is an easy one: experience first. Life first. Art second.

1.3. ON CREATIVITY

You do not have to be a painter or a sculptor to be an artist. You may be a shoemaker. You may be creative as such. And, if so, you are a greater artist than the majority of the painters whose work is shown in the art galleries of today.

—ALFRED STIEGLITZ

What is creativity? Before anything else, creativity refers to creation: the act of bringing something into existence. In this sense, especially in the domain of art, creativity is the opposite of direct imitation or objective representation (literally, re-presentation) of things already in existence. Almost anything produced by human beings can be considered at least to some degree as creative. Academic studies of creativity often distinguish between "little c" creativity (simple creative solutions to everyday problems) and "big C" Creativity (creative breakthroughs having significant, wide-ranging implications).

Alas, it has become common for artists to refer to themselves as "creatives" even if their work is not creative—in other words, it doesn't even meet the "little c" threshold, such as when someone copies a known work or, in photography, stumbles upon an unusual subject or event for which they can't take credit beyond, as the trope goes, "being in the right place at the right time."

There is some debate among artists and philosophers about whether art, or at least "good art," must be creative. Some definitions of art refer only to works requiring skill or possessing aesthetic appeal, while others call out creativity explicitly. This is to say that, depending on the definition you choose to use, not all art is necessarily creative, and not all creative products are necessarily art. This may seem a minor linguistic quibble, but it is not.

Much academic study of creativity in recent years, in fields like psychology and neuroscience, has revealed fascinating insights into the ways that creativity may shape and express your life and unique personality. This is to say, art that is not creative may still be art by some definitions, and may still be worthwhile as such, but it will not yield you the added rewards of creativity. This is part of the reason why the definition of art I chose to strive for in my own work[13] (and that I also consider as the most venerable definition by which to appreciate other people's art) specifically includes the word "creative" as one of its criteria.

"If creativity is to be a viable neuroscientific construct it should conform to several scientific conditions," wrote Rex E. Jung and Oshin Vartanian in their introduction to *The Cambridge Handbook of the Neuroscience of Creativity*. "First," they wrote, "it should have a definition that lends itself to scientific inquiry." So, what is the scientific definition of creativity?

The definition of creativity most often used in scientific research is this: "the production of something *novel* and *useful*." This is already a high bar, implying that a creative work must be at least to some degree original, and have some demonstrable benefit; however, creativity researcher Dean Keith Simonton proposed making the definition even stricter by adding a third criterion: *nonobviousness*[14]—the quality of being surprising and/or unexpected. He explained, "Creativity can be optimized just a single way: Simultaneously maximize originality, utility, and surprise. *If the idea is commonplace, useless, or obvious, or any combination of possible zero values, then an uncreative idea results.* Each exerts veto power over the rest." (Italics mine) He added, "A creative idea cannot originate via the straightforward application of well-established disciplinary procedures ... such ideas must be considered routine, reproductive, or habitual rather than truly creative."

Novelty is synonymous with originality, meaning that any creation that only reproduces something already done by someone else—no matter how skillfully or beautifully crafted—is, by definition, not creative. Usefulness may be easy to assess in domains such as science or industry, but may be trickier to apply to art. Therefore, some researchers of artistic creativity prefer using terms like "appropriate," "effective," "meaningful," or "expressive,"[15] instead of "useful." I think that's an unnecessary

---

[13] See page 29.

[14] Adding this third criterion aligns the definitions of creativity with considerations used by the U.S. Patent Office in evaluating whether to grant patents.

[15] For example, Teresa M. Amabile, Professor of Business Administration at Harvard Business School, wrote, "In other domains—the arts, for example ... work is generally considered creative if it is both novel and expressive of something, evoking a reaction (or range of reactions) in observers that the artist intended."

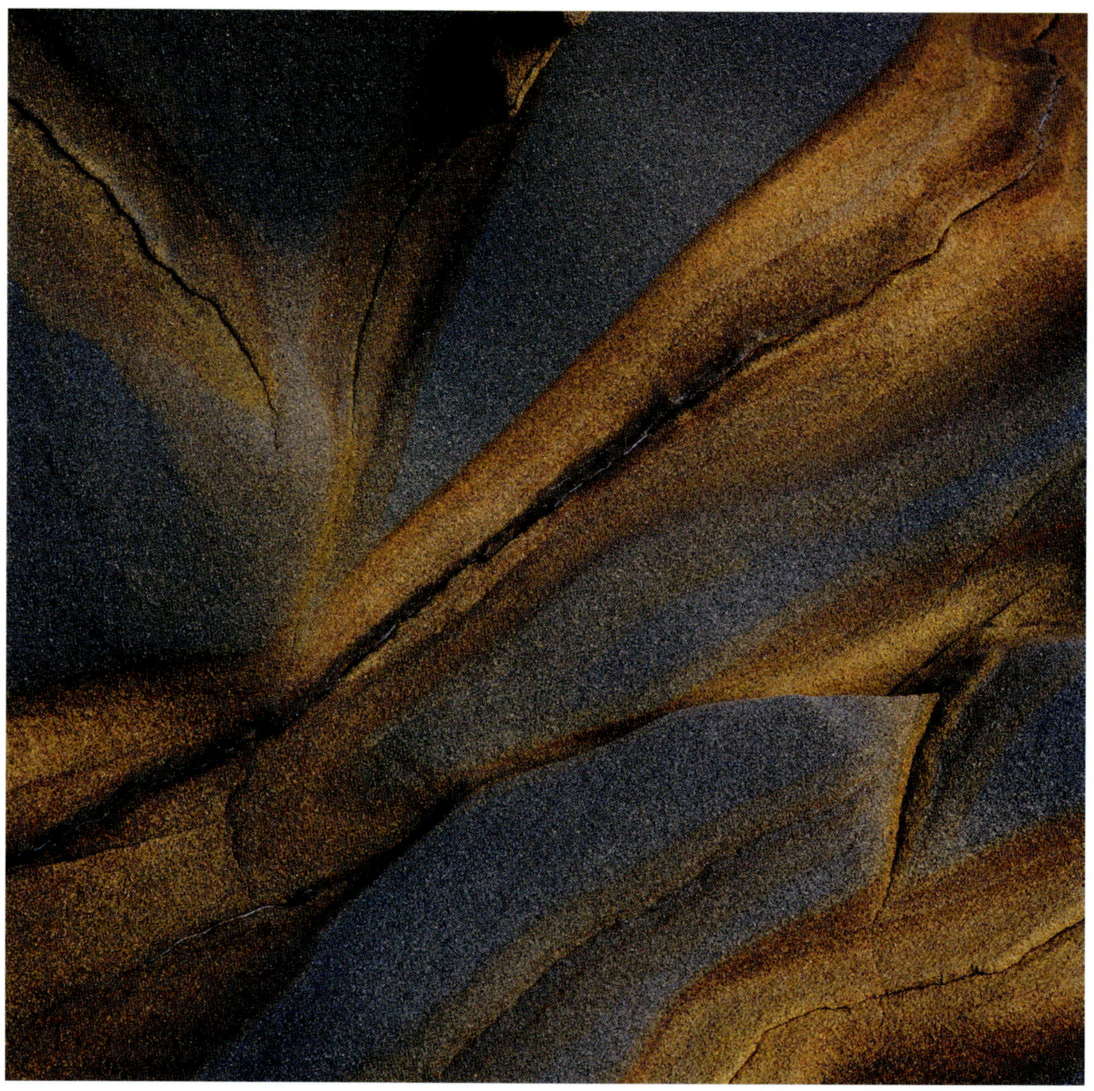

complication. Art is something people do by choice because it enriches their lives, and in almost every case also the lives of others, which makes art intrinsically useful.

Also, usefulness in art doesn't have to relate to the *products* of artistic work; it can also refer to the value one gets from engaging in the *process* of artmaking. This is to say that if a person values time spent creating art, then art may be considered useful even regardless of outcome. Put another way, when it comes to artistic creativity, unlike creativity in other areas, usefulness is built in, which leaves the criteria of originality and nonobviousness as the more important measures of artistic creativity.

No doubt, there is no such thing, in art or in other areas, as an entirely original product. Novelty, therefore, like nonobviousness, is not an either/or quality, but a matter of degree. Put another way, the measure of artistic creativity is not merely the fact that a new creation is somewhat different from former ones, but how far the new creation departs from former influences.

As neuroscientist Oliver Sacks put it:

> *All of us, to some extent, borrow from others, from the culture around us. Ideas are in the air, and we may appropriate, often without realizing ... What is at issue is not the fact of "borrowing" or "imitating," of being "derivative," being "influenced," but what one does with what is borrowed or imitated or derived; how deeply one assimilates it, takes it into oneself, compounds it with one's own experiences and thoughts and feelings, places it in relation to oneself, and expresses it in a new way, one's own.*

Although creativity, at least up to a point, is correlated with known cognitive and practical benefits, we must acknowledge that it also comes at a risk, and sometimes even with some pathologies. People with abnormal psychologies that make them less inhibited in generating new ideas and combining seemingly unrelated concepts will exhibit higher creativity but may also suffer various neuroses related to their condition.

In a practical sense, creative work, by virtue of being novel and nonobvious, may arouse resistance or fail to generate public interest. As philosopher José Ortega y Gasset put it, "Accustomed to ruling supreme, the masses feel that the new art, which is the art of a privileged aristocracy of finer senses, endangers their rights as men. Whenever the new Muses present themselves, the masses bristle."

To meet the usefulness criterion of the definition of creativity, it seems that creative work must not be "too novel" or "too nonobvious." But even within this vaguely defined range, there is no denying that creativity comes at a risk: There is no guarantee that the effort you invest in being creative will yield useful outcomes. Also, the more novel and nonobvious your work, the smaller will be the audience of people who may understand it, let alone be moved to pay for it. At the end of the day, as Henri Matisse put it, "Creativity takes courage."

So, why do it? Because creative expression is one of the most powerful ways of making your experiences—the building blocks of your life—meaningful as they happen, and instructive and memorable afterward. As psychologist and creativity coach Eric Maisel put it:

> *Creating is one of the ways they [creative people] endeavor to maintain meaning. In the act of creation, they lay a veneer of meaning over meaninglessness and sometimes produce work that helps others maintain meaning. This is why creating is such a crucial activity in the life of a creator: It is one of the ways, and often the most important way, that she manages to make life feel meaningful.*

ON EXPRESSION AND SELF-EXPRESSION

Every production of an artist should be the expression of an adventure of his soul.

—W. SOMERSET MAUGHAM

The *Merriam-Webster Dictionary* defines expression as, among other things, "a mode, means, or use of *significant representation* or symbolism … the quality or fact of *being expressive.*" (Italics mine) The same dictionary defines the word expressive as, "effectively conveying *meaning or feeling*," and the term self-expression as "the expression of *your* thoughts or feelings especially through artistic activities." (Again, italics mine) Note the qualification "your" separating expression in the general sense from self-expression, which is specifically the expression of things *you* felt (i.e., not made-up meanings or someone else's feelings).

Consider the implications of conveying "meaning or feeling," as opposed to, say, appearances or descriptions. Meanings and feelings are subjective. Expressing them is not the same as capturing objective appearances or relaying aesthetic appeal already inherent in the subject. Art intending to express meaning and feeling must go beyond just showing others that you visited certain places, or got lucky to see certain things, or copied someone else's work expressing their meaning or feeling. Self-expression is about things you felt—your own subjective inner experiences. It's about things you consider to be not just beautiful or interesting, but also personally meaningful in some significant way.

Federico Fellini said, "All art is autobiographical." This is the same as saying that all art is self-expressive, or, conversely, that a work that is not self-expressive is not art. Along the same lines, Tolstoy wrote, "Art is a human activity, consisting in this, that one person consciously, by certain external signs, conveys to others *feelings he has experienced*, and other people are affected by these feelings and live them over in themselves." (Italics mine)

As with creativity, there are definitions of art that do not require self-expression to be worthy of the name, which is to say, again, that it's up to you to choose the definition of art you wish to aspire to in your own work. Not all are equally venerable or demanding. Something can be considered as art strictly in the sense that it is beautiful to behold or created with great skill, but without being expressive. Such works may still possess value as decorative items or as works of fiction. Expressive art, however, is valuable not only because of its physical characteristics, but also because it meets Danto's definition of art as "embodied meaning." By this simple characterization we can say that art that is not expressive does not convey meaning—it is literally meaningless. Photographer André Kertész expressed this point using a poignant metaphor. He wrote:

> *If you want to write you should learn the alphabet. You write and write and in the end you have a beautiful, perfect alphabet. But it isn't the alphabet that is important. The important thing is what you are writing, what you are expressing. The same thing goes for photography. Photographs can be technically perfect and even beautiful, but they have no expression.*

Whereas creativity may be something to aspire to in measure (i.e., too much creativity may indicate a cognitive disorder, or come at the cost of social isolation and lack of public interest), expression has no such downsides. Simply stated, if you wish for your art to be meaningful, strive to make it expressive. If you wish for your art to be as *personally* meaningful as it can be, then strive to make it *self*-expressive.

Although not necessarily downsides, there are some practical challenges to self-expression. The most obvious one is that you must avoid planning your artistic productions in advance. This is for the simple fact that you can't know in advance when inspiration to create will find you or how you will feel when it does. Instead, you must remain open to experiences and respond to them creatively as they happen. You may plan generally to situate yourself in places and at times when you may be more likely to experience inspiration, but you should not plan the works that may ensue from these experiences.

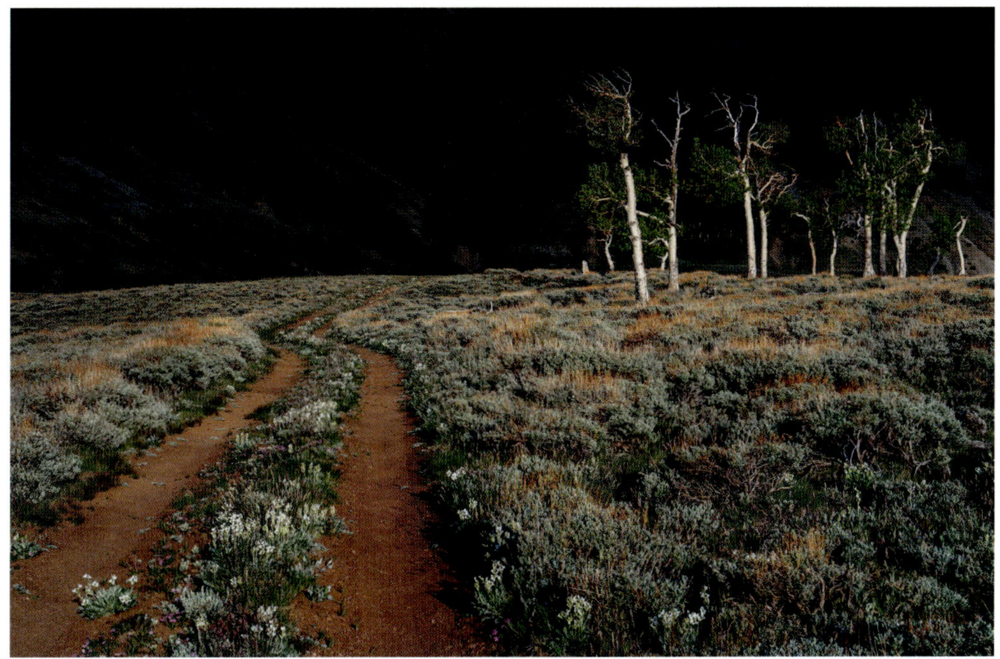

Keen photographers may wonder whether self-expression contradicts the idea of visualization (or, as some refer to it, "previsualization"): seeing in the proverbial "mind's eye" a final image before making an exposure. The answer: It can, but it doesn't have to. If you visualize your final image before leaving the house, then certainly it is unlikely your images will be self-expressive. But if you defer visualizing until you experience an "aha!" moment of inspiration and allow your feelings to guide your visualization, then your images will absolutely be self-expressive. In fact, it is the only way they can be self-expressive.

To dispel yet another common misconception: The purpose of self-expression is not necessarily (or at all) to have other people understand exactly what you wished to express. That can be accomplished more effectively in reportage (e.g., documentary images or factual writings) than in creative art. Also, if you strive for your work to be easy to understand, you may end up restricting yourself to a limited range of commonly relatable experiences and expressions—a low common denominator that may limit your creativity and your capacity to discover or to evolve novel ways of artistic expression. It is better to think of self-expression as a habit, rather than as a goal: as a way to make yourself more mindful of your inner feelings and their meaning, and intuitively seek ways to express them when they happen using your chosen medium, subjects, and materials.

PART 2: PRACTICAL ADVICE

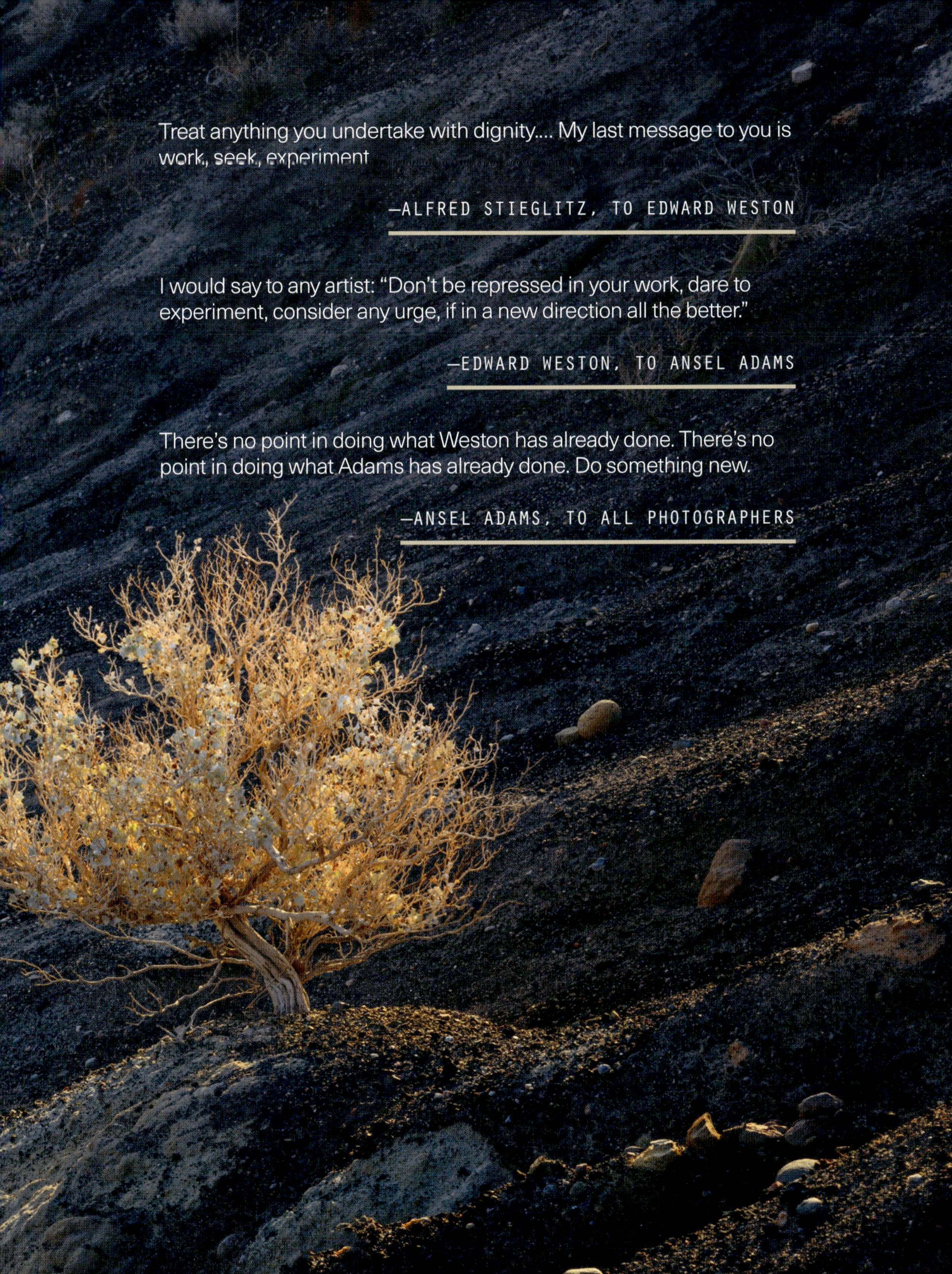

Treat anything you undertake with dignity.... My last message to you is work, seek, experiment

—ALFRED STIEGLITZ, TO EDWARD WESTON

I would say to any artist: "Don't be repressed in your work, dare to experiment, consider any urge, if in a new direction all the better."

—EDWARD WESTON, TO ANSEL ADAMS

There's no point in doing what Weston has already done. There's no point in doing what Adams has already done. Do something new.

—ANSEL ADAMS, TO ALL PHOTOGRAPHERS

Building on the theoretical foundations in Part 1 of this book, this part is dedicated entirely to suggestions on how you may put some of the theory into practice. I am not interested in simply rehashing common tropes and platitudes (in fact, I believe some common bits of advice given to artists are often useless if not outright false). The advice I offer here is not just repeated from other sources; it is founded in choices I have made, my reasons for making them, and the lessons I've learned on my own journey.

The idea for this book came from my publisher, Rocky Nook, who suggested I write a book of advice themed after a book titled *Letters to a Young Poet*, which consists of an epistolary exchange that occurred in the early 1900s between an aspiring poet named Franz Xaver Kappus and the great poet Rainer Maria Rilke. Since I did not have my own letters from a young artist to respond to, I decided to write this book as if I was offering advice to one such artist I happen to have known personally: my younger self. Inevitably, this means that at times my advice may come across as didactic, or preachy, or even as tough love. I hope this doesn't dissuade you from considering it seriously, even if you may deem some of it unsuitable to you.

My goal is not to convince you that my way is necessarily right for you or anyone else, but to prompt you to think about your own decisions (artistic and other) as parts of, and as inseparable from, the lifelong pursuit of learning and becoming who you are—your own unique personality, circumstances, and goals—rather than to accept as given any advice or guidance that happens to be popular or convenient. As some of what I suggest here may involve making profound and consequential (perhaps even risky) life choices, I encourage you to question everything I say and to research for yourself anything that may pique your interest, including—especially—things you may disagree with me about.

To be clear, my advice here is not intended as recipes for success or happiness. Some of the most meaningful times and lessons in my life involved risk, discomfort, doubts, and occasionally coming to terms with the consequences of what in hindsight turned out to have been bad choices. At times, learning these lessons came at the cost of personal sacrifices and involved enduring periods of doubt and aimlessness before I could fully appreciate their importance, meaning, and rewards. In hindsight today, I consider these ostensibly negative experiences as parts of the unavoidable "cost of entry" to meaningful living. Without them, my life may have been easier, more comfortable, and more predictable, but likely also stunted, limited, and far less interesting.

BECOME WHO YOU ARE

You will never find yourself unless you quit preconceiving
what you will be when you have found yourself.

—ROBERT HENRI

You have no responsibility to live up to what other people think
you ought to accomplish. I have no responsibility to be like
they expect me to be. It's their mistake, not my failing.

—RICHARD FEYNMAN

Pretend that I am someone you know well and trust completely asking you this question: Who are you, really? I'm not asking for your name, what you look like, where you live, or what your cultural background is. I'm not asking about your profession or your relations to other persons. I'm not asking about what you have *in common with* others. I'm asking about the individual person that you—and only you—are: the unique, singular combination of traits, skills, knowledge, experiences, preferences, quirks, oddities, circumstances, and aspirations that make you *different from* others.

What are some adjectives you would use to describe yourself if you did not have to worry about how anyone else might judge or perceive you? How are these adjectives reflected or expressed in the way you live and in the art you create? Which of these adjectives do you choose to share or conceal when you present yourself to the world?

What do you like or dislike about yourself? What are you proud of or embarrassed about? What do you wish others knew about you? What do you hope nobody will ever find out about you? Which of these things have you always known or believed about yourself? Which have you come to learn or accept about yourself later in life? Are you content being who you are? Are there things you wish you could change about yourself? Is there another person you wish you could be more like, or perhaps even trade places with?

How much of who you are is borrowed from others around you? How much have you accepted unquestioningly to fit in with the beliefs and customs of your tribe, culture, or community, or to avoid conflict? To what degree do your ethical values match those of the society and place you happened to have been born into, rather than having been chosen freely and objectively by comparing them against alternatives? To what degree was your choice of profession driven by your passions or by the need to make ends meet or to ensure a comfortable lifestyle? To what degree did you resign yourself to living and working as you do because you didn't (or don't) believe you could do better?

How confident are you in any of your answers to the questions above? I ask because various philosophies have emphasized the importance of knowing, learning, and becoming who you are, suggesting that not everyone does, and that even those who do may not always guide their life choices by this knowledge.

Would you like your life and work to be more closely aligned with your own personality, desires, and values? If so, what's stopping you?

KNOW THYSELF

For who will do his own work aright will find that his first lesson is to know what he is, and that which is proper to himself; and who rightly understands himself will never mistake another man's work for his own but will love and improve himself above all other things, will refuse superfluous employments, and reject all unprofitable thoughts and propositions.

—MICHEL DE MONTAIGNE

"Know thyself" was one of three maxims carved above the entrance to the Temple of Apollo in Ancient Greece, home of the high priestess Pythia—the legendary Oracle of Delphi. Surely, if people knew themselves intuitively, there would be no reason for this stern admonition.

Knowing yourself—who and what you are—is difficult for various reasons. To a large degree, who you are is determined by factors beyond your control, perhaps even beyond your awareness: your genes; traits you inherited from your forebears; parental, social, and cultural influences in your life; and how you were shaped by your own life experiences. The effects of these factors may not become evident to you until you have lived long enough to recognize—sometimes only in hindsight and with deliberate effort—the ways in which you are different from others. Thus, self-knowledge is not so much a singular accomplishment, but an ongoing process of discovery and adaptation. Although there are aspects of yourself that are fixed from the moment of your birth, there are also parts of yourself that change as you mature, as you gain knowledge and experiences, as you react—consciously or intuitively—to various stimuli, events, and circumstances.

Self-knowledge can be a great source of wisdom and inner peace. It can also be a great source of misery. When you learn what aspects of yourself are beyond your ability to change, you may use this knowledge to better yourself or at least to accept yourself as you are. If you possess useful traits or abilities, you may feel grateful for your good fortune, but you may also realize you have no reason to feel vain—you just got lucky. On the other hand, if you learn things about yourself that you dislike or that limit you in some ways, you may find peace in the knowledge that it is pointless for you to feel guilty, resentful, or regretful about them. In more formal terms, knowing yourself will help you appreciate and leverage your gifts and find adaptive[16] ways of transcending your challenges in meaningful ways.

Self-knowledge will also help you make good long-term choices according to your own nature, recognizing that what may be best for you is not necessarily what is best for someone else. Some people benefit greatly from certain professions, activities, and ways of life that may lead others to despair. Some people are comfortable fitting into certain social roles while others feel more comfortable as individualists and outsiders. Self-knowledge is critical in making such consequential decisions as who or whether to marry, whether to have children, where to live, what career path to take, or whether to accept the traditions of the society you happened to have been born into or seek alternative ways of life—decisions that, once made, may profoundly and irreversibly affect how rewarding and meaningful the rest of your days may be, what opportunities and freedoms your future self may have (or be denied), and so on. The right choices in such matters are not universal. They depend, for any given person, as much on circumstances as on the unique combination of traits that make each of us a unique individual.

According to the American Psychological Association (APA), the term *personality* "refers to the enduring characteristics and behavior that comprise a person's *unique* adjustment to life, including major traits, interests, drives, values, self-concept, abilities, and emotional patterns." (Italics mine) To the point of this book: the opposite of being unique is being ordinary. Thus, to embrace and to become your own unique self is to become extraordinary.

Personality psychology is founded on the idea that we are each at least in some ways unique (i.e., extraordinary individuals). This uniqueness may lead to differences

---

[16] In psychology, adaptive behavior means adjusting to situations in ways that produce long-term positive outcomes even if difficult in the short-term, as opposed to maladaptive behavior, which may lead to long-term problems even if it makes you feel better in the short-term.

in our preferences, temperament, attitudes, and various cognitive abilities relative to others. Although often not stated overtly, personality psychology also explains why so many popular maxims and traditions often claimed as universally true for all people should never be taken unquestioningly as the most appropriate for every individual. This is especially true of maxims, traditions, norms, and opinions relating to things that a person does by choice (such as artmaking), rather than by necessity, submission, or coercion. This may seem like a benign and obvious statement, but only until you stop to consider that many of us have a choice (even if very difficult or risky) in such matters as conforming with traditions and ways of life, living up to other people's expectations or judgments, and loyalty to various ideologies or tribes just because we happen to have been born into them or because they are dominant among our peers, rather than independently chosen.

"Man's main task in life," wrote psychologist Erich Fromm, "is to give birth to himself, to become what he potentially is. The most important product of his effort is his own personality." Do you know what your personality is? The science of personality psychology can help you find the answer.

Moreover, personality psychology, which reveals commonalities and differences among individuals, is compatible with the philosophy of existentialism, which is founded in the idea that people who wish to live authentically must choose (to the degree they have the freedom to do so) their own ethics and actions according to their temperaments, sensibilities, and consciences, regardless of any traditions and expectations they happened to have been born into or that are considered appropriate, honorable, desirable, or dutiful by their society or by influential persons. As psychologist Abraham Maslow put it in his book *Toward a Psychology of Being*:

> *It is possible that existentialism will not only enrich psychology. It may also be an additional push toward the establishment of another branch of psychology, the psychology of the fully evolved and authentic Self and its ways of being.*

A commonly used model in personality research is the *Five-Factor Model* (FFM), also known as the *Big Five* model of personality. According to the FFM, every individual personality is a unique blend of these five traits: *openness to experience, conscientiousness, extraversion, agreeableness*, and *neuroticism* (making up the acronym OCEAN). Different people may rank differently relative to others in each of these traits, and the combination of the five yields one's unique personality.

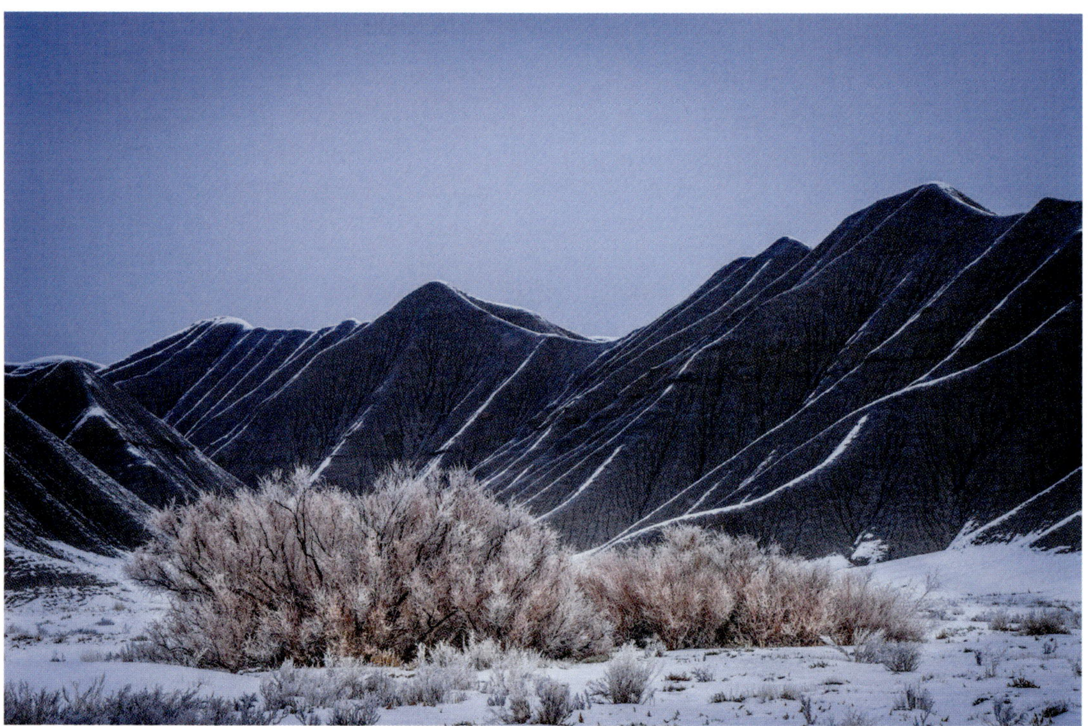

Broadly speaking, extraversion (and its corollary, introversion) is a measure of how outgoing and social a person is; agreeableness relates to a person's capacity for sympathy, tolerance, and cooperation with others; neuroticism relates to a person's predisposition to such things as anxiety, worry, pessimism, and guilt; openness to experience (often shortened to just "openness") relates to a person's richness of imagination, adventurousness, degree of curiosity, and resistance to authority; and conscientiousness relates to a person's tendency to be efficient, organized, disciplined, focused on achievement, and prone to long-term planning.

Openness is the personality trait most closely correlated with creativity. This doesn't mean that people who are less open than others are not creative or that they should not practice art; it only means that the kind of art that may be most enjoyable to an "open" person (experimental, abstract, personal, etc.) may not be the same as the art that will be most enjoyable for a person who scores low on openness (and may therefore be more conservative and prefer sticking to pure, traditional methods, styles, and subjects). Similar analyses can be made regarding other FFM traits (see table opposite).

So, do you wish to truly know thyself? If you don't already know how you rank on each of the FFM traits, I suggest you stop here for a moment and look up one of many freely available online FFM tests, just to give you a general idea. If you want a deeper understanding of yourself, I suggest looking up an expert in psychological testing in your area (many psychiatric institutions have them on staff) to conduct a formal test and help you interpret the results. Odds are, it will be a useful eye-opener for you.

Trait	High	Low
Openness	Emphasis on creativity (originality); keep trying new things; combine multiple media.	Emphasis on technical perfection; become highly specialized in a certain technique or style.
Conscientiousness	Work in projects; design and publish books; plan your work ahead.	Start a lot of things, see what "sticks." Keep your options open. *Don't* commit to long-term or complex projects.
Extraversion	Find a like-minded community; join clubs; compete; attend public events.	Seek solitude; read a lot; spend a lot of time thinking about and processing your work; avoid contests.
Agreeableness	Make a lot of friends; become a public speaker; teach classes.	Avoid people and upsetting distractions; give *honest* expert critique.
Neuroticism	Find familiar and comfortable places to work; observe the world from a distance.	Explore far and wide; engage directly with your subjects.

Some ways in which the Five Factor Model may inform your art.

If you wish to drill even deeper, see if you can find an expert in your area who may also be able to run you through the *Minnesota Multiphasic Personality Inventory* (MMPI) test, which takes a different approach to personality testing from the FFM, and may also be useful in diagnosing certain psychological predispositions or disorders. (Note that MMPI tests are not generally conducive to self-testing and require trained expertise to interpret.)

Other, more common types of personality models, such as the *Myers-Briggs Type Indicator* (MBTI) or the *Enneagram* model, may also be useful and revealing. I recommend trying them, if only because they are easy to self-administer, often available for free, and may offer you valuable insight into yourself and others. However, keep in mind that the accuracy of these models, while generally higher than pure intuition, doesn't meet scientific standards, which is why they are rarely used in academic research and may not necessarily give you an accurate representation of your personality. This latter point is important because these models come with the risk of drawing incorrect or inaccurate conclusions about your personality. So, take their results with a grain of salt.

A common subject of debate among personality researchers is whether and to what degree personality is a fixed quantity: how much of it may be influenced or determined by genes, early life experiences, and other external factors. At the risk of oversimplification, this statement is not generally in dispute: Much of what determines your personality (especially aspects modeled in the FFM and similar models) is a product of external factors and cannot be changed, at least not to a great degree. For example, a person who is an introvert may consciously (even convincingly) act as an extravert in some situations and for certain periods of time, but such a person cannot become an extravert. However, most personality researchers believe that there is also room for people to shape their own personalities using various practices.

Having the results of a scientifically backed personality test may be extremely liberating. It can help you understand yourself better as well as explain yourself better to others. For example, if you score high on openness and low on conscientiousness, as I do, you may be tired of people badgering you to become organized, to keep your desk clean or your books alphabetized, to finish projects you start, to adhere to deadlines, or to establish a daily routine. I take comfort and validation in knowing that some of the smartest and most creative people in history were famous (or infamous, depending on whom you ask) for being messy, forgetful, disorganized, heedless of deadlines, and prone to leaving works unfinished to pursue new interests. For people like me, having this combination of traits, strict routines, having to maintain a clean workspace, and stressing over deadlines may in fact have a detrimental effect on our capacity to come up with creative ideas.

Likewise, consider your measures of extraversion and neuroticism, whether you feel an incessant need to always interact with or appease other people or, conversely, whether you feel uncomfortable around people and prefer to live and work in solitude. Some people thrive in one extreme, some in the other, and some may be comfortable finding a balance in between. If you are an introvert, don't feel bad if you are not the life of the party or if you don't want to accept invitations to socialize. If you are an extravert, don't feel you have to defend to anyone your inability to enjoy solitude. Whatever your personality, find a way of life that fits with it. Pretending or wishing to be more (or less) social than your temperament is comfortable with, whether for your own sake or to live up to other people's expectations, will make you miserable.

Nihil inimicius quam sibi ipse[17].

—MARCUS TULLIUS CICERO

The hell to be endured hereafter, of which theology tells, is no worse than the hell we make for ourselves in this world by habitually fashioning our characters in the wrong way.

—WILLIAM JAMES

In the previous section, I advised you to get to know better your closest friend and ally: yourself. Now, let me introduce you to your worst enemy: also, yourself. The reason? Much as we'd like to believe otherwise, we humans are not always rational in our perceptions and decisions. We are susceptible to external influences and confirmation bias more than we often realize or care to admit. As Fromm put it:

> *Most people are convinced that as long as they are not overtly forced to do something by an outside power, their decisions are theirs, and that if they want something, it is they who want it. But this is one of the great illusions we have about ourselves. A great number of our decisions are not really our own but are suggested to us from the outside; we have succeeded in persuading ourselves that it is we who have made the decision,*

---

[17] Latin for: "Nothing is more hostile [to a person] than himself." Also commonly translated as, "Man is his own worst enemy."

*whereas we have actually conformed with expectations of others, driven
by the fear of isolation.*

We are often blind to our own faults and shortcomings and may try to rationalize
them when we become aware of them because they may seem intuitive, but we do so
without examining our intuitions rationally to see if they are correct. In the words of
Samuel Johnson:

> *No weakness of the human mind has more frequently incurred ani-
> madversion than the negligence with which men overlook their own
> faults, however flagrant, and the easiness with which they pardon them,
> however frequently repeated.*

Self-knowledge can help you recognize situations when your gut instincts may lead
you astray: situations where acting against your intuition or even against your short-
term comfort may be preferable to what may seem obvious—situations when doing
things "the hard way" may yield you greater freedom and more meaningful living in the
long-term.

Much of our behavior, perceptions, emotions, and beliefs, are shaped by factors we
implicitly take for granted or fail to question and to justify rationally: factors like false
intuitions; the temptations of convenience, ease, or popularity; resistance to unravel
complexities; the desire to conform, placate, impress, or imitate others; overblown
estimates of risks or rewards; and irrational fears (such as fear of offending others,
being misunderstood, becoming isolated, or failing; or fear of missing out (FOMO) on
what other people are doing, often at the cost of missing out on useful and meaningful
things we could be doing).

We often accept as given pseudo-knowledge considered as "common sense," even
when it is demonstrably at odds with evidence or probabilities. Our instincts, shaped
by evolutionary selection to ensure our survival in a different world than the one we
live in today, sometimes cause us to favor the safety of going along with the tribe even
when such allegiances may conflict with our interests as individuals. Platitudes such
as, "better safe than sorry," when taken to an extreme, may in hindsight make us feel
greater sorrow for having chosen the safe route than the sorrow we would have felt if
we had taken a risk and failed.

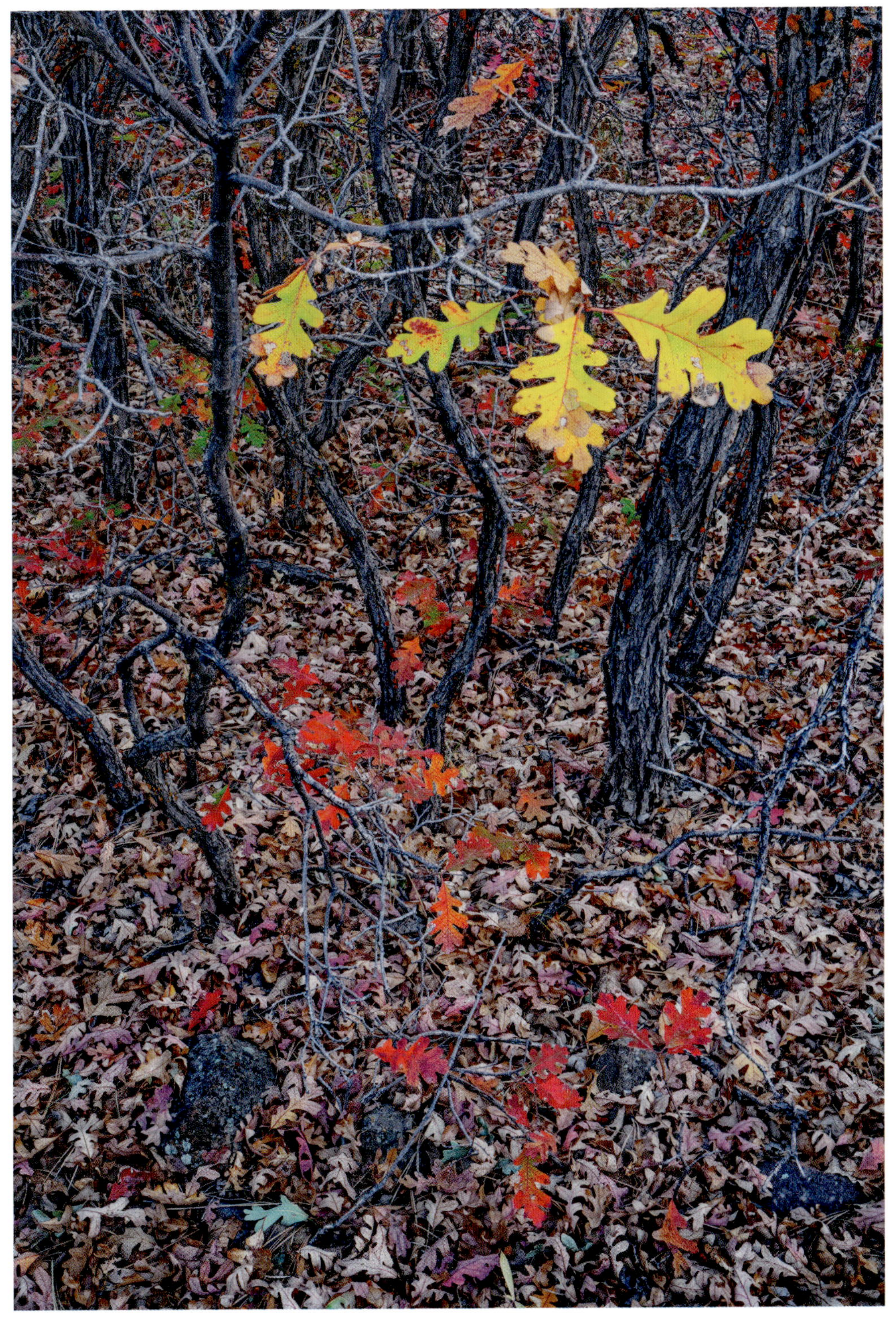

Most unfortunate, by sticking to and refusing to deviate from some common customs, sensibilities, and traditions that may no longer serve useful purposes—and may even diminish our welfare for no rational reason—we may end up denying ourselves opportunities for authentic living in trade for the lesser benefit of avoiding short-lived discomfort or conflict, or for those averse to solitude, finding a community that is more closely aligned with our own values.

This is especially true of artistic activities, which we are ostensibly free to pursue according to our own sensibilities and philosophies, largely or entirely free of coercion or risk, for the sheer purpose of elevating our own lives—activities that, if we are willing to engage in them seriously, invest time and effort in them, and accept certain degrees of calculated risk, may reward us with such profound inner states as flow, awe, a sense of self-worth, fulfillment, and well-earned pride in our creations, regardless of anyone else's judgment or understanding of them.

Common areas where artists often fail to act in their own best interests and opt instead for compliance and lesser rewards include conformity, preconception, impatience, laziness, distraction, plagiarism, club mentality, and competition. I will expand on these in other parts of the book, but I'll highlight here a few factors that are shared among some or all of them.

One of these factors is *hedonic adaptation*, which I mentioned in the essay on happiness.[18] Hedonic adaptation is the tendency to return to a baseline of happiness after each accomplishment. No matter how attractive something might seem or how happy you feel once you have it, it will soon become less satisfying. This effect, known as the *hedonic treadmill*, is reminiscent of what Schopenhauer referred to as "the will"—the force of endless, purposeless striving that drives all natural phenomena. Since there's no limit or final goal to this striving, no matter what you accomplish you will always find yourself wanting more. Hedonic adaptation, like Schopenhauer's will, is also a source of much misery because if you always want more than you have, you will never feel satisfied. Artist and mystic William Blake offered this bit of relevant wisdom: "You never know what is enough, until you know what is more than enough." In his *Meditations*, Marcus Aurelius suggested this simple exercise to help resist the will (i.e., the hedonic treadmill):

> *Don't imagine having things that you don't have. Rather, pick the best of the things that you do have and think of how much you would want them if you didn't have them.*

---

[18] See page 7.

It takes effort and willpower to force yourself off the hedonic treadmill, to resist the natural drive to always want more—more popularity, more income, more gear, more awards, more fame, bigger, faster, newer, shinier ... even when, considered objectively, they serve no practical purpose and have no lasting effect on your overall satisfaction and sense of meaning in life. The alternative: Seek meaningful experiences that may reward you with intangible rewards such as flow, contentment, and lasting memories. Also, once you accustom yourself to states of mind like mindfulness and immersion in creative activities, these rewards will become more frequent and predictable, and will not require you to compromise your own sensibilities and priorities to appease any judge or audience, nor to oversimplify your work to appeal to other people's expectations and common tastes. Odds are, they will also make you happier by saving you time and money.

Another example of being your own enemy is allowing other people too much power to control your behavior and feelings—for example, caring too much about how you may appear to others and pretending to be (or even convincing yourself that you are) someone who is not truly *you* just to fit in with some community or club or to stay current with some fleeting fashion. As Nietzsche put it, "We are like shop windows in which we are continually arranging, concealing or illuminating the supposed qualities others ascribe to us—in order to deceive ourselves."

In his play *Huis Clos* (No Exit), Sartre famously wrote, "L'enfer, c'est les autres" (hell is other people). The expression is often misinterpreted to mean that other people, by their petty actions and demands, may cause us anxiety and discomfort. But that's not what Sartre meant. What he meant was this: We make ourselves miserable when we judge ourselves according to what we believe other people think of us. A good way to avoid this effect is to remind yourself of the words of Michel de Montaigne:

> *No one but you knows whether you are cowardly and cruel or loyal and devout. Others never see you; they only guess about you by uncertain conjectures. They do not see your nature so much as they see your artifice. So do not cling to their judgments; cling to your own.*

Another, often more entertaining, way of ridding yourself of feeling beholden to other people's opinions is to remind yourself that they, too, like all people, are flawed and irrational in their own ways, even if they conceal it well. So, why would you take them seriously? "Who are these people whose admiration you seek?" asked Epictetus.

"Aren't they the ones you are used to describing as mad? Well, then, is that what you want—to be admired by lunatics?"

Be wary also of aspiring too much for perfection or to prove yourself "better" than others for sheer vanity. In art, "better" is always—and can only be—a relative and subjectively determined qualification. More important, it is a meaningless qualification if it causes you to sacrifice your artistic sensibilities and aspirations to impress others. Instead of aspiring to be *the* best, aspire instead for your own personal best— your own highest level of achievement that accords with your personality, resources, opportunities, and inner rewards. You don't have to beat an Olympic runner to gain great personal benefits from jogging. You don't have to outdo a celebrated chef to enjoy cooking. You don't have to be a professional bestselling artist to gain the emotional, elevating benefits of artmaking.

One of the greatest bits of wisdom of Stoic philosophy is this: The only thing better than to have something is to not need it. "Whenever you see another man holding office, set against this the fact that you have no need to hold office," wrote Epictetus. "If someone else is wealthy, see what you have instead. For if you have nothing instead, you are miserable; while *if in place of wealth you have no need of wealth, know that you possess something more than he does, and much greater in value.*" (Italics mine)

Is an artist who feels in competition with others—who is constantly courting galleries and publications hoping to win the approval of juries or editors or social media fans, and who may be driven to despair and self-doubt if failing to gain these things— better off than an artist who genuinely doesn't care about such things and is satisfied entirely with the inner rewards of making art? The former must always consider the opinions and tastes of other people when creating, and likely will feel jilted if other artists' works are deemed more worthy than their own. Why give other people such power over your welfare? The latter, on the other hand, is free from such concerns and may create in peace and follow the muses wherever they may lead without fear of judgment or failure.

Of course, those who must earn a living in art have to produce works that others will consider worth paying for. But there's no rule that says an artist must choose between making popular art and personal art. You may make some work meant for sale or to draw public interest, and other work meant to elevate your life. The two don't necessarily need to overlap. Just as an engineer or an accountant may spend part of their time working to benefit others while still making time to pursue their personal, creative work for its own sake, so can professional artists.

BECOME A PHILOSOPHER

> Every work of imagination must have a philosophy; and every philosophy must be a work of art.
>
> —T. S. ELIOT

> To be a philosopher is not merely to have subtle thoughts, nor even to found a school, but so to love wisdom as to live according to its dictates, a life of simplicity, independence, magnanimity, and trust. It is to solve some of the problems of life, not only theoretically, but practically.
>
> —HENRY DAVID THOREAU

Whether you are aware of it or not, every aspect of your living is rooted in a philosophy you have evolved by learning, experiencing, and being influenced by others' thoughts. Some of your philosophy may even reflect instincts evolved by long-extinct life forms from which our species has ensued, predisposing us to certain behaviors and perceptions, to favoring some things over others, to liking or fearing certain things. No conscious person can get through a day or even make a single decision without having a philosophy: a sense of the nature and purpose of life, a moral compass, goals, aspirations, beliefs, views about other people, estimates of the possible consequences of certain choices, and so on.

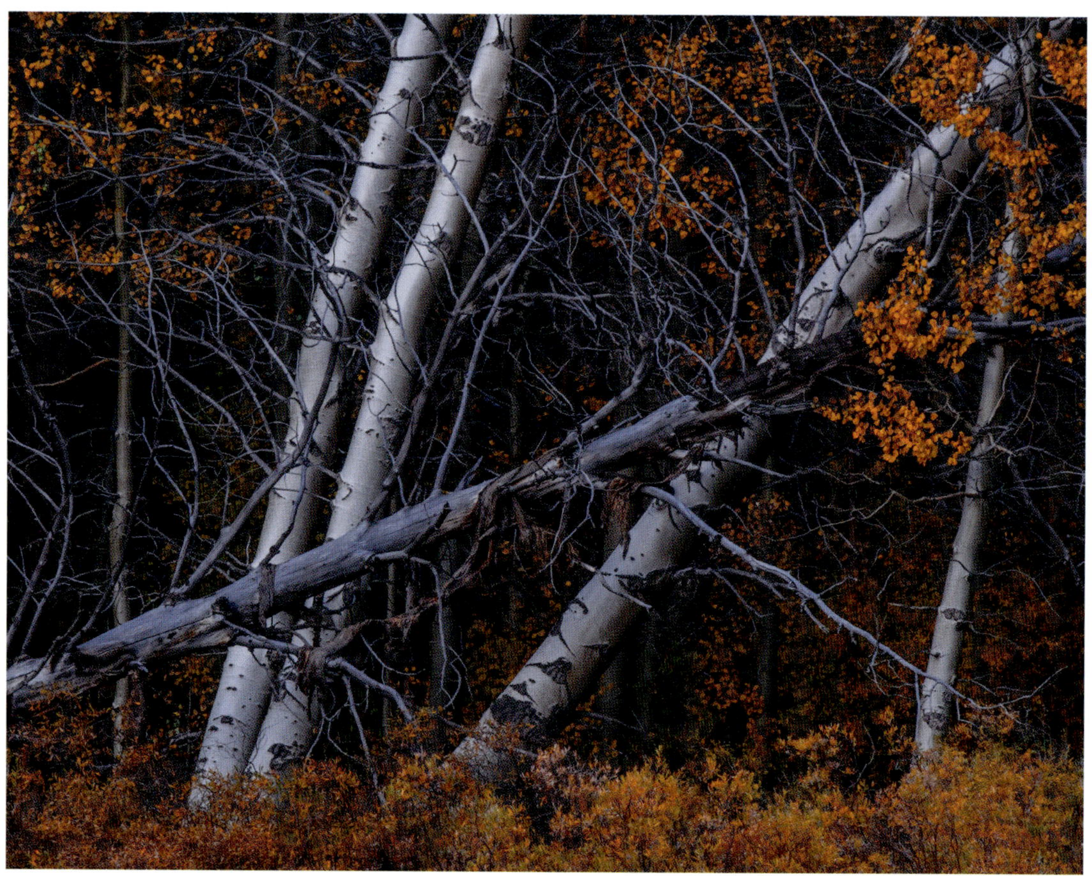

To become a philosopher—in the literal sense, a lover (and therefore seeker) of wisdom—doesn't necessarily mean studying philosophy in the academic sense. It means taking charge of shaping your life consciously: considering as much information as you can to decide your values, your beliefs, your ideas, even some aspects of your personality, rather than leaving these things to chance or accepting them uncritically from others. In this pursuit, it can be invaluable to consider what some of humanity's greatest thinkers had to say about important subjects. We each only get a limited time to live and limited access to the vast body of knowledge humanity has accumulated throughout history. None of us can come close to figuring out all these things by ourselves. Why not benefit from so much great wisdom freely available to us—wisdom conceived, refined, questioned, debated, and tested by some of the greatest minds that ever existed, over thousands of years?

It is tempting to take for granted ideas considered as "common sense" based on gut feelings—ideas that are too often accepted implicitly as correct because they are common, not necessarily because they make sense. The first thing you'll realize when you set out to study philosophy is that there are always more ways than one to think about things, and that nothing is as simple as it may first appear to be. Philosophical thinking will challenge, sometimes in jarring ways, practically all assumptions of certainty. You'll have to get over your fear of asking about quintessentially important things such questions as, "how do I know that?" "what if I'm wrong?" or "what will I do if I find out that some of my core beliefs are untenable?" To a philosopher there is only one obvious answer to such questions: Knowing is always better than not knowing.

Although absolute knowledge is not possible, the tools of philosophy can still help you decide which of several possible answers to an important question is most likely to be correct. You will find this attitude reflected in the words of many great philosophers in all eras and traditions. For example, Socrates famously proclaimed that an unexamined life is not worth living. René Descartes, considered the father of modern philosophy, wrote, "If you would be a real seeker after truth, it is necessary that at least once in your life you doubt, as far as possible, all things." Immanuel Kant, on the cusp of the Age of Enlightenment, wrote, "The duty of philosophy was to abolish the semblance arising from misinterpretation, even if many prized and beloved delusions have to be destroyed in the process." Bertrand Russell, a pioneer of analytic philosophy, declared, "The demand for certainty is one which is natural to man, but is nevertheless an intellectual vice." Simone de Beauvoir wrote, "I tore myself away from the safe comfort of certainties through my love for truth—and truth rewarded me."

Inevitably, when you realize there are different, sometimes even contradicting, ways to think about things, some ways will emerge as better than others—more rational, more probable, more meaningful, more effective, more rationally consistent, more rewarding, or more closely aligned with your personality, goals, and circumstances. In this sense, one of the greatest benefits of becoming a philosopher is that it will give you choices you may not have even known to consider otherwise: ways to think about life and about how to conduct yourself in the world, as well as ways to examine your choices and make informed decisions that best fit your life and temperament. Having a deeper understanding of the nature and implications of various choices that may be open to you will give you the confidence and courage to face life's most difficult and consequential decisions. It will also help you help others who may be struggling with difficult choices.

To not contemplate your own philosophy—to surrender unquestioningly to common, convenient beliefs without examining their rationality and how they stack up against alternatives—is also a choice, and despite being ostensibly easy, it is in fact a very severe one. Whether you choose a philosophy for yourself or allow others to choose your philosophy for you, once you settle on a philosophy you implicitly forfeit and deny yourself other possible philosophies, and whatever differences they may make in your life. By failing to make a conscious, informed, honest choice of a philosophy to live by, you don't avoid choosing; you are only ceding the choice to circumstances and other people, who may not always know better than you or have your best interest in mind. Existential philosophers refer to avoiding making your own choices as living in "bad faith" (which is the opposite of living authentically, or in "good faith").

Do you need to be a philosopher to be an artist? The answer depends on your definition of art. Certainly, you don't need to study philosophy to be an artist, perhaps even a successful one. But philosophy can help you better understand what *kind* of artist you may wish to become if you hope to reap the greatest rewards from both practicing and experiencing art.

Without philosophy you can still be an artist, albeit in a compartmentalized and specialized sense, separate from other aspects of life. Without philosophy, you may still enjoy being an artist; you may still be able to satisfy your professional aspirations in art; you may still make beautiful and popular works, and you may compete successfully with other artists. However, without philosophy, your art will be just that, your art, which would be a shame since art can be much more than that—much more than just a process for producing aesthetic and/or commercially sellable artifacts. With the help of philosophy, art may elevate and enrich your life in ways that no material rewards or externally conferred honors can—ways you may not even know are possible without philosophy.

Without philosophy, you may unwittingly deny yourself some of the *greatest* reward that art can offer you. Art can be a means to learning about, living as, expressing, and growing your true self. Among these rewards are such elevated and life-affirming states of mind as transcendence, awe, contentment, ecstasy, flow, a sense of purpose and deep satisfaction in good times, and "an asylum ... into which no tyranny can force its way" (Nietzsche's words) in challenging times.

As Samuel Taylor Coleridge wrote in his *Biographia Literania*, "No man was ever yet a great poet, without being at the same time a profound philosopher. For poetry is the blossom and the fragrance of all human knowledge, human thoughts, human passions, emotions, language."

If your only interests in art are extrinsic—to satisfy or impress others, earn income, become famous, compete, win awards, or share a hobby with a like-minded community—then certainly you can get by, and even become materially successful, without philosophy. But if your interests in art are, at least in part, intrinsic—to elevate the quality of your experiences; to arouse and sustain powerful, gratifying, or even cathartic feelings; to evolve and to strengthen your emotional resilience; to soothe a troubled mind or a wounded heart; to nurture calmness and confidence; to keep yourself creative, imaginative, and eager to learn for your entire lifetime, rather than succumb to boredom, rote, or apathy; to open yourself up to profound inspiration and spiritual revelations—you *need* philosophy.

So, become a philosopher. By this, I don't necessarily mean that you should become a professional or academic philosopher (although those may be very rewarding), but a philosopher in the literal sense of the term: a lover of wisdom.

> Enlightenment is man's leaving his self-caused immaturity. Immaturity is the incapacity to use one's intelligence without the guidance of another. Such immaturity is self-caused if it is not caused by lack of intelligence, but by lack of determination and courage to use one's intelligence without being guided by another. Sapere Aude![19] Have the courage to use your own intelligence!
>
> —IMMANUEL KANT

Recall that philosophy is the love of wisdom. But is wisdom enough? Specifically, is there a point to wisdom if it does not guide your life and manifest in your beliefs and choices? For wisdom to affect meaningful change in your life, another ingredient is needed: courage. My next bit of advice to you is therefore this: Become not just a philosopher, but a courageous philosopher—a philosopher who seeks after wisdom not just for its own sake, but also with the goal of having wisdom guide your life. As Kant put it: *Dare* to be wise. Wisdom is of limited use if it does not translate into action. In some cases, acting wisely may be easy, enjoyable, and immediately rewarding. In other cases, it may be difficult, risky, and not guaranteed to reward beyond knowing that you are living in the most honest and authentic way you can.

---

[19] Latin for "dare to know," or "dare to be wise."

Becoming a philosopher may open the door for you to a richly meaningful and satisfying life. But if you do not also find the courage to step through this door—to live your philosophy—then becoming a philosopher may instead lead you to a life of regret and dissatisfaction, knowing or speculating about what you may be missing, perhaps even suspecting that it can be within your reach, if only you had the courage to try it. This in turn may make you bitter and cynical, and color even your finest moments with regrets and what-ifs.

"Life," wrote Anaïs Nin, "shrinks or expands in proportion to one's courage." Existential psychologist Rollo May concurred. "Courage," he wrote, "is not a virtue or value among other personal values like love or fidelity. It is the foundation that underlies and gives reality to all other virtues and personal values."

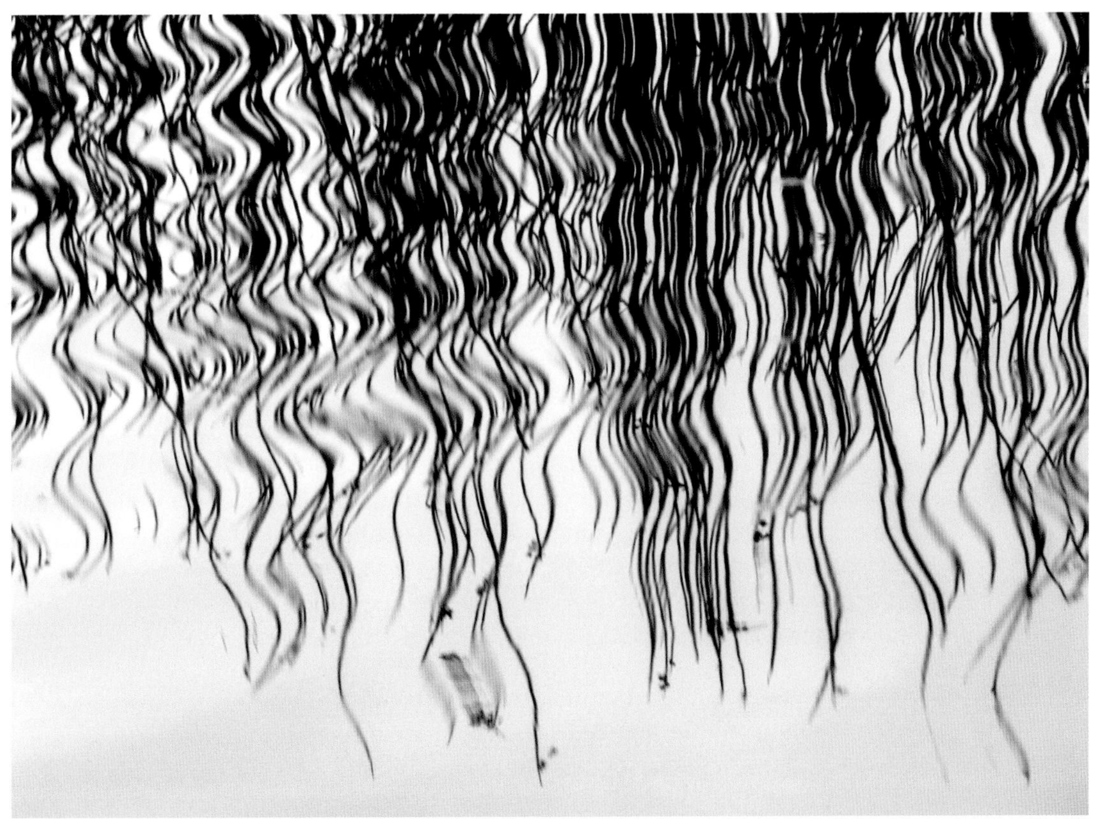

Of course, courage is no guarantee of success. Sometimes, courageous decisions may leave you in some ways worse off than you were before making them. But that doesn't mean they are without value. To know you have tried—that you have it in you to make courageous decisions—is a great and lasting reward in itself. "There is no comparison," wrote Francis Bacon, "between that which is lost by not succeeding and that which is lost by not trying." And John Updike, reflecting on the courage of J. D. Salinger, wrote, "The refusal to rest content, the willingness to risk excess on behalf of one's obsessions, is what distinguishes artists from entertainers, and what makes some artists adventurers on behalf of us all."

Beyond the importance of courage in guiding your life, courage is also important in how you practice your art. In his book *The Courage to Create*, May emphasized the importance of courage to both artists and society in making creative (i.e., original) and self-expressive art. He wrote, "If you do not express your own original ideas, if you do not listen to your own being, you will have betrayed yourself. Also you will have betrayed our community in failing to make your contribution to the whole." Courage in art, according to May, is also needed because (despite so many rosy platitudes promoted by self-appointed "creativity coaches") living and working creatively is not always fun. As May put it, "I believe in life, and I believe in the joy of human existence, but these things cannot be experienced except as we also face the despair, also face the anxiety that every human being has to face if he lives with any creativity at all."

Maslow made similar statements, linking courage with the inevitable risks involved in striving for novelty—for work and ideas that may depart from established traditions and from other people's expectations. He wrote:

> *Every one of our great creators, our god-like people, has testified to the element of courage that is needed in the lonely moment of creation, affirming something new (contradictory to the old). This is a kind of daring, a going out in front all alone, a defiance, a challenge. The moment of fright is quite understandable but must nevertheless be overcome if creation is to be possible. Thus to discover in oneself a great talent can certainly bring exhilaration but it also brings a fear of the dangers and responsibilities and duties of being a leader and of being all alone.*

Beyond anything else, it takes special courage, once you have learned who you are, to be that person—your extraordinary self. It should go without saying that to be extraordinary is to depart from what is ordinary.

"The real fool, such as the gods mock or mar," wrote Oscar Wilde (to his former lover who betrayed him), "is he who does not know himself. I was such a one too long. You have been such a one too long. Be so no more. Do not be afraid. The supreme vice is shallowness." Shallowness—lack of depth—means going about life at surface level, not just presenting a convenient façade to the world, but believing yourself to be no deeper than that façade, ignoring or deliberately suppressing deeper and more complex aspects that nonetheless exist in any human personality. This is what Wilde meant by shallowness being a "supreme vice": pretending to be something other or lesser than you really are or can be—someone you (or others) feel you *should* be. The price you may pay for such shallowness is literally your life. You may still draw breath, but the life you live will be the life of a fictional—shallower—character who is not you, or at least not all of you.

When it comes to courage in art, perhaps no one put it as succinctly as Henri Matisse who said, "Creativity takes courage." He also wrote in a letter to Léon Degand, "An artist is an explorer. He has to begin by self-discovery and by observation of his own procedure. After that he must not feel under any constraint." Elsewhere, he wrote, "An artist should never be a prisoner of himself, a prisoner of manner, a prisoner of reputation, or a prisoner of success."

CHOOSE THE KIND OF ARTIST YOU WISH TO BE

The thing of course, is to make yourself alive. Most people remain all of their lives in a stupor. The point of being an artist is that you may live.

Many artists begin practicing their craft as hobbyists, imitating others. Once they accomplish a degree of technical proficiency, popularity, or financial success, they begin referring to themselves as artists, but largely continue to do things in the same way they did before. Perhaps they upgrade their equipment and materials along the way, but they rarely take the time to expand their knowledge of art or their chosen medium, to experiment with new styles, to seek inspiration in other art forms, to examine their motivations beyond just keeping up an enjoyable practice, or to deepen their philosophy. Why mess with success?

This attitude is unfortunate for two reasons: As an individual, it may cause you to miss out on some of the greatest rewards and most meaningful experiences that artmaking has to offer. Also, as a member of a society, it may limit your artistic contributions largely to "more of the same," sometimes perpetuating prejudices, styles, and obsolete ethics long after they have served their usefulness, making it harder for more innovative creators to become recognized or established.

My advice: Don't become an artist by passively (or retroactively) adopting a definition of art to fit the work you are already doing. Instead, take some time and put in the effort to learn about all the things that art can be, and then strive for the kind (and definition) of art that seems most meaningful to you. Likely, it will be a definition that will set a high and difficult bar for you to aspire to; demand greater investment of time, effort, and skill; be riskier to pursue than other definitions may allow for; and push you further than you already are along the continuum between just striving to have fun and striving for individuality, expression, and excellence.

Ansel Adams lamented the temptation of ease in photography. In his essay "A Personal Credo," he wrote, "I have often thought that if photography were difficult in the true sense of the term—meaning that the creation of a simple photograph would entail as much time and effort as the production of a good watercolor or etching— there would be a vast improvement in total output. The sheer ease with which we can produce a superficial image often leads to creative disaster."

Ted Orland (art teacher and Adams's former assistant) extended the same idea to all artistic work. In his book *The View From The Studio Door*, he wrote, "We recognize that someone has found their voice when their distinctive spiritual or emotional core becomes an inseparable part of their art. Reaching that threshold means letting the concerns and influences of others fall away, so that your own voice is heard clearly. *It takes a whole lot of dedication and conviction and hard work and talent and luck to make that happen—but most of all it takes time.*" (Italics mine)

Recall the definition of art I chose to apply in my own work: "the *expression* or application of human creative skill and imagination." (*Oxford Dictionary*; italics mine) It should be clear to you now that what I strive for in my own work is this: committing to invest as much of my time and attention as I can in learning and striving to become a learned, creative, and self-expressive person.

One implication of this definition is that it doesn't matter so much what you do or how good you are at it. It matters more that your work is challenging, engaging, and meaningful to you. Aspiring to creativity (i.e., striving to find novel concepts to express in your work and novel ways to do so) and self-expression (i.e., channeling your own authentic experiences into your work) checks all these boxes.

You will find that the very pursuit of these goals—creativity and self-expression— also goes hand in hand with learning and becoming who you are. Self-expression will force you to acknowledge and articulate consciously what you are feeling, why you are feeling it, and how to share it with the world. It will also motivate you to live such that you have feelings and experiences worth expressing. Creativity, being intrinsically tied to various personality traits, will prompt you to explore (and expand) the boundaries of your own innate abilities—your degree of openness and curiosity, the richness of your imagination, your capacity to innovate, your courage to depart from conventions. Albert Camus expressed this idea succinctly and poetically, long before the psychology of flow became the subject of scientific research. In *The Myth of Sisyphus*, he wrote,

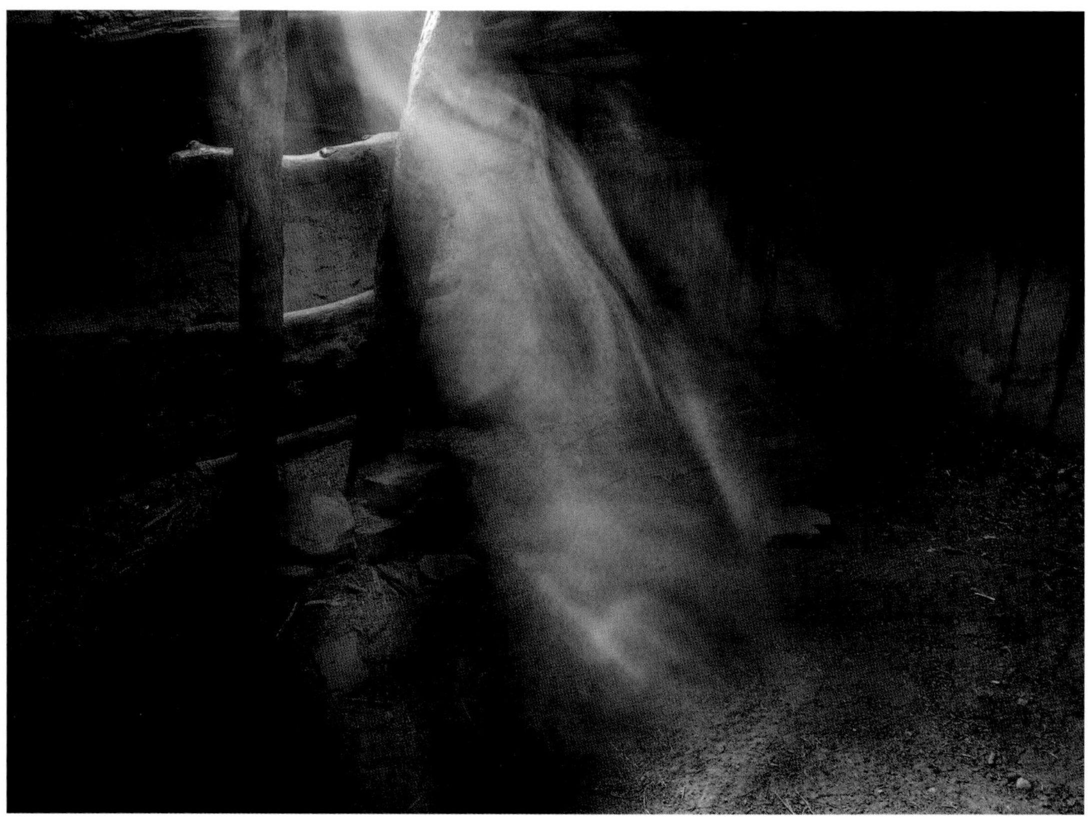

"To create is … to give a shape to one's fate. For all these characters [referring to creators], their work defines them at least as much as it is defined by them."

The word *art* comes from the Latin *artem*, which refers not to objects possessing aesthetic appeal, but to things created consciously and deliberately (as opposed to things occurring randomly or naturally). When you align your choices, in life and in art, with your own personality and freely chosen values (as existential thinkers suggest you should), you will in a sense create your own self and your own life. This is the premise behind my earlier recommendation to consider your own life as your most important work of art.

> The important thing for me, then, is not the "work," but my life. Life is not the means for the achievement of an esthetic ideal of perfection; on the contrary, the work is an ethical symbol of life.
>
> —THOMAS MANN

In the late eighteenth century, after a period of flourishing in science and rationalism helped the world emerge from the thousand-year period known as the Middle Ages (sometimes also referred to as the "Dark Ages") into what we now term the modern era, philosopher Immanuel Kant published his seminal book *Critique of Pure Reason*. You may fairly wonder why a brilliant philosopher (who literally penned an article defining the term Enlightenment, referring to that historic period) may object to the use of pure reason to understand the world and decide how to comport yourself in it (i.e., as a basis for ethics).

Kant's view, formally known as *transcendental idealism*, is that our minds give rise to a humanistic perception of the world that is not necessarily the same as the real world. In other words, we can never know, by reason or by any other method, what the absolute, complete reality of the world is; we can only know how this reality presents itself to us—to our human senses and intellect. This idea of distinguishing the world as it really is (what Kant called "noumena," or "things in themselves") from the way the world appears to us (what Kant called "phenomena") has revolutionized philosophical thinking ever since, and has been affirmed more recently by various scientific studies into the nature of existence (e.g., the picture of reality arising from Einstein's theory of relativity, and from quantum physics) and the nature of our consciousness and perceptions (e.g., studies in neuroscience and evolutionary biology attempting to decipher how and why consciousness manifests in the brain).

I mention this separation between our perceptions of reality and what things really are because it is an underlying theme in practically every other philosophy I refer to in this book. Indeed, the very notion that we have the power to choose how to interpret the world and to consciously shape our living experiences—to become who we are—is rooted in the idea that our mental image of the world has to be different from what the world "really is," which is beyond our ability to change (or, according to some philosophers, even to know).

In *Critique of Pure Reason*, Kant made this profound statement:

> *All interest of my reason (the speculative as well as the practical) is united in the following three questions:*
>
> *1. What can I know?*
>
> *2. What should I do?*
>
> *3. What may I hope?*

In response to his own first question, Kant offered an elaborate system of metaphysics. His response to his second question came in the form of his second book, *Critique of Practical Reason*. Alas, both are deeply esoteric and, despite their depth and profound influence on the works of later philosophers, beyond the scope and purpose of this book.

Kant's answer to the third question is perhaps most relevant to the advice I offer in this book. It consists of two parts: The first, according to Kant, is to consider that "all hope concerns happiness"; that is, we hope for things that will make our lives better. But he also added an important twist: We must not live for the sake of things that will make us happy; instead, we must live with "no other motive than the worthiness to be happy." Put another way, experiencing happiness should not be a goal in itself. To make our lives most meaningful, our goal must instead be to live such that we are worthy of happiness, and hope that happiness may find us at various points along our journey.[20]

---

[20] If you are an American, this idea may already be familiar to you. The United States Constitution guarantees the rights to life, liberty, and *the pursuit* of happiness, but not happiness itself. This shows the great prescience of the framers in realizing the greater importance not of happiness but of striving to be worthy of it.

The corollary to this view is also important: If we achieve some form of happiness by unethical means, or too easily, it will not satisfy.

Before offering you a very short summary of my own answers to Kant's questions, I urge you to now pause, think about, and write down your own. Your answers may guide you and may even change as you read through the rest of this book.

My answers:

1. I can know that I am a living, conscious being, only on this earth for a short period of time—i.e., that my allotment of moments in which I get to experience, to learn, to think, and to feel, is limited and precious. I can know what many great thinkers and artists have offered the world.

2. I should strive to understand myself, the nature of the world, the sources of meaning in life, and the experiences of other living beings, as honestly and objectively as I can. I should then use this understanding to guide my ethics and choices.

3. I may hope that as I grow older, I will also grow wiser. I may also hope that whenever I pause to reflect on my life, I may do so objectively, with few regrets, and with the sense that I put my limited supply of conscious, living moments to good use.

As my answers to these questions guide my choices in life, and as my artistic work aims to express my life experiences arising from these choices, the connection between my philosophy and my art should explain why, as I wrote in the introduction to this book, I consider my life my most important work of art, and why the most important bit of advice I have to offer you is this: Think of your own life as your most important work of art too. Make it as good and as meaningful as you can.

CULTIVATE INDIVIDUALISM

> What I must do is all that concerns me, not what the people
> think. This rule, equally arduous in actual and in intellectual
> life, may serve for the whole distinction between greatness
> and meanness. It is the harder because you will always find
> those who think they know what is your duty better than you
> know it. It is easy in the world to live after the world's opinion;
> it is easy in solitude to live after our own; but the great man
> is he who in the midst of the crowd keeps with perfect
> sweetness the independence of solitude.
>
> —RALPH WALDO EMERSON

In an age when mass media is more pervasive than ever, when the influence of celebrities, advertisers, pundits, politicians, or even random people on social media have the power to sway public opinions and tastes, staying true to yourself requires diligence and effort. It requires consciously protecting your "me time" from the addictive temptation of endless doom-scrolling, the constant distraction of unimportant alerts, and getting caught up in futile arguments. It requires awareness of, and resistance to, the very unfortunate effect of FOMO. It requires the discipline to disconnect occasionally from the onslaught of news, posts, status updates, advertisements, political skirmishes, celebrity gossip, and pointless bantering. It requires nurturing the courage and discipline to then use these disconnected times to affirm and invest in your own personality, interests, ideas, emotional well-being, and creative endeavors, regardless of outcome and what other people think or even know about how you choose to invest *your* time.

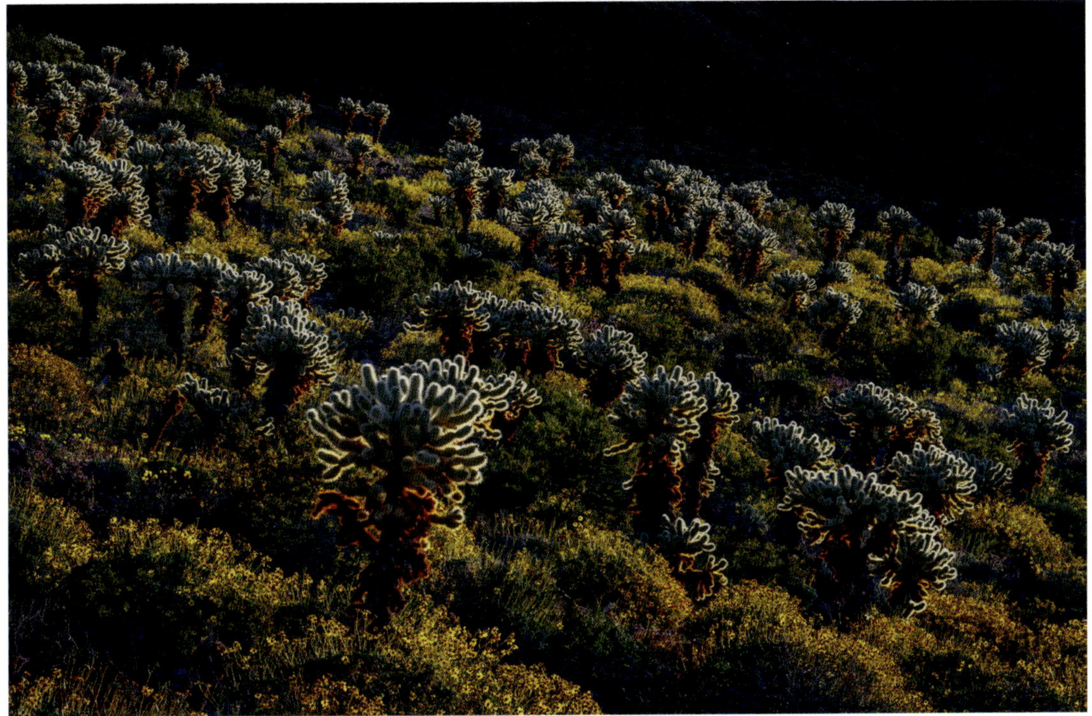

A common theme in the writings of many of the thinkers and artists I mention in this book is individualism—the quality of being to the best of your ability (which is always a matter of degree), an independent, self-reliant, free-thinking, and self-directed person.

This is especially the case when it comes to setting aside and protecting times for activities like artmaking, times in which you are free to pursue your work and interests on your own terms, without distractions, coercions, or the expectations of other people. As Oscar Wilde put it, "A work of art is the unique result of a unique temperament. Its beauty comes from the fact that the author is what he is. It has nothing to do with the fact that other people want what they want.... *Art is the most intense mode of individualism that the world has known.* I am inclined to say that it is the only real mode of individualism that the world has known.... But alone, without any reference to his neighbours, without any interference, the artist can fashion a beautiful thing; and if he does not do it solely for his own pleasure, he is not an artist at all."

Wilde was not alone in emphasizing the importance of individuality in art. For example, Johann Wolfgang von Goethe wrote, "Individuality of expression is the beginning and end of all art." Albert Camus wrote, "Any thought that abandons unity glorifies diversity. And diversity is the home of art." Bertrand Russell wrote, "It is this distinctive individuality that is loved by the artist, whether painter or writer. The artist himself, and the man who is creative in no matter what direction, has more of it than the average man."

"In his heart," wrote Friedrich Nietzsche, "every man knows quite well that, being unique, he will be in the world only once and that no imaginable chance will for a second time gather together into a unity so strangely variegated an assortment as he is: he knows it but he hides it like a bad conscience—why? From fear of his neighbor, who demands conventionality and cloaks himself with it.... Artists alone hate this sluggish promenading in borrowed fashions and appropriated opinions and they reveal everyone's secret bad conscience, the law that every man is a unique miracle."

An especially pernicious limitation to individualism in art is the false belief that you are only "allowed" to choose from among a small handful of possibilities: acceptable styles, methods, traditions, subjects, or from a finite set of "isms." This may give you the illusion of choosing freely without realizing there may be more possibilities available to you beyond the range of options acceptable to others. As Noam Chomsky explained it, "The smart way to keep people passive and obedient is to strictly limit the spectrum of acceptable opinion, but allow very lively debate within that spectrum. That gives people the sense that there's free thinking going on, while all the time the presuppositions of the system are being reinforced by the limits put on the range of the debate."

As an individual you are free to accept only some (or no) aspects of any ideology or tradition, and you are also free to come up with your own. Certainly, departing from the herd may result in some undesirable consequences, but so long as these are not too dire, then so what? As Russell put it, "One should respect public opinion in so far as is necessary to avoid starvation and to keep out of prison, but anything that goes beyond this is voluntary submission to an unnecessary tyranny, and is likely to interfere with happiness in all kinds of ways."

Being a true individualist doesn't necessarily mean being reclusive or antisocial (although these may be legitimate life choices if they align with your personality). Being an individualist is ultimately about three things: knowing what choices are available to you, having a way of comparing and prioritizing these choices according to your own values and sensibilities, and having the courage to choose the option that best fits you. Otherwise, feel yourself free to, as Walt Whitman put it, "dismiss whatever insults your own soul."

BECOME A MORE INTERESTED PERSON

Once they are through the process of education, most people
lose the capacity of wondering, of being surprised. They feel
they ought to know everything, and hence that it is a sign
of ignorance to be surprised at or puzzled by anything. The
world loses its characteristic of being full of wonder and is
taken for granted. The capacity to be puzzled is indeed the
premise of all creation, be it in art or in science.

—ERICH FROMM

Photographer Jay Maisel offered what I believe to be one of the best bits of advice for any artist. He said, "If you want to take more interesting photos, become a more interesting person." Taking the liberty of generalizing Maisel's statement beyond just the medium of photography, I think it remains just as true in this broader form: If you want to make more interesting *art*, become a more interesting person.

Keen readers may perhaps wonder whether I mistyped the title of this essay. I did not. People don't become interesting in a vacuum. To become a more interesting person, you must first become a more *interested* person: a curious person, an adventurous person, a thinker, a learner, a seeker, an experimenter, an inventor, a skeptic, an investigator, a rebel. You must be willing to examine your values and convictions, to consider them against other ideas and evidence, and to adapt, refine, or even change your views, your work, and your life if your examinations reveal errors in your thinking or better, more authentic ways of experiencing the world and making meaning of it.

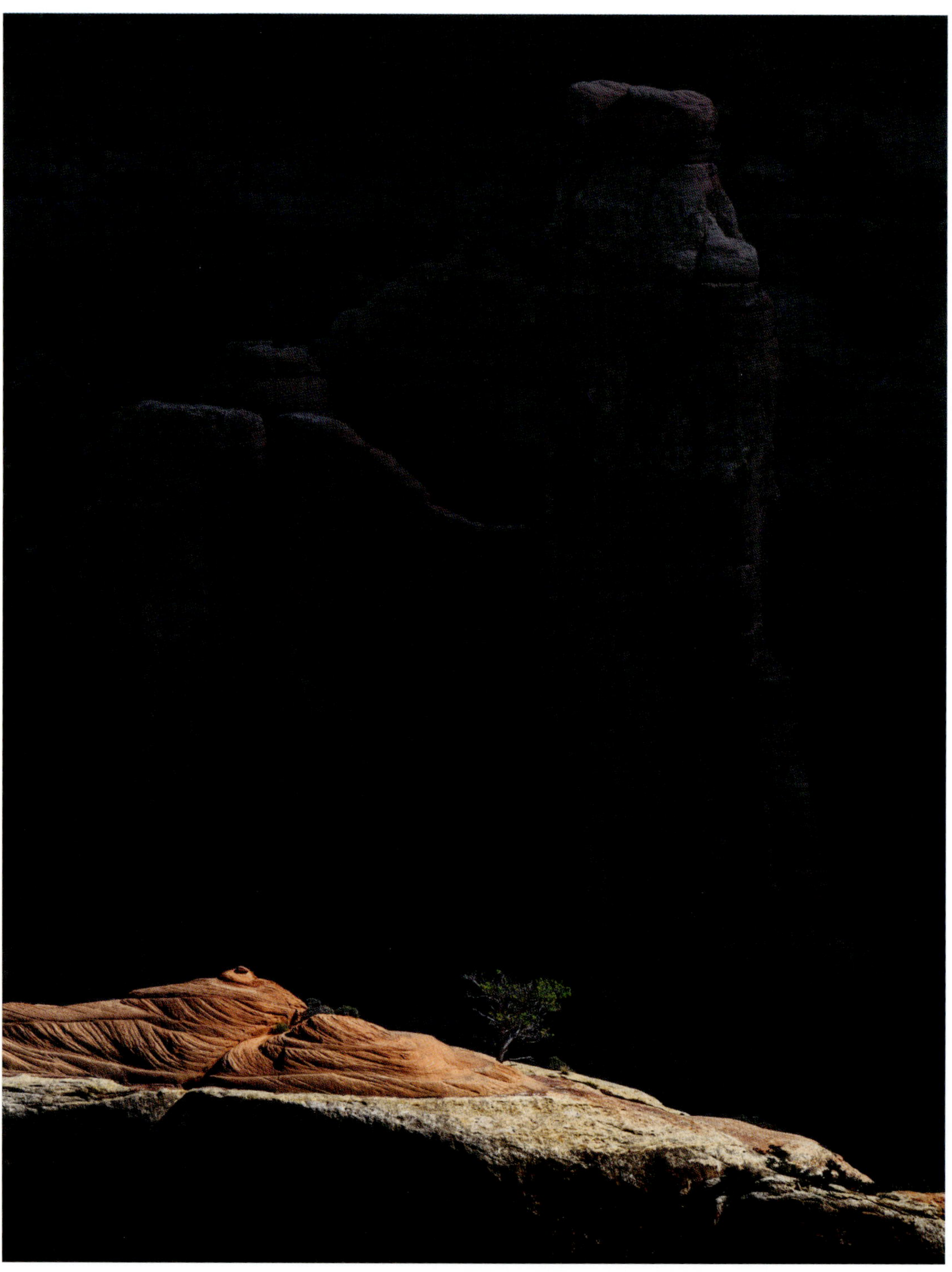

To become a more interested person is, to borrow a term from Rollo May, to evolve *creative courage*. In his words: "Whereas moral courage is the righting of wrongs, creative courage, in contrast, is the discovering of new forms, new symbols, new patterns…" Painter and educator Robert Henri expressed a similar sentiment in his book *The Art Spirit*. He wrote:

> *When the artist is alive in any person, whatever his kind of work may be, he becomes an inventive, searching, daring, self-expressing creature. He becomes interesting to other people. He disturbs, upsets, enlightens, and he opens ways for a better understanding. Where those who are not artists are trying to close the book, he opens it, shows there are still more pages possible.*
>
> *The world would stagnate without him, and the world would be beautiful with him; for he is interesting to himself and he is interesting to others.*

What interests you besides the technical or social aspects of your art? How much do you know about your subjects? The history of your medium? The musings of great artists and thinkers that came before you? Current thinking about art by subject matter experts? The science behind artistic expression? Correlations and differences between your medium of choice and other art media? Whatever it is, whether related directly to your work or not, dedicate time to study it in depth—to read about it, to think about it, to mine it for meaning as deeply as you can, and to consider its implications. But don't stop there. Once you have learned enough about one subject, switch to another.

Beyond just becoming familiar with known aspects of art and of your medium, also strive to introduce mystery into your life and work. Define the boundaries of your unknown and contemplate ways to investigate beyond them, to express your questions and doubts in your art, to contemplate what the answers might be and how you can make inroads toward exploring and discovering them. Ask yourself big questions about art and life, even questions you may not expect to find answers for. "The job of the artist," remarked Francis Bacon, "is always to deepen the mystery." Painter Georges Braque agreed, saying, "If there is no mystery, then there is no poetry, the quality I value above all else in art." Photographer Wynn Bullock explained the personal value of mystery:

*Searching is everything—going beyond what you know. And the test
of the search is really in the things themselves, the things you seek to
understand. What is important is not what you think about them, but
how they enlarge you.*

Schopenhauer, in his essay "The Wisdom of Life," explained why the most important factor in shaping your experiences—whether they are good or bad, shallow or
deep, meaningful or mundane—is your own personality. Similar circumstances may
lead different people to different interpretations, depending on their attitudes: whether
they are willing to open themselves up to powerful emotions; whether they are jaded or
cynical; whether they immerse themselves in their experiences and contemplate their
deeper meanings, or become distracted by other activities or concerns.

According to Schopenhauer, what a person *is*—the sum of a person's temperament, health, ethics, intellect, sensitivity, knowledge—is by far the most important
factor in determining the quality of a person's experiences, rather than such factors as
wealth or possessions, or the opinions of other people. Personality—what you are—is
also the one thread that runs through and binds all your experiences, and therefore
has the greatest effect on your sense of meaning and happiness in life. Explaining the
importance of taking deep interest in things to elevate your life, Schopenhauer wrote:

*The world in which a man lives shapes itself chiefly by the way in which
he looks at it, and so it proves different to different men; to one it is
barren, dull, and superficial; to another rich, interesting, and full of
meaning. On hearing of the interesting events which have happened in
the course of a man's experience, many people will wish that similar
things had happened in their lives too, completely forgetting that they
should be envious rather of the mental aptitude which lent those events
the significance they possess when he describes them.*

Open your eyes. Train yourself to become mindful of every nuance of your experience as it happens—your perceptions, your emotions, your senses—and seek the
deepest pleasure and meaning in it that you can find. Resist being distracted. Don't
casually dismiss any aspects of your experience that may seem on their face unimportant or unexciting. Research and study anything you come across that may be
relevant to your work or your experiences that you feel you should understand better.

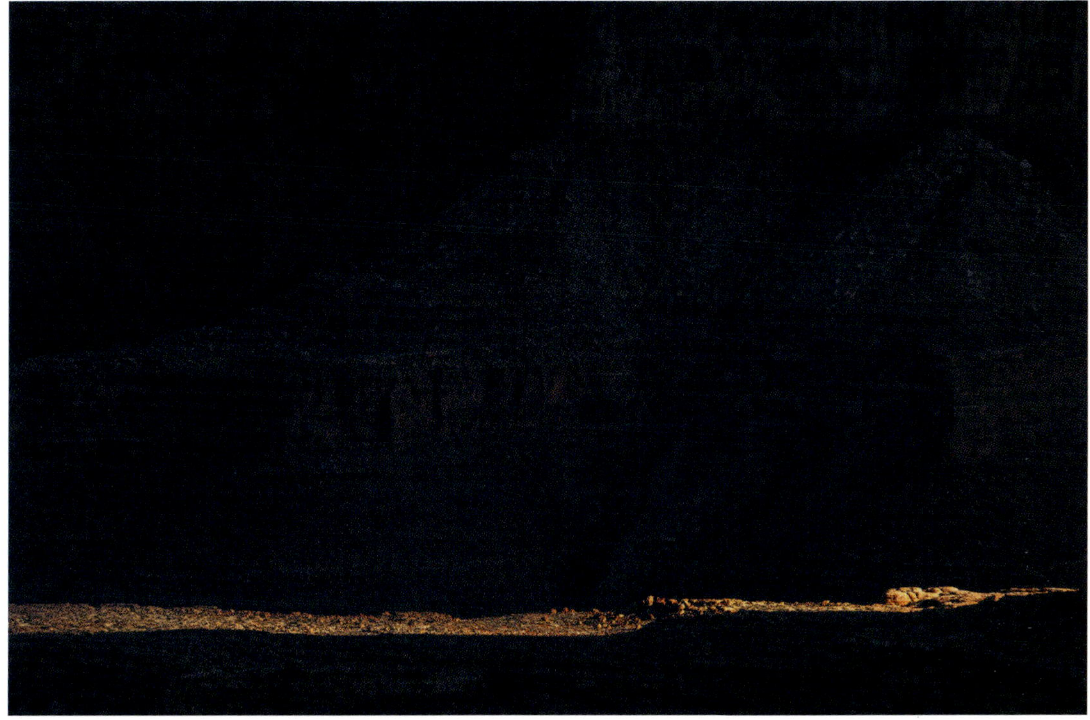

Consider that *you* get to decide for yourself whether anything is important, exciting, or interesting. Learn as much as you can, about whatever interests you, and always stay open to discovering—or developing—new interests.

Find out what the great thinkers—people with deeper knowledge, insight, or sensitivity than you, whether they are philosophers or scientists or artists or anyone who has discovered deeper meaning in anything—have, or had, to say. Assimilate from them whatever fits with your own personality and enriches your life.

Wonder about everything, no matter how ordinary or obvious it may seem. Find out how flowers grow, the meanings of words like "art" and "creativity," what scientists have learned about the nature of consciousness, what quantum mechanics is all about, why other people may have opinions and beliefs that are different from yours, or anything else that enters your mind that you wish you understood better or that just makes you go, "huh."

Become a more interested person and you will become a more interesting person.

> It is difficult for an artist to live in an environment in which everything is judged by its utility, rather than by its intrinsic quality. The whole side of life of which art is the flower requires something which may be called disinterestedness, a capacity for direct enjoyment without thought of tomorrow's problems and difficulties.
>
> —BERTRAND RUSSELL

What comes to your mind when you see a picture of a beautiful scene or object? Do you immediately wonder whether it really looked as it appears in the picture? Where it might be? What tools or techniques the artist used to produce such a compelling rendition? If so, you may be cheating yourself out of a deeper and more meaningful art experience.

Any object or experience presented to you as a work of art is, before anything else, exactly that, a work of art—something created by an artist for at least one of two possible reasons: to reward the artist with a meaningful creative experience and/or to convey to you, the beholder, a meaningful impression. Knowledge of what the artist saw or wished to express may help you understand the artwork better, which in some cases may help enrich your experience, but it should not be your primary interest. Your primary concern when encountering and beholding a work of art is to make *your own* experience as a beholder of art as rich and meaningful as it can be. Alas, most people sabotage themselves in this regard by allowing other interests to usurp or distract from their *aesthetic* experience: the experience of direct enjoyment of a work of art, independent of any other consideration.

No matter how curious you might be about such things as the subjects portrayed in an artwork or about how or why the artist created it, since your attention is a finite resource, attempting to satisfy this curiosity must come at the cost of distracting you, partly or entirely, from appreciating the artwork for its own sake, as an object in itself. This is why Kant, in his book *Critique of Judgment*, recommended that we strive to avoid associating our aesthetic experiences—our pure, undistracted enjoyment of a work of art—with any other interest. This attitude is known as *disinterestedness*.

Kant explained, "The delight which we connect with the representation of the real existence of an object is called interest.... Now, where the question is whether something is beautiful, we do not want to know, whether we, or anyone else, are, or even could be, concerned in the real existence of the thing, but rather what estimate we form of it on mere contemplation (intuition or reflection)." Put another way, reality may inspire art, but art must not be expected to represent things in reality. To make the most of your aesthetic experience, you must set aside any interest you may have regarding the objects depicted in an artwork.

The skill of appreciating a work of art as an aesthetic object and not as a depiction of other objects is not innate nor easy to evolve. Our interest in objects portrayed in an artwork arises naturally in our minds and doesn't intuitively feel "wrong." It may require training our minds over time to disregard these interests as we behold art if our goal is to experience to the fullest the most rewarding and profound effects the artwork can inspire.

Disinterestedness is especially difficult to accomplish when considering artistic photography. With other media, we tend to assume that some departure from reality is to be expected and accepted. However, in viewing photographs, we intuitively assume that (or want to know if) the objects in a photograph really looked "like that," where they might be, whether we might see (and photograph) them ourselves, and whether the photographer manipulated the captured image to achieve certain aesthetics. Disinterestedness requires that when we view photographic *art*, we knowingly ignore all these things (which may be relevant and useful in other forms of photography), and not allow them to influence our appreciation of the artwork's pure aesthetics.

Photographic purists and traditionalists have succeeded in convincing viewers that photographs must be "authentic," not in the philosophical sense of expressing a person's true thoughts, feelings, and personality, but in the simplistic sense of representing things as they would appear to a random person who might be standing next to the photographer. Even if we suppose this is possible, and even if we accept that such fidelity to realistic appearances is important in some genres and uses of photography (i.e., photography used for documentary or evidentiary purposes), we must also accept that such expectations are irrelevant to art. In fact, what makes a photograph artistic—in the literal sense of being a *created artifact*—is that it expresses the (philosophically authentic) feelings, sensibilities, and creative imagination of the artist. As Henry Peach Robinson explained:

> *A method that will not admit of the modifications of the artist cannot be an art, and therefore is photography in a perilous state if we cannot prove that it is endowed with possibilities of untruth.... All arts have their limits, and I admit that the limits of photography are rather narrow, but in good hands it can be made to lie like a Trojan. However much truth may be desirable in the abstract, to the artist there is no merit in a process that cannot be made to say the thing that is not.*

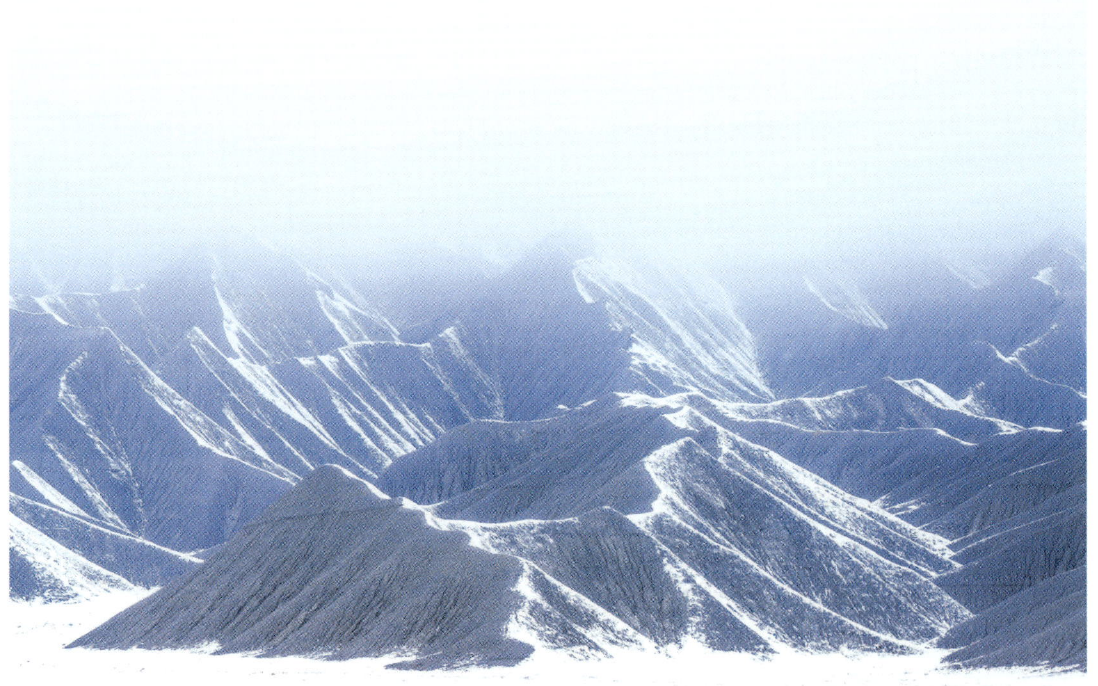

Disinterestedness means engaging fully with an artwork as it is, for what it is, as the artist intended to present it, without distractions. Purism—sticking to traditions and dogmas for their own sake, even in cases where they are not relevant to the artist's intent—is a common and often severe form of distraction among viewers of artistic photography. It is also arrogant and selfish in the sense that a purist presumes to know better than the artist what the artist's job is "supposed to be," or how to do it "the right way." As art critic John Ruskin wrote:

> *The world is full of vulgar Purists, who bring discredit on all selection by the silliness of their choice; and this the more, because the very becoming a Purist is commonly indicative of some slight degree of weakness, readiness to be offended, or narrowness of understanding of the ends of things.*

If you wish to gain the most from making and beholding art, embrace and practice disinterestedness and don't be a purist (vulgar or other). Reserve your "interested" attitudes for situations where it is appropriate (i.e., when looking at work whose intended purpose is to represent reality rather than to be appreciated as creative and/or expressive art), and train yourself also to suspend these interests when looking at art, in the same way that you've learned to suspend your expectation of realism and factual representation when reading a fictional novel or poem (as opposed to, say, a guidebook or newspaper article), or when watching a fictional movie or television show (as opposed to a documentary or investigative reporting). "Art," as Albert Camus put it, "lives only on the restraints it imposes on itself, and dies of all others."

Keep in mind that the primary beneficiary of adopting a disinterested attitude toward art is you. By suspending irrelevant interests when appropriate and relaxing your expectations of what an artwork should be, and striving instead to experience an artwork for what it is—as an aesthetic experience, rather than a copy of reality—you open yourself up to learning and understanding art and artists better, and your experiences of the beauty and meaning embodied in an artwork will be purer and more intense. Likewise, if you fail to approach art with a disinterested attitude, and instead expect the art to represent faithfully real objects, you will sabotage your own experience by failing to maximize your aesthetic experience, and perhaps even make yourself the victim of self-inflicted disappointment if your misplaced expectations of realism are proven false.

What usually destroys the experience of a photograph is to start criticizing it.

—MINOR WHITE

Critics have always been people less susceptible than other men to the contagion of art. For the most part they are able writers, educated and clever, but with their capacity of being infected by art quite perverted or atrophied. And therefore their writings have always largely contributed, and still contribute, to the perversion of the taste of that public which reads them and trusts them.

—LEO TOLSTOY

In the age of social media, it has become a habit among artists, especially photographers, to approach all shared artworks (their own and others') with the mindset of critics. Instead of aiming to behold art with the goals of experiencing elevated, reverent feelings, finding meaning or solace in it, becoming liberated by it from other—pettier and more mundane—aspects of life, viewers instead become preoccupied with things like subject matter, realism, whether certain "rules" were followed (or not followed), and flawed or praiseworthy use of certain techniques.

While these aspects of the work may be considered important in some contexts, they may also diminish or eliminate entirely the possibility of having a rich, emotional aesthetic experience that could arise from engaging fully with an artwork for its primary function, which is (paraphrasing Berthold Auerbach's reference to music) to "wash away from the soul, the dust of everyday life." That is unfortunate. Just as unfortunate, many viewers, especially if they are also artists, assume it to be their role to provide critical feedback to the artist, whether solicited or not.

If you look at any work of art with the primary interest of analyzing it as a critic would, you may unwittingly and ironically deny yourself the greatest benefit that you may gain from it: the inner experience of feeling yourself, as Susan Sontag put it, "involved with a work of art," which she described further as "the experience of detaching oneself from the world," followed by the sense that the art (again in Sontag's words) "returns us to the world in some way more open and enriched."

My advice: Make yourself conscious of the temptation to analyze works of art with a critic's mindset before first experiencing them intuitively and emotionally and making an honest attempt to contemplate their meaning and intent. Don't allow your attention to be hijacked by irrelevant details and technical minutiae that may deny you the deeper rewards of experiencing artworks as sources of elevated feelings, as respites and departure from the ordinary and mundane: as aesthetic experiences. As philosopher Roger Scruton put it (expressing the essence of what Kant meant by the attitude of disinterestedness), "What demarcates aesthetic interest from other sorts is that it involves the appreciation of something for its own sake."

Becoming mired in technical aspects of an artwork may serve you well in your early attempts at making your own art, during the (hopefully short) period of acquiring and honing your own artistic skills. However, for the sake of your own joy in experiencing art, strive to move beyond this stage as quickly as possible.

Art historian E. H. Gombrich wrote, "There is no greater obstacle to the enjoyment of great works of art than our unwillingness to discard habits and prejudices." Another historian, Renaissance scholar Walter Pater, wrote, "For art comes to you proposing frankly to give nothing but the highest quality to your moments as they pass, and simply for those moments' sake." If viewing art does not reward your moments with such high qualities, perhaps it may be time to discard some habits and prejudices.

If your interest in the technical aspects of other people's art, even if for the sake of improving your own skills, ends up numbing the emotional effects of art and prejudicing you against such things as creative novelty, you will become the unwitting victim of your own inner critic. It would be like learning to cook so you can criticize

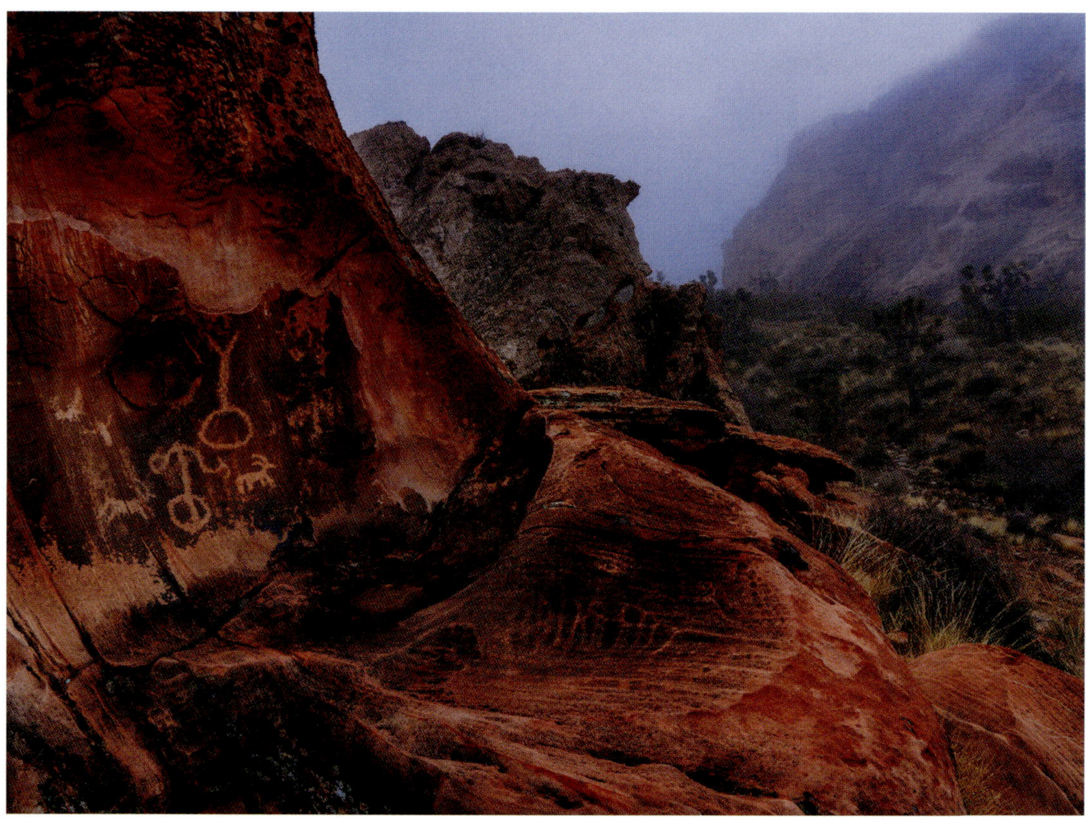

other people's culinary skills at the cost of losing your own capacity to enjoy eating good food.

Instead, make a clear distinction between times when critical thinking may be useful for improving your own skills or, if explicitly asked, to offer constructive feedback to others, and times when it's best to set aside your personal interests and critical mindset and open yourself up to experiencing art with no ulterior purpose other than to let it "speak" to you, inspire you, and wash away "the dust of everyday life."

BECOME A LION, BECOME A CHILD

> Many people feel they are powerless to do anything effective
> with their lives. It takes courage to break out of the settled
> mold, but most find conformity more comfortable. This is why
> the opposite of courage in our society is not cowardice, it's
> conformity.
>
> —ROLLO MAY

In his book *Thus Spoke Zarathustra,* Nietzsche described three "metamorphoses of the spirit," or stages of personal development that people may pursue if they wish to live their lives to the fullest, which, according to Nietzsche, means to live according to your own values, with the greatest degree of freedom that your circumstances allow—the idea that later philosophers considered as living *authentically.* Nietzsche described the three stages as analogous to adopting the attitudes of a camel, a lion, or a child.

According to Nietzsche, most people go about life with the attitude of a camel. A camel by this analogy is one who accepts its imposed burdens willingly and obediently, without rebelling or attempting to free itself. Camels are strong and docile, willing to work hard and tackle difficult tasks when needed. The camel, Nietzsche wrote, "kneels down ... wanting to be well loaded."

A camel accepts the burdens of life dutifully and unquestioningly. It does not lament its fate or try to fight for greater freedoms than are afforded it by its masters and community. A camel wishes to be of service, to love and to help others, to not "rock the boat." The camel is Nietzsche's analogy for people who accept as given the burdens, responsibilities, expectations, and values imposed on them by their society, and are willing to fulfill their predestined roles honorably and helpfully; people who are generous toward others and perform whatever labors are expected of them—even if difficult—to the best of their abilities, often setting aside their personal interests.

It's easy to see how Nietzsche's metaphor of a camel relates to common attitudes toward art. Many artists are content fitting into the greater "art community," without questioning or challenging its norms, values, and judgments. They feel satisfied in creating their work according to well-established styles. They are willing to invest time, money, and effort to pursue technical excellence rather than creative breakthroughs, even if their only reward is the approbation of their peers and community. They have no aspiration to venture beyond the status quo, or challenge themselves to make personally expressive work (certainly if such work may depart from common sensibilities or fail to satisfy common tastes).

The downside of a camel's attitude is not that it lacks in personal rewards. The problem is the opposite: Conformity and popularity reward individuals abundantly—in mutual admiration, in social bonding, in acceptance, in avoiding conflict, in a sense of belonging to community founded in shared values—which is why most never feel any desire to question or justify these values, to consider whether these values may conflict with their own, let alone to challenge them. Most don't realize that these ample satisfying rewards come, at least to a degree, at the cost of some personal freedom to push boundaries, experiment, innovate, or consider possibilities beyond what has already been done and vetted.

Some camels, however, when out "in the loneliest desert" (Nietzsche's words)— away from the watchful eyes of society—find themselves contemplating their own values and desires and may come to realize that the established norms of their community are too limiting to them, or even contradict their own knowledge or beliefs. They may grow to feel confined and frustrated by (or entirely at odds with) the way things are. They may question their willingness to continue to accept tacitly and limit themselves to just doing "more of the same." They may feel a yearning for greater freedom to live and create according to their own sensibilities and ethics, which may differ from or contradict those of their community. These camels, if they find within themselves the courage to do so, may morph into lions.

Lions are those who, when they realize their own values differ from those of their community, decide to liberate themselves. To do that, they must face and defeat their ultimate enemy: a dragon named "Thou Shalt." Nietzsche describes the dragon Thou Shalt as a beast covered in golden scales, each engraved with the words "thou shalt," and each corresponding to a precept, ethical judgment, or tradition dating back to humanity's earliest days. The lion, who was once a camel who may have loved and revered the dragon Thou Shalt and the values inscribed in its scales, must now find within itself the courage to slay the dragon and free itself—an act that Nietzsche described as, "the most terrifying assumption for a reverent spirit that would bear much."

Describing what a lion's attitude may mean to an artist, Nietzsche wrote (in an earlier article about his admiration for the composer Richard Wagner), "An artist who possesses this power over himself [the courage to defy common tastes and expectations] subjugates all other artists even without wanting to do so. To him alone ... his friends and adherents, represent no danger or limitation: whereas lesser characters who seek support from their friends generally lose their freedom through them."

Echoes of Nietzsche's lion attitude can be found in the writings of many rebellious artists and thinkers. For example, poet William Wordsworth wrote, "Every great and original writer, in proportion as he is great and original, must himself create the taste by which he is to be relished." Robert Henri advised, "Do whatever you do intensely. The artist is the man who leaves the crowd and goes pioneering. With him there is an idea which is his life."

Ansel Adams, when asked in an interview about Henri Cartier-Bresson's mocking comment that he and his friend Edward Weston were "photographing rocks" as the world was "going to pieces," demonstrated a lion's attitude when he responded defiantly, "I would never apologize for photographing rocks. Rocks can be very beautiful." Photographer Cecil Beaton likewise expressed a lion's attitude when he advised, "Be daring, be different, be impractical, be anything that will assert integrity of purpose and imaginative vision against the play-it-safers, the creatures of the commonplace, the slaves of the ordinary."

Existential philosophers borrowed much of their worldview from Nietzsche, and the lion's attitude is often evident in their writings. For example, Sartre wrote, "We are not lumps of clay, and what is important is not what people make of us but what we ourselves make of what they have made of us." Camus defended the freedom of artists when he wrote, "The aim of art, the aim of a life can only be to increase the sum of freedom and responsibility to be found in every man and in the world. It cannot, under any circumstances, be to reduce or suppress that freedom, even temporarily." Simone de Beauvoir wrote, along the same lines, "In order for the artist to have a world to express he must first be situated in this world ... at the heart of his existence he finds the exigency which is common to all men; he must first will freedom within himself and universally; he must try to conquer it."

Lions must resist societal impositions to win their freedom. Their attitude therefore must sometimes be confrontational, subversive, aggressive, defiant, and sometimes—by necessity, not by will (or even against their will)—offensive to others. Defying traditions and expectations may also make lions isolated and lonely. For Nietzsche and the existentialists, these were costs one must be willing to pay in order to live authentically, according to one's own values. In fact, Nietzsche believed that the suffering that arises from living defiantly is ultimately a good thing, being the only way that a person may experience the most elevated feeling possible: the feeling of transcendence that can only come from mustering the strength to endure pain and to confront challenges.

It may seem that one must be either a camel or a lion—either one who conforms with public opinions and expectations, or one who rebels against these things at the risk of antagonizing others. But Nietzsche suggested that there is a third way. After triumphing over the dragon Thou Shalt, a lion may continue its spiritual metamorphosis by transforming itself into a child. What Nietzsche meant is that a child by nature doesn't feel itself encumbered by traditions and norms; it just assumes itself free to pursue whatever feels "right." A child is by default creative, open to new experiences and possibilities, willing to try new things and learn new things, not in defiance against other people's norms, but simply because these things seem worthwhile and interesting.

Where a lion says "no" to social norms that restrict it, a child says "yes" to anything it considers interesting, exciting, beautiful, or proper, without worrying about how other people may judge its actions. In Nietzsche's words, "The child is innocence and forgetting, a new beginning, a game, a self-propelled wheel, a first movement, a sacred 'Yes.' For the game of creation, my brothers, a sacred 'Yes' is needed: the spirit now wills his own will, and he who had been lost to the world now conquers his own world."

Expressing the essence of Nietzsche's child attitude, photographer Lilo Raymond wrote:

> *Photography for me is a way of avoiding grown-ups, boredom and going to the laundromat. It allows me to live in another world, intensified and of my own finding. I assume the right to stare long and hard, to be blunt, loving and unselfconscious. I attempt to find a kind of poetry that eludes me in other more sober activities. It has become a continuous search with no shining end in sight except to go on trying.*

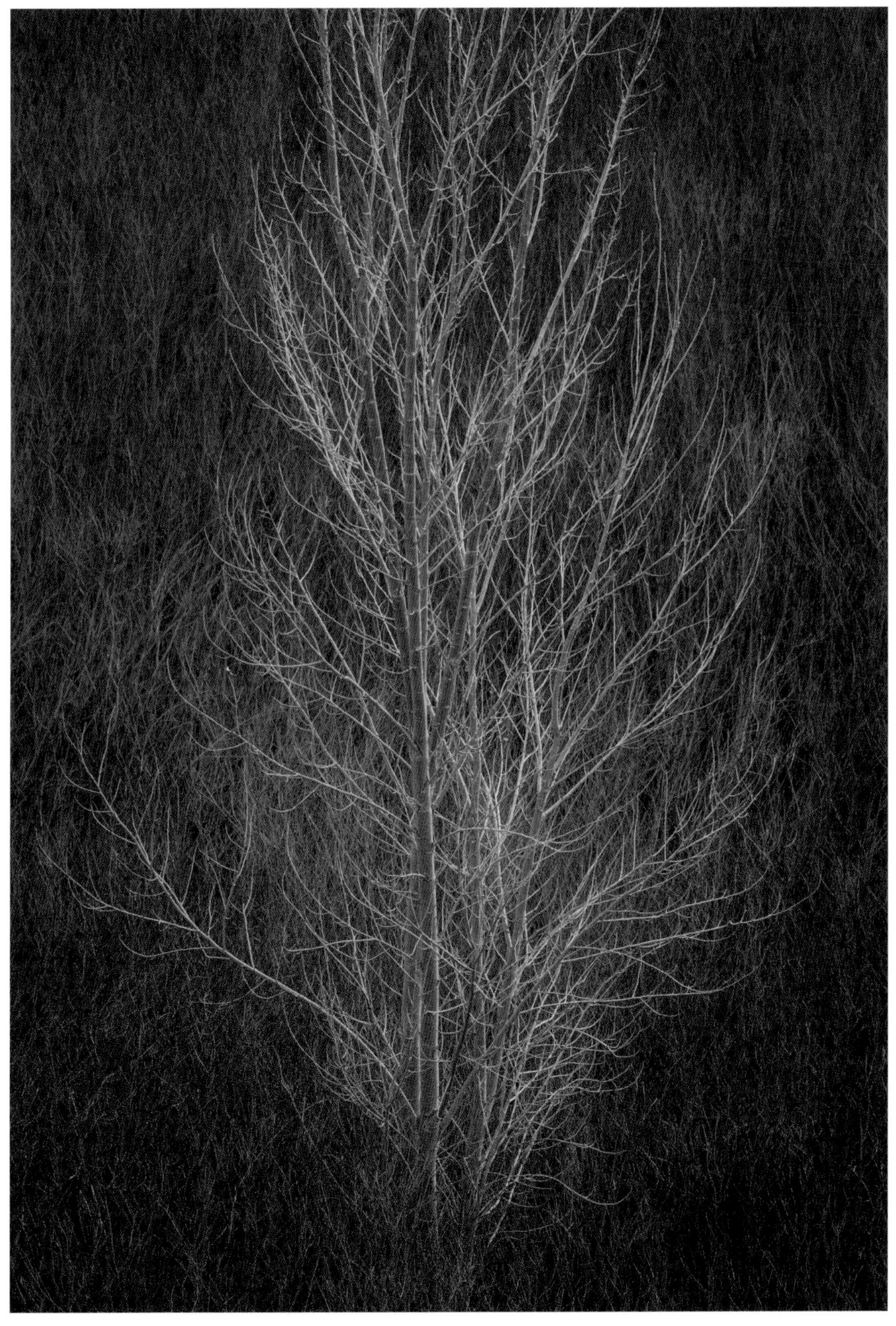

To be sure, going through life with the attitude of a lion, let alone finding the strength and discipline to transcend your circumstances and to live as Nietzsche's child, may be difficult and challenging. But in the realm of art, it is much easier to do. As Einstein put it, "The pursuit of truth and beauty is a sphere of activity in which we are permitted to remain children all our lives." All you have to do is resist conformity and pursue your work in your own way, according to your own values. You may still rub some people the wrong way, but it's unlikely you'll face any severe consequences for doing so. What you gain from creating your work authentically—according to your own personality and sensibilities—will far outweigh what you may have to sacrifice in terms of creative freedom and inner satisfaction to appeal to a low common denominator for the sake of satisfying others. As the defiant Paul Cézanne expressed, "The work which goes to bring progress in one's own subject is sufficient compensation for the incomprehension of imbeciles."

BE CREATIVELY PROMISCUOUS

Not to be strong enough to withstand an influence without weakening is proof of impotence.... For my part, I have never avoided the influence of others, I would have considered it cowardice and lack of sincerity toward myself. I believe that the artist's personality affirms itself by the struggle he has survived. One would have to be very foolish not to notice the direction in which others work.

—HENRI MATISSE

It is no surprise that openness—the personality trait described in the *APA Dictionary of Psychology* as referring to "individual differences in the tendency to be open to new aesthetic, cultural, or intellectual experiences"—is the one personality trait most closely correlated with creativity. Creativity doesn't happen in a vacuum; it involves coming up with novel (i.e., original) ways to combine, expand on, or repurpose existing ideas and knowledge. A person who is not open to new experiences, therefore, will likely accumulate much fewer "raw materials" (ideas, inspirations, influences, knowledge) from which to formulate creative ideas than a person who is preternaturally eager to learn, experience, and consider new things and new ways of thinking.

It is one thing to lack a natural predisposition to openness, but quite another to deliberately suppress it. This seems to be, at least implicitly, the goal of a trend in photography characterized as "photographic celibacy"—going out of your way to avoid seeing other people's photographs for fear that you may not be able to resist the urge to copy them instead of asserting your own creative and expressive skills.

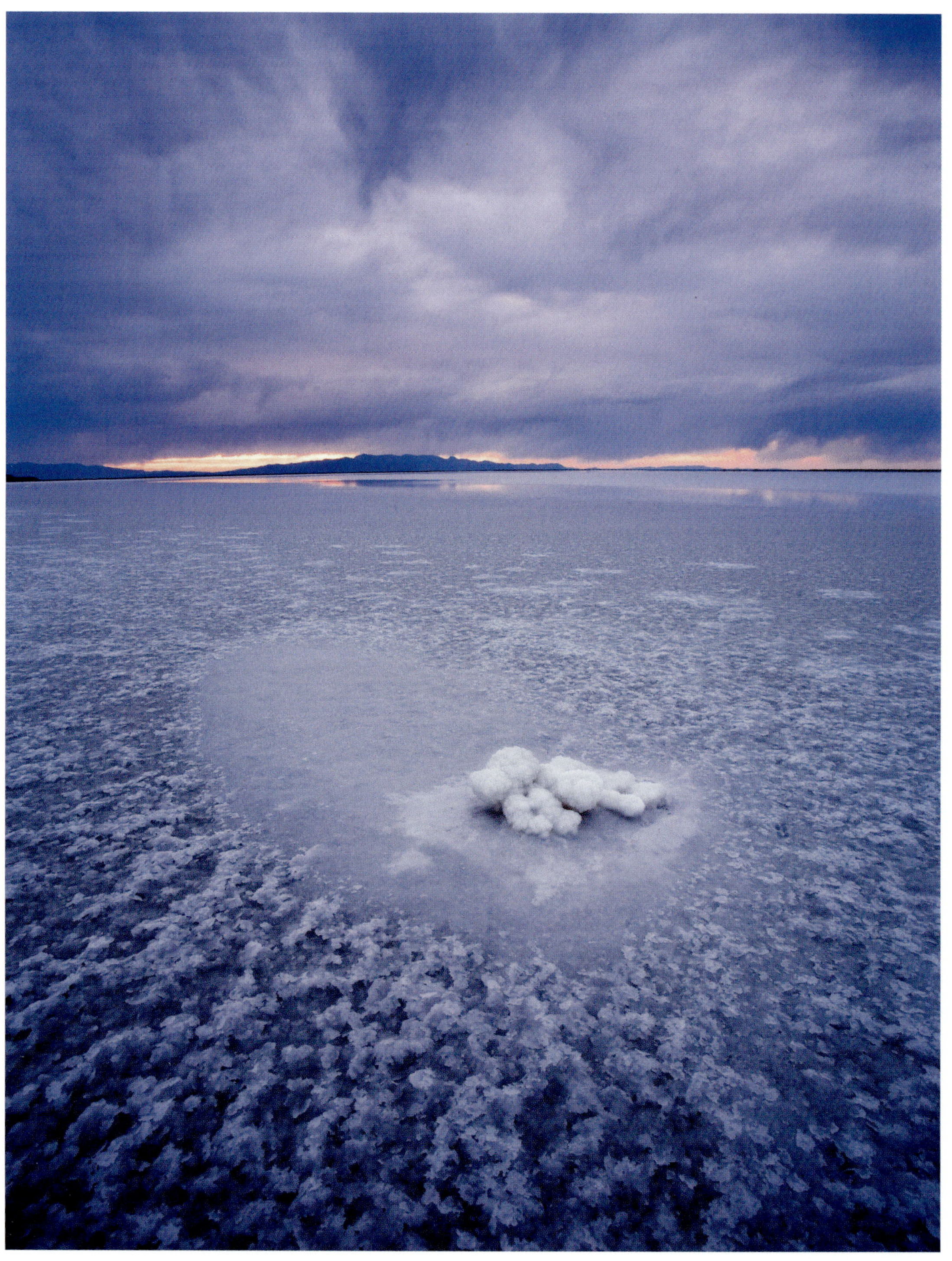

In his 1953 book *Man's Search for Himself*, Rollo May dismissed the "celibate" attitude as an indicator of personal weakness. He wrote:

> *It is the persons who are weak in the sense of their own personal identity*
> *who are overcome by the power of tradition, who cannot stand in*
> *its presence, and who therefore either capitulate to it, cut themselves*
> *off from it, or rebel against it. This is graphically illustrated by some*
> *modern artists who are afraid to look at Renaissance pictures for fear*
> *they might be influenced. One of the distinguishing marks of strength as*
> *a self is the capacity to immerse one's self in tradition and at the same*
> *time be one's own unique self.*

The temptation to copy other people's work is not unique to photographers. It is found in other art forms too. Fear of pursuing original, creative, expressive ideas is understandable for a person who seeks in art primarily extrinsic rewards (sales, popularity, recognition, validation, etc.). It's easy to see why such a person would consider it safer and more profitable to repeat formulas already proven to yield such rewards, rather than risk producing personal work that, for all its intrinsic rewards, may be misunderstood or unpopular. As Fyodor Dostoevsky wrote, "Lack of originality, everywhere, all over the world, from time immemorial, has always been considered the foremost quality and the recommendation of the active, efficient and practical man."

However, if you aspire to make art for the sake of elevating your own creative experiences, and not deny yourself the great joys to be found in other people's art, then any form of celibacy seems a very poor strategy. Avoiding other people's art will only impoverish your life by placing hard limits on the range of knowledge, ideas, and inspiring influences you may receive from other creators. As photographer Robert Mapplethorpe put it, "The more pictures you see, the better you are as a photographer." Of course, his words hold equally true for other art forms too.

Also, if you aspire to contribute something meaningful of your own to society, you are less likely to be able to do so without knowing what has already been done by others. As E. H. Gombrich put it, "If you want to do anything new you must first make sure you know what people have tried before." Or, as T. S. Eliot put it, more poetically:

> *No poet, no artist of any art, has his complete meaning alone. His sig*
> *nificance, his appreciation is the appreciation of his relation to the dead*
> *poets and artists. You cannot value him alone; you must set him, for*
> *contrast and comparison, among the dead.*

Art, like science and philosophy, progresses not by imitation and repetition of what has already been done by others, but by building on the legacies of others. Historically, we know that art does not generally evolve in a steady, linear fashion, but in sudden, revolutionary leaps brought about by creative individuals seeking new ways to express in their works aspects of their own extraordinary minds: their own ideas, experiences, perceptions, goals, philosophies, and aesthetic sensibilities.

The (in my opinion, far better) alternative to artistic celibacy is creative promiscuity: to learn as much as you can about those who came before you and what your peers are doing. Who knows what inspiration and pleasures you might find in so much great and diverse art as we are fortunate to have available to us today?

Seeing what other people are doing and have done—assuming you have it in you to muster a modicum of self-discipline, original thinking, and respect for the creative effort of others—can only help you identify what sets you apart: what you may have to say that has not already been said. It will also give you a good foundation of ideas upon which to build your own worldview and to apply toward your own creative ideas.

Keep in mind also that building on others' ideas and legacies doesn't necessarily mean evolving, refining, or expanding on these same ideas. It may also mean coming up with alternatives, counterpoints, or extensions to these ideas, or even repudiations of them. Therefore, beyond just not copying others, don't feel yourself obligated to maintain allegiance to any tradition or community, no matter how powerful, popular, or supportive.

The choice is yours. Choose your pigeonhole. Where in
society would you like to live? Or, would you choose to, dare
to, stay aloof from the boundaries and be better able to accept
or jump on new ideas, new philosophies, that are direct
outgrowths to let you explore and demonstrate your very own
personality, your sensitivity, your willingness to communicate?
To in fact, maybe, really make art.

—AL WEBER

In the previous section, I explained that becoming who you are is not something to accomplish once and for all and then check the "became who I am" box. Rather, it is an ongoing process of constant learning and evolving by various means: by introspection (self-examination), by trial and error, by keeping up with relevant research (especially in fields like personality psychology and other cognitive sciences), by considering what great thinkers (i.e., philosophers) have, or had, to say about such things as human nature, happiness, and ethics (i.e., how to live most meaningfully and virtuously).

It is no surprise, given the complexity of the human mind and the limitations of human knowledge, that you may at times find conflicting opinions about important aspects of life, or encounter evidence that may challenge or contradict your prior knowledge, intuitions, or beliefs. It is ultimately up to you to seek information and understanding, to recognize what "being who I am" means to you, to acknowledge that it may mean different things at different times, and ultimately to find the courage to become that person, even if it is not the person you previously thought you were or wanted to be, or the person other people expect you to be.

Despite so many platitudes about the need to "find yourself," learning something about who you *really* are is not necessarily an opportunity for self-improvement. Often, it may just as well be an opportunity for self-acceptance. Knowing when one is more appropriate than the other is ultimately a matter of being honest with yourself. It is true that none of us is perfect, but it is also true that none of us is free from biases and prejudices, especially about ourselves.

Certain kinds of art and attitudes toward art can assist you in the process of learning about and becoming who you are. For example, making creative art requires tapping into your ability to come up with original ideas, reflecting and training certain aspects of your personality (such as openness to experience). Making self-expressive art—art that gives tangible form to your own feelings—can help you discover who you are by making you consciously aware and mindful of your thoughts and emotions, contemplating and articulating them as you strive to find ways to express them in your artwork. Also, striving to express meaningful thoughts, feelings, and experiences will motivate you and perhaps give you the courage to seek out and pursue elevated experiences and states of mind worth expressing in your art. Knowing who you are can be immensely helpful in identifying what kind of life, work, and artistic considerations (choice of media, process, goals) are most suitable and rewarding to the unique person that is you (even if they may not be so for others).

Achieving self-knowledge is no doubt difficult, but it is not the end of the road. It is like climbing a steep mountain to gain a long view. The next step, which may be just as difficult (in some ways, more difficult) is to apply this knowledge: to convert theory into practice; to chart a course to your next destination; to live, work, and create as the person that you are, or at least as close to it as your circumstances allow.

Knowing who you are and *living* as this person are two destinations connected by a bridge, which is courage. The bridge of courage is constructed of various materials, such as risk aversion, grit[21], resilience, susceptibility to external influences, desire to please or to defy others, capacity for long-term planning. Like other aspects of personality, different people possess different degrees and qualities of these materials. The point is not to make yourself as courageous as someone else is, nor to envy the courage of someone else. The point is to be honest with yourself about the true extent of the materials available to you, and then to use your stock to its limits—to not hold back—to build the best bridge you can between knowledge and action. Don't hold

---

[21] The quality of being able to endure difficulties and setbacks without losing your motivation to keep pursuing your long-term goals.

any materials in reserve. Why? Because they are perishable. If left unused for too long, they decay into such toxic substances as guilt, regret, remorse, frustration, and self-recrimination.

"No one can construct for you the bridge upon which precisely you must cross the stream of life, no one but you yourself alone," wrote Nietzsche, "There are, to be sure, countless paths and bridges and demi-gods which would bear you through this stream; but only at the cost of yourself: you would put yourself in pawn and lose yourself. There exists in the world a single path along which no one can go except you: whither does it lead? Do not ask, go along it."

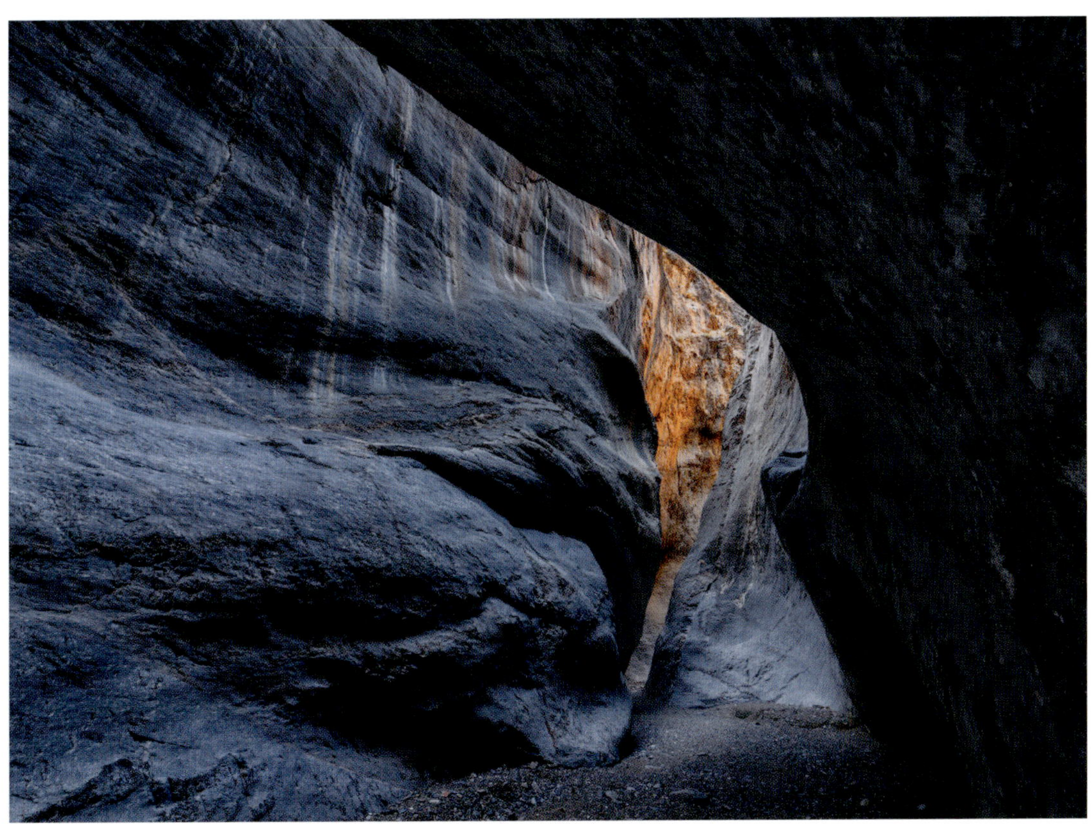

AMOR FATI

> My yearning no longer paints dreamy colors across the veiled
> distances, my eyes are satisfied with what exists, because
> they have learned to see. The world has become lovelier than
> before.
>
> The world has become lovelier. I am alone, and I don't
> suffer from my loneliness. I don't want life to be anything other
> than what it is.

—HERMANN HESSE

The term *amor fati* is Latin for "love your fate." It was most prominently used by Nietzsche to describe his attitude toward life. In his autobiography, *Ecce Homo* ("behold, the man"), he wrote, "My formula for greatness in a human being is *amor fati*: that one wants nothing to be different, not forward, not backward, not in all eternity. Not merely bear what is necessary, still less conceal it … but love it." According to Nietzsche, loving your fate—your circumstances (those you can control and those imposed on you)—is more than just resolving to accept and endure what life throws at you; it is striving actively to make the most of any situation, no matter how good or bad. As painter Francis Bacon expressed, "You must understand, life is nothing unless you make something of it."

Various philosophies, such as Stoicism and Buddhism, admonish not to become too attached emotionally to anything you might lose.[22] Nietzsche's approach, in

---

[22] For example, Epictetus advised that you should feel no worse about the death of a child or a spouse than you would about the breaking of a cup, because it is the nature of humans to die and of cups to break. This is reminiscent of the Buddhist practice of *nekkhamma* (renunciation), which includes avoiding becoming attached to impermanent things, including people, objects, and ideas, which may cause you suffering if you lose them.

contrast, is "to be only a Yes-sayer." Hesse, who was deeply influenced by Nietzsche's philosophy, described this attitude in his book *Wandering*. He wrote:

> *You can't be a vagabond and an artist and still be a solid citizen, a wholesome, upstanding man. You want to get drunk so you have to accept the hangover. You say yes to the sunlight and your pure fantasies, so you have to say yes to the filth and the nausea. Everything is within you, gold and mud, happiness and pain, the laughter of childhood and the apprehension of death. Say yes to everything, shirk nothing, don't try to lie to yourself. You are not a solid citizen, you are not a Greek, you are not harmonious, or the master of yourself, you are a bird in the storm. Let it storm!*

Nietzsche based his advice—to love your fate, no matter what it is, and to accept the consequences of your choices, no matter how dire—on his theory of "eternal recurrence." In his mind, if time is infinite, then it is likely that all possible situations will ultimately recur, over and over, perhaps infinite times. It's not clear whether Nietzsche believed that things *will*, in fact, recur (which is a possibility arising from certain interpretations of the laws of thermodynamics and other scientific theories), or whether he suggested it as a useful thought experiment: to pause for a moment and to ask yourself, as he put it, "Do you desire this once more and innumerable times more?"

Your fate will be what it will be. If you don't love it, you will find yourself at various times feeling frustrated, indignant, bored, or outright miserable. But if you make the effort and shape your attitude toward life consciously to make the best of whatever comes your way, to rewrite the story of any situation such that you see it in a positive way—the opportunities it presents you, the challenges you may endure and transcend, the lessons you may learn, whatever beauty you may witness—then on the whole you will make your life story, in all its ups and downs and plot twists, deeply meaningful.

No doubt, it is easy to love your fate in happy times, and much harder when life bears down. But when you shape your attitude such that you seek something to love about *all* your experiences, including the painful and challenging ones, then your times of happiness will become elevated, too, since you will know how they compare against the difficulties you have endured. "If we affirm one moment," Nietzsche wrote, "we thus affirm not only ourselves but all existence ... and if our soul has trembled with happiness and sounded like a harp string just once, all eternity was needed to produce this one event—and in this single moment of affirmation all eternity was called good, redeemed, justified, and affirmed."

> A man who sets out to justify his existence and his activities
> has to distinguish two different questions. The first is whether
> the work which he does is worth doing; and the second is
> why he does it, whatever its value may be.
>
> —G. H. HARDY

Why do you create art? Why do you create the kind of art you do? Why do you do it in the way that you do? Why did you decide to become (or not become) a professional artist? Why do you work in the medium you do? Was it a deliberate, considered choice involving comparison with others, or an accident of fate? How confident are you that you can articulate your answers to these questions clearly and unambiguously? That you have considered them rationally, and determined them to be the most appropriate choices for *you*?

I've had to face some uncomfortable realizations when attempting to answer these questions. I became a photographer because I loved being in and photographing natural scenes. In time, I came to appreciate the rewarding effects of creative thinking and their capacity to enrich some of my favorite experiences, in my favorite places, and later having tangible, beautiful mementos of these peak experiences. In time, I have accumulated a sufficient collection of usable images, gotten some of them published, and began to earn income and public recognition as a photographer. It seemed appropriate to me then to start referring to myself as an artist, which in a sense I was, although it was not in the same sense in which I consider myself an artist today.

In a moment of reckoning, after having been a photographer for more than three decades, as I was writing an article intending to defend photography as an art form on equal footing with other media, the question suddenly bubbled up in my mind: If I knew at a younger age that I wished to be an artist in the sense I consider myself one today, and if I wanted to dedicate my life to excelling in one art form, would I have chosen photography? I could feel my brain buzzing in protest as the inevitable answer formed itself in my mind despite my attempts to resist it: No, I likely would not have chosen to become a photographer. Perhaps a musician, perhaps a painter, perhaps a poet.

Now what?

"They" say it's never too late to start a new career. "They" are wrong. Making any kind of new start involving a high degree of risk, especially after a certain age, requires much more than unbridled optimism that "it's not too late." Realism, often tending toward pessimism, has always served me better than naïve hopefulness as a practical attitude toward life, especially when facing important, consequential decisions. (In fact, as I write these words, I feel vindicated in my pessimism by a recently published study asserting that, "Optimism bias is partly a consequence of low cognition."[23])

Existential philosophers use the term *facticity* to refer to the sum of factors that are beyond your ability to change: the hard facts constraining or preventing your freedom to make independent choices. Being a photographer today, at my age, is part of my facticity, as is my lack of time and desire to embark on a new career as I'm fast approaching my seventh decade of life.

When an ideal choice is not possible or feasible within your facticity, what do you do? One answer I already touched on is this: You listen to Nietzsche—you find a way to love your fate (*amor fati*). Difficult as it may seem, don't become discouraged by your inability to do what you want. Instead, resolve yourself to, as Nietzsche put it, "want nothing to be different."

When striving to make peace with seemingly difficult circumstances, the first thing to recognize is where your facticity ends and your freedom to choose—the things within your control—begins. This is as much about acknowledging your limitations as it is about recognizing choices that, despite being extremely difficult or risky, are nonetheless open to you. The point is to assess rationally the degree of difficulty and risk of making certain fateful choices (e.g., deciding to leave a place or tribe, quitting a good but unrewarding job, or ending a relationship) against the magnitude of cumulative misery you may have to endure if you fail to make these choices. Only in making a conscious choice about which is the better (or least bad) option can you claim to live

---

[23] Dawson, C. (2023). Looking on the (B)right Side of Life: Cognitive Ability and Miscalibrated Financial Expectations. Personality and Social Psychology Bulletin, 0(0). https://doi.org/10.1177/01461672231209400

authentically. Much as you may want to, you can't avoid choosing. Failing to make a choice is the same as choosing to persist in your current state.

The second thing to recognize is that among the things that are within your ability to change, the most important one is this: your own attitude. As Epictetus put it, "It is not the things themselves that disturb men, but their judgements about these things." Or, in the words of Marcus Aurelius, "External things are not the problem. It's your assessment of them. Which you can erase right now."

Reframing my previous questions, now accounting for my facticity (i.e., that I am at an age where starting over in a new medium I have little or no skill or knowledge in would almost certainly lead to disappointment), I then asked myself this: If there is no feasible way for me to change my artistic medium, what *can* I change—about myself and about the way I work—that might get me to a point where I can love what I do and, as Kant advised, make myself worthy of happiness, of eudaemonia: being content with my choices.

With eudaemonia as my goal (rather than "being a musician" or "being a famous photographer"), my answers to the questions at the beginning of this essay seemed clearer. Research shows that creative work is most satisfying when driven primarily by *intrinsic*, rather than *extrinsic*, motivations; by seeking rewards in the work itself—in the *process* of conceiving and creating the work—rather than by rewards offered by others for the *product* of the work, such as popularity, sales, or awards.

Why not both? Certainly, both intrinsic and extrinsic rewards can be very satisfying, but the most rewarding kind of work is one that would be meaningful and worth doing even if it *only* results in intrinsic rewards. As Teresa M. Amabile of the Harvard Business School wrote, "people will be more creative when they are motivated primarily by the interest, enjoyment, satisfaction, and challenge of the work itself—and not by extrinsic motivators or constraints."[24]

The conclusion: Even though music, poetry, or other creative products may impart a more powerful, expressive effect on their audience than photographs can, the intrinsic rewards to be found in all art forms result from an artist's attitude, not from any medium or product. Put another way, so long as you approach your art, in whatever form, aiming to invest as much effort, seriousness, dedication, attention, and time toward producing creative and personally expressive work, the medium becomes secondary, no matter what anyone else may think about the art you produce.

With the attitude of seeking to maximize my intrinsic rewards, I chose to care less about the fact that my medium ended up (by an accident of history, rather than by deliberate comparison with other media, which were beyond my knowledge and

---

[24] Amabile, T. M. (2018). Creativity and the labor of love. In R. J. Sternberg & J. C. Kaufman (Eds.), The nature of human creativity (pp. 1–15). Cambridge University Press. https://doi.org/10.1017/9781108185936.003

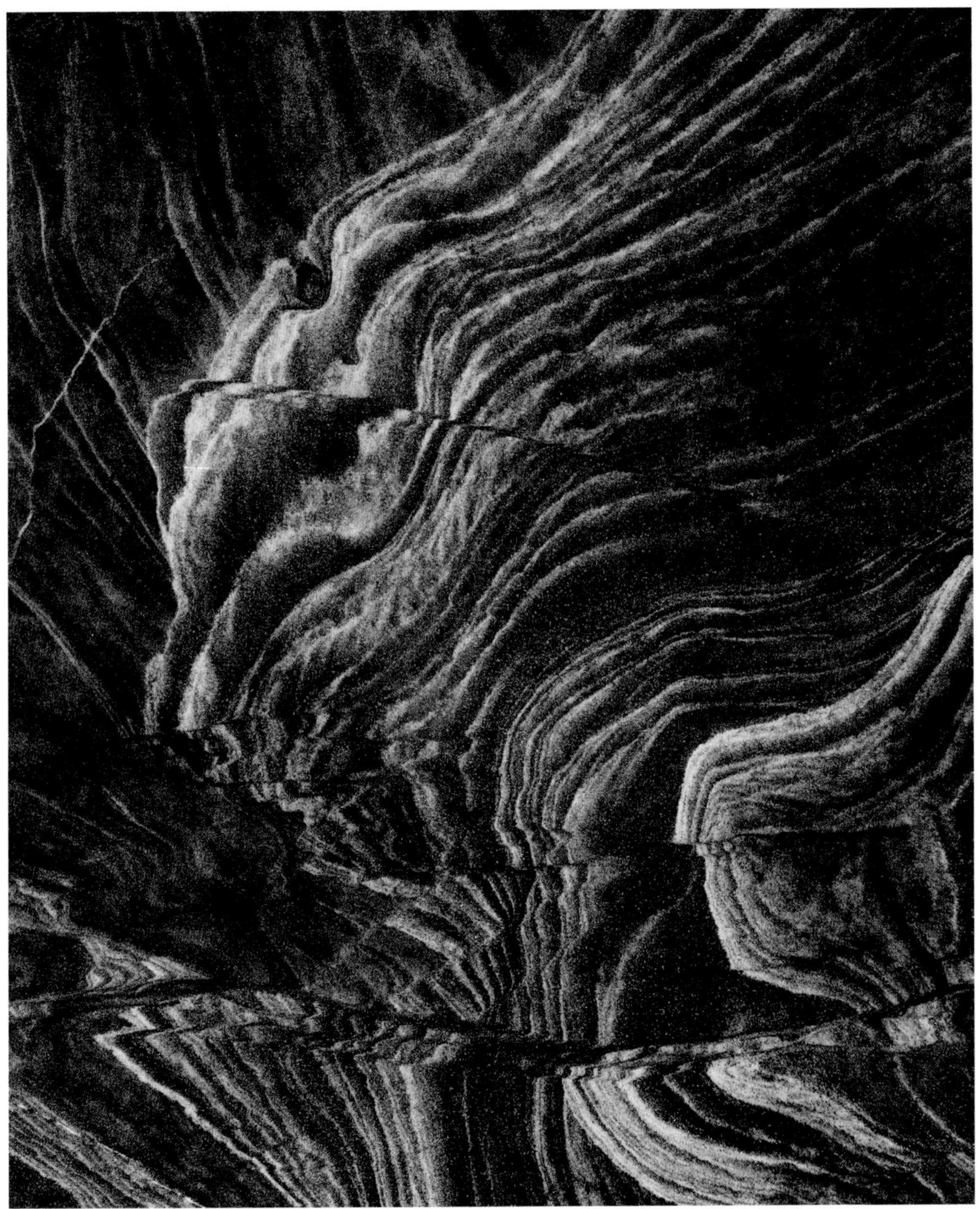

ability when I made my choice) being photography. While a part of me wishes I could compose music or write poetry with the same skill I have accomplished in photography, this (extrinsic) motivation is not sufficient to offset my (intrinsic) motivation to photograph what I want, how I want, and the inner rewards I experience when immersed fully in my work, among places and things I love, steeped in wonderful sensations—natural smells, sounds, and sights, the feeling of sun or rain or the movement of air on my skin, and so on.

"The object," as Robert Henri put it, "is intense living, fulfillment; the great happiness in creation." With this in mind, I considered my motivations to pursue my work—the things, the experiences, the rewards that are most important and meaningful *to me*. Photography has become much more meaningful and enjoyable to me than it was in times when I felt myself arbitrarily bound to pursue "fine-art nature photography" according to anyone else's expectations or ethics, or with the goal of being rewarded by others.

Certainly, I enjoy it when other people like and purchase my work, and I could not have earned a living in art and writing without these rewards. But if I could not make a living in creative work, I would still pursue it in the same way and with the same goals as I do now; I would just need to find a different way to earn a living. Since there are safer and more lucrative vocations than art, you should only practice art for a living if the art that is meaningful for you to make also happens to be sellable. Otherwise, pick a different profession and don't compromise your art. As Rilke advised the aspiring young poet Franz Xaver Kappus, who turned to him for help:

> *I know no advice for you save this: to go into yourself and test the deeps in which your life takes rise; at its source you will find the answer to the question whether you must create. Accept it, just as it sounds, without inquiring into it. Perhaps it will turn out that you are called to be an artist. Then take that destiny upon yourself and bear it, its burden and its greatness, without ever asking what recompense might come from outside.*

Kappus never became a professional poet, but he also never gave up writing poetry.

Now, reconsider the questions at the beginning of this essay, but first list your motivations and desires to practice whatever art form you choose. If you find that most of these are extrinsic (i.e., dependent on other people), I suggest you strive consciously to rethink your mode of work, resist the temptation to persist in what you already know and do, and instead strive to make intrinsic rewards your highest priority.

LIVE ETHICALLY, NOT AESTHETICALLY

What I wanted was to show how, in the mixed regions, far from depriving life of its beauty, the ethical precisely imparts beauty to it. It affords to life peace, assurance and security, for it is constantly crying out to us: *quod petis, hic est.*[25] It saves one from all infatuations that would exhaust the soul and it brings to it health and strength. It teaches us not to overvalue the fortuitous or to idolize good fortune. It teaches one to be happy in good fortune, and this is something the aesthete is incapable of, for good fortune in itself is an infinite relativity. It teaches one to be happy in misfortune.

—SØREN KIERKEGAARD

In his novel *Either/Or*, Søren Kierkegaard distinguished between living *aesthetically* and living *ethically*.[26] "Aesthetic" is Kierkegaard's term for people who never consider their choices, go along with what is popular, and spend their lives in pursuit of ease, superficial beauty, and pleasure. "Ethical" people, on the other hand, strive to live authentically (a term that was not common in Kierkegaard's time, but that later became a tenet of existential philosophy), even at the cost of enduring difficulty, isolation, and suffering.

---

[25] Latin term, originally by Horace, meaning "what you are seeking is here."

[26] In later writings, Kierkegaard added a third category: *religious* living. However, I'll leave it to readers who may be interested to research and consider this aspect of Kierkegaard's philosophy on their own, as it is beyond the scope of this book.

Most people live aesthetic lives: They just want to have fun, not overthink things, and seek to entertain and distract themselves to avoid boredom and conflict. Aesthetes are preoccupied primarily with satisfying their immediate desires and don't look (or think to look) for deeper moral meaning in their lives. In contrast, those who choose to live ethical lives often must make hard choices to live up to their own values. They think about the meaning and consequences of their actions and experiences, and stick defiantly to their own sense of what is noble and worthy, even if other people may feel differently from them or fail to understand them.

Kierkegaard suggested that living ethically, despite being harder, is ultimately much more rewarding than living aesthetically. Although it may seem that an ethical life may lack in beauty (i.e., aesthetics), it, in fact, includes all the beauty of aesthetic living, and also yields greater and worthier rewards that come from finding and living as one's true self: deepening one's emotional experiences, having a greater appreciation for life, love, and transcendence. Part of what makes ethical living difficult is that asserting your freedom to choose, rather than always reaching for what seems obvious and immediately enjoyable, inevitably comes at a cost: anxiety. When you consider yourself free to choose and weigh the moral implications of all possible choices open to you, every decision you make becomes more difficult. This is because some choices, upon close examination, will always seem more ethical than others, and the most ethical options are not always the ones that are most obvious or easiest to make. Thus, in Kierkegaard's famous words, "anxiety is the dizziness of freedom."

Consider the simple example of shopping for a common item at a grocery store. If you see only one variety of this item, there is no need to choose or compare. But if you find yourself facing shelves filled with myriad versions of the same item, the decision becomes harder. Now think of more difficult examples, such as having to choose whether to spend your life within the place or community you were born into or consider other places and walks of life that may be more satisfying; whether to pursue a safe career in a profitable field or strike out on your own in a profession that may be more exciting or give you more leisure time, but that may also require you to make peace with various risks or inconsistent income; whether to settle down and start a family or maintain your freedom to live a nomadic, solitary life; and so on.

In almost every situation, possibilities that are not obvious or that may involve various degrees of risk and uncertainty, are nonetheless still available to you to choose. Taking the time to consider all your choices seriously—to wonder what you may miss out on by choosing one way instead of another, how much more exciting and beautiful your life might be if you tried and succeeded in some risky endeavor, or whether the choice that seems most appealing to you may disappoint people you care about—can no doubt be a source of deep anxiety, not only before you make your decision, but potentially afterward in the form of regrets, recriminations, or isolation. As William James put it, "There might be some anguish in looking back from the pinnacle of prosperity (necessarily reached, if not by eating dirt, at least by renouncing some divine ambrosia) over the life you might have led in the pure pursuit of truth." An aesthete may never stop to consider such choices seriously. To an ethical person, serious consideration of all possible options is taken as a duty—the only way one may feel justified in one's choices, even if these choices may result in undesirable consequences.

Thus, in one sense, we may consider aesthetes simply as "ordinary people" who live according to established customs, expectations, and vetted templates, and never venture too far from well-trodden paths and socially acceptable norms. This raises the obvious question: What's wrong with being ordinary? According to Kierkegaard, being ordinary—accepting social norms without question, striving to fit into commonly acceptable roles, obeying rules set by others without questioning their validity or their greater moral implications, pursuing simple pleasures without overthinking them, avoiding conflict and discomfort—comes at a very steep cost: the cost of losing yourself, the unique individual that you are ... or can be, if you so choose.

Lest you dismiss this perception of ordinariness—of being "normal"—as just the opinion of one anxious and unhappy individual (which Kierkegaard certainly was), consider that other revered thinkers have expressed similar notions. For example, Abraham Maslow wrote:

> *Certainly it seems more and more clear that what we call "normal" in psychology is really a psychopathology of the average, so undramatic and so widely spread that we don't even notice it ordinarily. The existentialist's study of the authentic person and of authentic living helps to throw this general phoniness, this living by illusions and by fear into a harsh, clear light which reveals it clearly as sickness, even tho widely shared.*

Likewise, Erich Fromm wrote:

> *It is naively assumed that the fact that the majority of people share certain ideas or feelings proves the validity of these ideas and feelings. Nothing is further from the truth. Consensual validation as such has no bearing whatsoever on reason or mental health.... The fact that millions*

Indian philosopher and mystic Jiddu Krishnamurti also made the same point, bluntly and succinctly, when he wrote, "It is no measure of health to be well adjusted to a profoundly sick society."

Aesthetes live much (or all) of their lives behind masks, never revealing their true selves, never questioning their values, taking it for granted that others have already done the "heavy lifting" on their behalf, or that their intuitions (shaped to a great degree by the society they live in or by influential figures in their lives) will not lead them astray. Whenever they are free to do so, they pursue ease and hedonic pleasures (as opposed to eudaemonic happiness), avoid deep and complex thoughts, and rarely

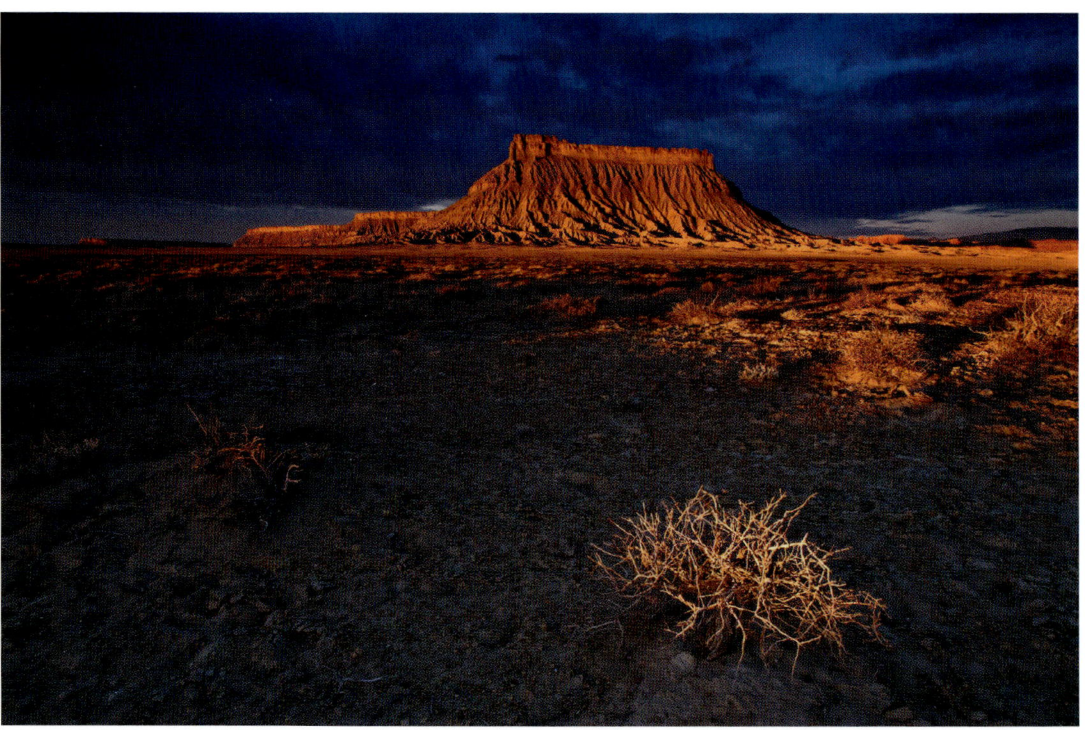

consider the moral implications of what they do or believe. Why complicate things if you don't have to?

Inevitably, however, by failing to seriously consider and choose their own values, aesthetes' public personas are always, at least to a degree, different from what they would be if they did not feel compelled to meet other people's expectations. Put another way, aesthetes don't consider themselves entirely as individuals responsible for every choice they make, but as members and representatives of tribes, communities, nations, or cultures that they did not knowingly choose for themselves or that they happened to have found by happenstance and came to feel comfortable and welcomed in, and they delegate some or all of their moral choices to what the collective they belong to deems appropriate.

The cost of aesthetic living is that, while aesthetes may feel happy simply pursuing pleasures and avoiding challenges, there will eventually come (in the words of Kierkegaard's fictional character Vilhelm, who represents an ethical person) a "midnight hour," in which the mask must come off and one must reveal one's true self. When this hour comes, an aesthete may finally realize the true cost of living without ethical consideration: having no true self to distinguish them as unique individuals. As Kierkegaard expressed, again through his character, Vilhelm:

> *I have seen people in real life who deceived others for so long that in the end their true nature could not reveal itself.... There is, in every person, something which to some degree prevents him from being completely transparent to himself; and this can be on such a scale that he is so inexplicably woven into the circumstances of life which lie outside him that he is almost unable to reveal himself. But he who cannot reveal himself cannot love, and he who cannot love is the unhappiest of all.*

Henry David Thoreau expressed a similar sentiment, more powerfully and bluntly, in his book *Walden*. Explaining his reason for choosing to live a solitary life in the woods, he wrote, "I went into the woods because I wished to live deliberately, to front only the essential facts of life, and see if I could not learn what it had to teach, and not, when I came to die, discover that I had not lived."

Kierkegaard suggested that choosing to be ethical, even if difficult, is the same as choosing to be your true self, to be authentic—to not wear a mask; to not just be your true self, but to also be willing to give your true self to another, which is his definition of true love. He also claimed that, contrary to intuition, an ethical life is more beautiful than an aesthetic life, since it includes all the beauty of the aesthetic life and adds to it. Again, Kierkegaard, in the voice of Vilhelm:

> *The personality, through choosing itself, chooses itself ethically and excludes the aesthetic absolutely; but since it is, after all, he himself the person chooses, and through choosing himself does not become another nature but remains himself, the whole of the aesthetic returns in its relativity ... and you shall see that only then is life beautiful, and that only in this way can a person succeed in saving his soul and gaining the whole world, in using the world and not abusing it.*

Finally, by becoming an ethical person—a person who consciously chooses to be authentic and to act according to their own values—you allow your personality to evolve, to become what you truly are, rather than pretend to be someone else, at the risk that after doing so for too long, you may no longer even know who you really are.

~ ~ ~

What does the distinction between aesthetic and ethical have to do with art?

For aesthetes, art serves, for the most part, as just a source of sensory pleasure or amusement, unencumbered with such things as deep contemplation, search for meanings, understanding, intellectual challenge, powerful or complex emotional experiences, or personal expression.

An obvious present-day example of aesthetic living is the way most people use social media: viewing endless streams of short-lived anecdotes to avoid boredom, hoping for the occasional minor reward—a "dopamine hit" ensuing from a "like" or a short comment. Aesthetes look for simple, surface-level beauty and rarely, if ever, stop to contemplate a given work—whether an image or a piece of writing—hoping to find meaning in it, noticing unobvious details or nuances, or hoping to learn or to gain insight about the world beyond perhaps learning that something pretty exists somewhere (Kant's characterization of "interest").

When encountering artwork on social media, few people pause to savor the experience or invest prolonged attention in it such that they may experience effects like awe or flow. Fewer, still, take the time to research the artwork further, read an artist's statement, visit the artist's personal website, read their books, or purchase the artwork for further enjoyment or to support the artist's work.

This mode of shallow and short-lived engagement with content (dubbed by some "doom scrolling") may seem a harmless distraction from the chores of the day. At least until one considers studies showing that in developed countries people spend on average (at the time of this writing) around three to five hours a day—a third or more of their waking time—on social platforms. Considering what time is left over for professional, family, and other obligations, the conclusion is clear: Most people today make no time at all for contemplative, individualistic experiences in their lives, and thus may never experience such things as awe, flow, transcendence, or powerful "aha!" moments (akin to the Zen concept of a "satori," defined by D. T. Suzuki as, "acquiring a new viewpoint for looking into the essence of things").

Alas, another unfortunate example of the aesthetic attitude is the way many photographers approach their work. They arrive at a prescribed place, at a prescribed time, go through a scripted and practiced succession of mechanical steps to capture a preconceived composition, and then quickly move on to something else after having "gotten the shot." They aim to maximize their productivity rather than to engage themselves with their work and subjects in the kind of prolonged experience that may give rise to flow, or even lead to reverential (dare I say, spiritual) states of mind. Rather than treat their artistic endeavors as self-expressive, life-enriching activities (which they can be), these photographers instead treat their work more as something fun to do—an activity preferable to boredom. For such photographers, photography is something separate from the routine of everyday life—a distraction from the drudgery of the mundane. They don't realize that creative and expressive photography (indeed, all creative and expressive pursuits) may be an invaluable source of meaning in life (or worse, they may be unwilling to invest the effort needed to make it so, even if they know it is possible).

The irony of living an aesthetic life is that it reduces most experiences to benign, superficial, irreverent anecdotes. In a sense, aesthetes are destined to remain stuck on the "hedonic treadmill": always seeking the next thrill, then quickly losing interest, becoming bored, and seeking the next one. Aesthetes are never satisfied with anything for very long, and very rarely experience deeper emotions than simple pleasure. They miss out on emotions inspired by such states as awe, flow, reverence, revelation, and transcendence, which may be much more rewarding in the long-term, even if they are not always immediately pleasant and often demand effort, fortitude, grit, endurance, or even sacrifice. They fail to consider and to choose consciously a more rewarding path: the path that Kierkegaard characterized as "ethical."

Unwittingly, by avoiding deeper engagement with the world, aesthetes become desensitized and oblivious to the most meaningful and beautiful aspects of living. They may believe they are enjoying themselves and living full lives because they are constantly stimulated and busy, but by being constantly busy they also miss out on experiences that demand significant investment of time and effort—experiences that require what may seem from the outside like idleness (i.e., "unproductive" mindful times free of interferences[27]). According to Kierkegaard:

> *Idleness, it is usually said, is a root of all evil. To prevent this evil one recommends work. However, it is easy to see from the remedy as well as the feared cause that this whole view is of very plebeian extraction. Idleness as such is by no means a root of evil; quite the contrary, it is a truly divine way of life so long as one is not bored.*

When you are busy, you don't take the time to savor your experiences to the fullest: to give them your complete attention. You don't invest cognitive resources in making yourself mindful and aware of nuances, subtleties, feelings, or creative epiphanies, contemplating deeper meanings in things than just their obvious surface appearances.

It's easy to fall into the trap of pursuing ostensibly enjoyable activities—such as rushing to visit various photogenic places on a short vacation, intending only to make preconceived photographs there—aiming no higher than to seek distractions from the drudgery of "ordinary" life without giving serious thought to the opportunity costs of such activities: all the things you could do to invest your time in more lasting and meaningful ways, in cognitively richer multisensory experiences (which may also reward you later with more profound and lasting memories). As Sontag observed, "A way of certifying experience, taking photographs is also a way of refusing it—by limiting experience to a search for the photogenic, by converting experience into an image, a souvenir. Travel becomes a strategy for accumulating photographs."

In contrast to aesthetes, people who live what Kierkegaard termed "ethical" lives, while still enjoying aesthetic experiences (e.g., beautiful art or fun activities), don't stop there. They also consider consciously their experiences and actions in the greater context of living authentically, all the ways they may invest their limited resources of time, attention, abilities, and opportunities in the most profitable ways, according to their own values and goals, aiming to reap the greatest long-term rewards for their choices,

---

[27] In their book *The Distracted Mind*, Adam Gazzaley and Larry Rosen offered this useful breakdown: "Four types of interference threaten to derail you [from achieving even a simple goal like having a meaningful conversation with a friend] … internal distraction, external distraction, internal interruption, and external interruption." According to Gazzaley and Rosen, distractions occur when you spend time dealing with irrelevant information, whereas interruptions occur when you are trying to do more than one thing at a time (i.e., to multitask).

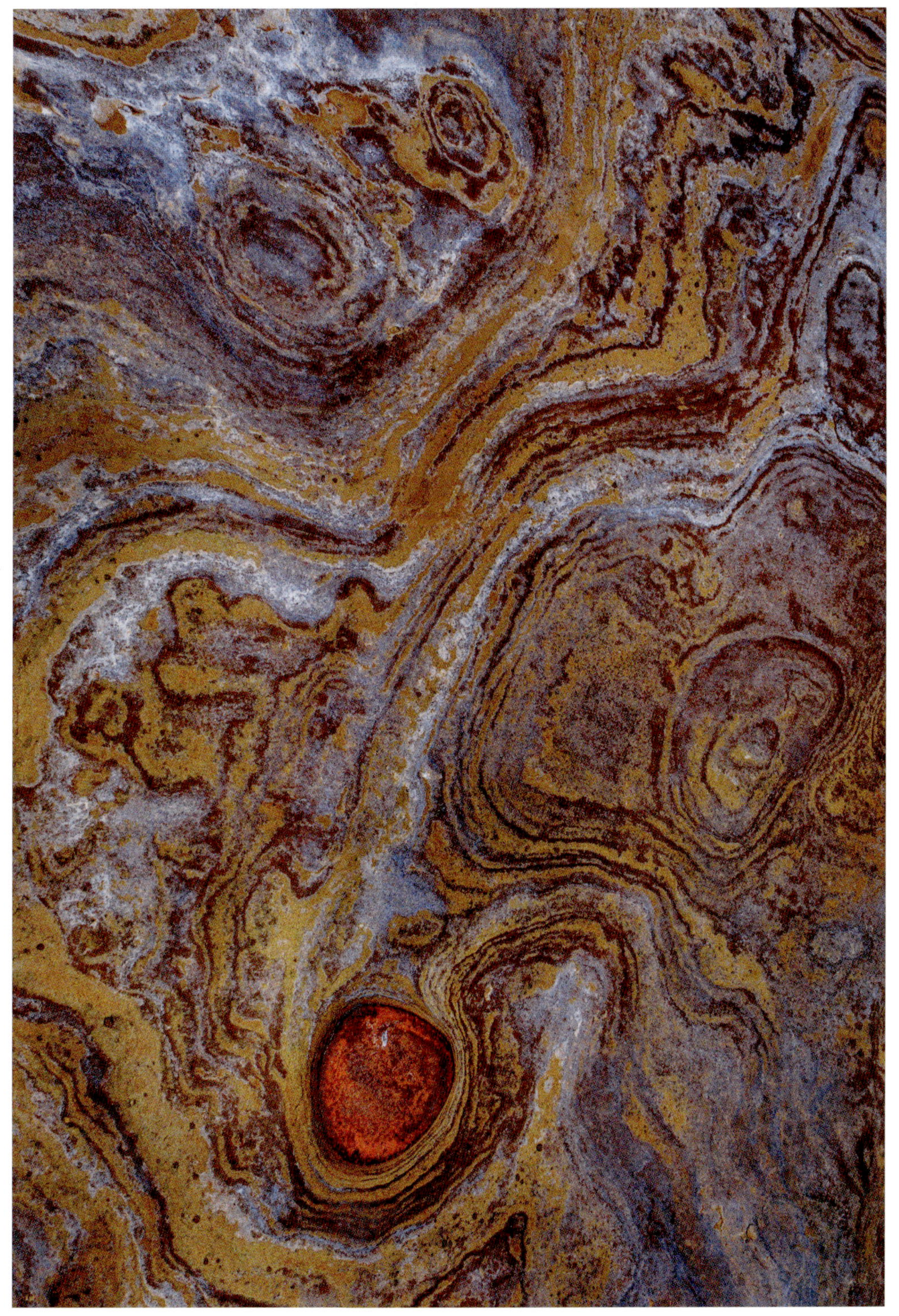

beyond just ceaseless striving to satisfy their immediate desires, yielding to tempting distractions, or avoiding being bored.

~ ~ ~

Although Kierkegaard discussed art mostly in the context of an aesthetic life, he also offered some thoughts on how people who are committed to living ethical lives may approach art. One way he suggested to maximize enjoyment from art is to take time to consider what an artwork has to offer beyond the obvious and expected. "The art of sculpture," he wrote, "can represent much more than human beauty, and yet this is its absolute object;[28] painting can represent much more than celestially transfigured beauty, and still this is its absolute object. The important thing in this respect is *to be able to see the concept in each art, and not let oneself be put off by what it can do besides.*"[29] (Italics mine)

Concepts are deliberate expressions of thoughts and feelings embodied in works of art by their creators. Practically speaking, Kierkegaard's advice to "see the concept" applies not only to studying more closely other people's art; it also means striving to be expressive in your own work and not just to document things you come across, or stop at mere aesthetic appeal. Consider what deeper meanings—what ideas, emotions, moods, or personal interpretations—you wish to express, and for your viewers to find, in your work. Also, make it your goal to learn constantly, by experimentation, reading, imagining creative possibilities, and hearing what other artists have to say about how to express meaning in artistic creations.

Aesthetes who see your work—and who may even be the majority of those who see it—may not always find or even think to look for greater meaning in your art than just obvious aesthetic appeal. But those who aspire to live ethical lives very well may. More important, your work will be more meaningful to *you* if you commit yourself to living ethically, and extend this commitment to art-making, aiming to find transcendent, meaningful, lasting, creative experiences in your work.

---

[28] Consider "absolute object" to mean "most commonly assumed purpose."

[29] Kierkegaard was just a teenager when photography was invented. Understandably, he did not give much thought to it as an art form. Still, his statements regarding sculpture and painting can easily be extended to photography. Paraphrasing his words, we can say that the art of photography can represent more than just realistic appearances, despite such representation being photography's "absolute object." Kierkegaard's conclusion above applies just as much to photography as it does to other media; the important thing is to be able to see *the concept* in a photograph, and not let yourself be put off by what it can "do besides" (i.e., besides just capture mimetic appearances).

BE MINDFUL

> I seek out places where it can happen more readily, such as
> deserts or mountains or solitary areas, or by myself with a
> seashell, and while I'm there get into states of mind where I'm
> more open than usual. I'm waiting, I'm listening. I go to those
> places and get myself ready through meditation. Through
> being quiet and willing to wait, I can begin to see the inner
> man and the essence of the subject in front of me.
>
> —MINOR WHITE

To become mindful is to consciously focus your attention on things happening in the present moment. Conversely, to become mindful is also to deliberately and ruthlessly deny attention to any thoughts not directly related to your present experience. Mindfulness can thus be defined as the skill of controlling attention: the ability to direct or deny attention at will and keep attention focused on things of your choice for as long as you wish it to remain so (i.e., to avoid attention being hijacked by distracting errant thoughts). It is not an easy skill to learn, and it requires constant practice to sustain.

"Things happening in the present moment" fall into two categories: sensory perceptions of the world outside of you (sights, scents, sounds, tactile sensations), and thoughts, feelings, and sensations occurring within you. To be mindful therefore requires training yourself to become acutely aware of things around you and within you. You must also become capable of examining these things consciously and choosing how to feel about and respond to them.

Becoming a mindful person will, in time, empower you to choose to focus your attention on useful, inspiring, and elevating aspects of your experiences, thus deepening and enriching these experiences as they happen. Also, it will empower you to consciously detach yourself from, or reduce the effects of, negative emotions, such as anxiety, dissatisfaction, regret, anger, or unproductive ruminations.

Beyond the obvious benefits to emotional wellbeing, evolving the ability to control attention is very useful in artistic activities—especially creative and self-expressive activities. Being mindful and conscious of your inner thoughts and feelings as they arise is vital to expressing and articulating them in your artwork. Given the nature of the creative process, which requires being open to new ideas some of the time and focusing on skilled work in other times, it's no surprise that the most creative people are those who can choose consciously when to allow their minds to wander and to consider a diversity of ideas (this is known as "divergent thinking"), and then, when a creative idea presents itself, to corral and focus attention on the tasks required to bring this idea to fruition (this is known as "convergent thinking").

The most effective way to train yourself to become mindful—to hone your ability to notice things occurring around you and within you, and to control your emotional responses to them—is the practice of mindfulness meditation. Dedicating even just a few minutes a day to meditation can noticeably improve your ability to become mindful within just a few weeks. I suggest giving meditation an honest try, either by yourself or with a guide, before deciding whether to stick with it. If after trying meditation you conclude that it does not appeal to you, there are other ways to train yourself to become mindful. I explain a couple of them—keeping a journal and making inventories—later in the book.

Like any other skill, the longer and more regularly you practice, the better you will get and the greater the rewards you'll be able to reap from mindfulness.

READ

I could never have dreamt that there were such goings-on
in the world between the covers of books,
such sandstorms and ice blasts of words,
such staggering peace, such enormous laughter,
such and so many blinding bright lights,
splashing all over the pages
in a million bits and pieces
all of which were words, words, words,
and each of which were alive forever
in its own delight and glory and oddity and light

—DYLAN THOMAS

Looking back, one of the things I am most profoundly grateful for is that I got to grow up in a world without the internet, so-called smart devices, and social media, and with abundant natural open spaces where I spent much of my time as a child. Another aspect of my childhood I'm grateful for is having access to a well-stocked town library. Since my formative years, and to this day, there have been almost no times in which I was not making my way through a book, sometimes more than one.

Beyond just being repositories for stories, information, and ideas, books require that you, the reader, become an active participant in accessing, assimilating, and applying the content you receive. In this sense, books are superior to other media, even if the reading experience may be less exciting and more demanding than engaging in other media. As Dana Gioia, former Chairman of the National Endowment for the Arts (NEA), put it:

> *Reading a book requires a degree of active attention and engagement. Indeed, reading itself is a progressive skill that depends on years of education and practice. By contrast, most electronic media such as television, recordings, and radio make fewer demands on their audiences, and often require no more than passive participation. Even interactive electronic media, such as video games and the Internet, foster shorter attention spans and accelerated gratification. To lose such intellectual capabilities—and the many sorts of human continuity it allows—would constitute a vast cultural impoverishment.*

These words accompany a 2004 publication titled, *Reading At Risk: A Survey of Literary Reading in America*, which points out exactly this kind of impoverishment. Alas, during the writing of this book, the NEA released a new survey[30] showing "a sharp decline in reading over the last decade."

Unlike other media, which may offer a richer sensory experience, reading demands that you fill in sensory experiences using the powers of your own imagination, and enrich the information you acquire by drawing on other knowledge you may already possess. Reading a book is a workout for your cognitive abilities, including skills useful in the creation of art, such as uninhibited imagination, the capacity to combine and reformulate seemingly unrelated concepts, and the ability to sustain focused attention for prolonged periods.

Developing a daily reading habit, even if difficult to establish, is one of the greatest investments you can make in yourself. Like any investment strategy, it also benefits greatly from diversification, which is to say, don't limit yourself in terms of genres, topics, or levels of difficulty. If you are looking for good stories, don't limit yourself just to fiction or to just nonfiction. If you are interested in art, read about a variety of arts, not just about your own medium. If you are interested in science or philosophy or poetry, cast a wide net, and be sure to consider the "big picture." Become a sponge for knowledge, for great writing, for advancing your reading skills and deepening your understanding.

Books, essays, poems, and other forms of creative writing may transport you to worlds of profound beauty, of which you become a co-creator along with the author as

---

[30] See: https://www.arts.gov/news/press-releases/2023/new-data-reveal-how-adults-participated-arts-during-covid-19

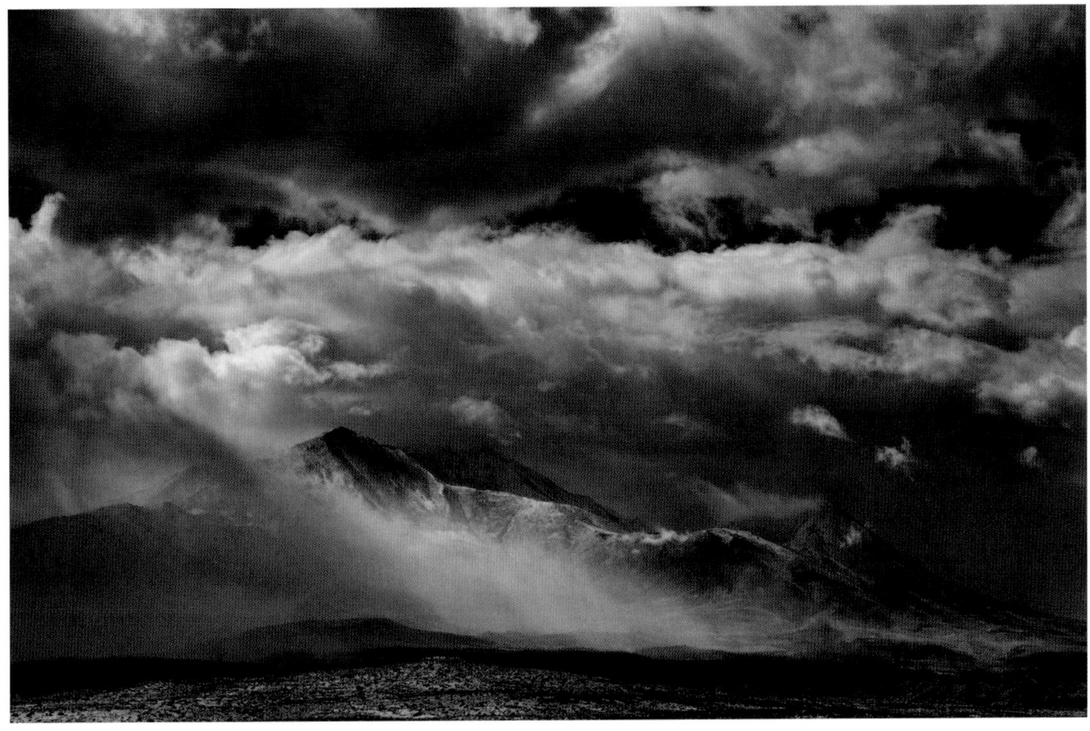

your guide. Poetry may move you to powerful emotions and to a deeper understanding of life as others experience it, sometimes in ways you may wish to adopt yourself and become better for it. As sources of knowledge, books set you free, making you less dependent on the opinions, beliefs, and ways of thinking of other people, allowing you to learn about and consider multiple points of view and to choose among them freely, according to your own best understanding and ever-growing breadth of knowledge. The more knowledge you gain, the more choices will be open to you to explain and understand things, whether phenomena in the world or aspects of your own personality. To have choices is to have freedom.

Becoming a skilled reader will also open for you worlds of experiences that you may not be able to access in other ways: places, people, ideas, and phenomena beyond your reach. It will also enable for you experiences not available to others: experiences that yield profound pleasures and a sense of meaning in life by engaging your attention, imagination, and intellect to their fullest extents. This will give you an advantage especially in this age where most people opt for the ease of relying on technology to think for them and serve them with ready-made solutions they have no need to understand, only to accept as given.

It has become common in the internet age for people to proudly claim to do their own research, often with unfortunate consequences. Doing your own research is an admirable and desirable thing, but it comes with an important caveat: The results of your research reflect the quality of your sources of information and your skill as a researcher. If either or both are lacking or guided by bias, doing your own research is a sure way to lead yourself to errors.

In his book *The Modern Dilemma*, Loren Eiseley lamented:

> *The technology which, in our culture, has released urban and even rural man from the quiet before his hearth log, has debauched his taste. Man no longer dreams over a book in which a soft voice, a constant companion, observes, exhorts, or sighs with him through the pangs of youth and age. Today he is more likely to sit before a screen and dream the mass dream which comes from outside.*

When asked in any public forum if I have a "word of advice," my go-to answer is, "read." By this I mean invest in yourself, free yourself, enlarge your world, and reward yourself with great pleasures of the mind.

EXPERIENCE FIRST

> Between ourselves and actual experience and the actual
> environment there now swells an ever-rising flood of images
> which come to us in every sort of medium—the camera
> and printing press, by motion picture and by television.
> A picture was once a rare sort of symbol, rare enough to call
> for attentive concentration. Now it is the actual experience
> that is rare, and the picture has become ubiquitous.
>
> —LEWIS MUMFORD

Some photographers make photographs spontaneously in response to, or as visual expressions of, meaningful life experiences. Other photographers do the opposite; they plan their experiences specifically with the goal of making photographs. The former group—which I will refer to as "experience-first photographers"—are a small minority of which I am a proud member. The second group—which I will refer to as "photograph-first photographers"—make up most camera enthusiasts.

The reason we see so much repetition, derivation, and outright plagiarism in photography is that most photographers, sometimes without considering the alternative, take the photograph-first approach; they plan their activities with the goal of making photographs. You can only plan for things you already know: things you have already seen, or things you deliberately set out to copy.

Experience-first photographers go about life seeking elevated and personally mean-ingful experiences, prepared to make photographs when circumstances are conducive to visual expression, but never feeling compelled to make photographs; nor are they disappointed when an otherwise rewarding experience did not yield any photographs. Photograph-first photographers, who plan their experiences explicitly with the goal of making photographs, likely will consider their excursions as failures or as wastes of time, and feel disappointed if returning from a planned outing without photographic trophies.

For photograph-first photographers, other qualities of experience come second to photography. Some photograph-first photographers even go so far as to brag about difficulties and hardships they endured to "get the shot." For experience-first photographers, on the other hand, photography comes second to other, more elevated, qualities of experience. These qualities, often ignored by or perhaps even unknown to photograph-first photographers, are in themselves sufficient reason to engage in an activity: to spend time in certain places or with certain subjects; to set aside mundane preoccupations for a time; to become immersed in peace, silence, and beauty for their own sake, without feeling under any pressure or obligation to return with anything other than a clear mind and a fond memory. Experience-first photographers may well avoid some activities, places, and subjects that could yield "good" photographs but fail to reward in other, deeper ways.

My reasons in making the distinction between experience-first and photograph-first photographers are twofold: First, I hope that at least some readers who are of the photograph-first mindset may be moved to consider the benefits of the experience-first attitude, not only as a means of making photographs, but as a life practice. Second, I wish to dispel the common myth that meaningful experiences are by necessity limited to positive, joyous, fun, or easy activities.

Photograph-first photographers, who rely on planning or on replicating the styles and works of others, implicitly forfeit, or at least diminish, their capacity to experience such things as flow, mindfulness, serendipitous discovery, and the great pride that ensues from having accomplished an original creation. Their attention is focused on their planned, preconceived outcomes, so even if the potential for an exciting and unexpected new photograph may exist before their eyes, they are likely to miss it due to inattentional blindness[31] or because their time is limited, governed by a schedule or preconceived idea that is their only measure of success.

Experience-first photographers—especially if they are mindful of their surroundings, their thoughts, and their emotions, and are practiced in maintaining a beginner's mind[32]—having time and attention to spare, free of the tyranny of expectations and preconceptions, and of the anxiety that comes from feeling compelled to photograph

---

[31] Defined in the *APA Dictionary of Psychology* as "a failure to notice unexpected but perceptible stimuli in a visual scene while one's attention is focused on something else in the scene."

[32] The attitude referred to in Zen Buddhism as *Shoshin*, requiring openness to novel ideas, lack of preconception, and willingness to learn, no matter what one's level of expertise is.

something at any cost, are more likely to notice things that photograph-first photographers might miss. Experience-first photographers are also more likely to feel at ease spending time experimenting, accepting the risk that their efforts may not always be fruitful, knowing that these experiences are still rewarding and worthy for their own sake.

It may seem obvious that photograph-first photographers will favor working in known locations—so-called "honey pots," where successful photographs are all but guaranteed—as a safer alternative to venturing into new territory or exploring new subjects or styles. Less obvious, perhaps, is what these photographers may be missing by focusing on such locations: the great joys in simple experiences such as just sitting on a rock and listening to the sound of the breeze for a bit, witnessing animals engaged in playful behavior, noticing signs of the changing seasons, savoring subtle sensations, allowing the mind to wander, and letting go of the frenetic goal-driven mindset that characterizes so much of everyday living. Beyond the narrow concern for making photographs, such experiences may be profoundly peaceful, clarifying, rejuvenating, and therapeutic.

It seems pointless to bring the same stressful and anxious attitudes that torment people in the daily pursuit of careers, studies, social obligations, and other prescribed, unsatisfying, repetitive, competitive, or just plain boring activities into your creative, artistic endeavors. If you can't use "free" time to free yourself literally from the daily grind, from the tedium of the mundane, can this time be truly regarded as free?

It may come as a surprise to some to learn that I almost always go to wild places with no other aim than to pursue good experiences or to have a good cry; contemplate in peace not only my good fortunes, but also my sorrows and challenges; seek strength and solace when I'm plagued by difficult feelings or circumstance; grieve a loss; or to prepare myself for challenges that may lie ahead.

"An artist," wrote Francis Bacon, "must be nourished by his passions and his despairs." What I have found after decades of coming to nature for solace, inspiration, and clarity of mind, is that all feelings—good, bad, happy, sad, sublime, or outright terrifying—may, if I approach them with the right attitude, give rise to beauty in some form. All emotions, when channeled consciously toward elevated states of mind, and—when circumstances allow—toward artistic expression, always deepen and dignify my experiences, whether they are blissful or painful. These elevated experiences, in turn, always arouse gratitude for the good, alleviate the bad, and leave me better than I was, even in my low times when hope is hard to come by, even if just for acknowledging and recalling my good fortune to have experienced so many extraordinary things in my lifetime. If this is not reason enough to practice my work with an experience-first attitude, what is?

I feel ever so strongly that an artist must be nourished by his passions and his despairs. These things alter an artist whether for the good or the better or the worse. It must alter him. The feelings of desperation and unhappiness are more useful to an artist than the feeling of contentment, because desperation and unhappiness stretch your whole sensibility.

—FRANCIS BACON

It is no coincidence that the first item on the list of Buddhism's Four Noble Truths is the acknowledgement that *dukkha*—suffering—is an innate part of life. I believe this is true, although I disagree with the Buddhist and Stoic belief that to avoid suffering we must numb ourselves to the powerful emotions that may cause us to suffer (what Buddhists refer to as *tanhā*). Certainly, a life devoid of intense feelings and challenges may spare us *some* suffering, but it's not worth the cost of depriving ourselves also of intense experiences, which inevitably go hand in hand with powerful emotions— experiences like love, awe, astonishment, caring deeply, persevering hardship, and triumphing over adversity. These experiences, despite involving suffering, are known to strengthen various personality traits, such as resilience, grit, and empathy, that may make the rest of life more deeply meaningful. As Oscar Wilde put it, "to have become a deeper man is the privilege of those who have suffered."

Nietzsche's philosophy on this matter aligns better with my thoughts and experience. He believed that in many cases, enduring (sometimes severe) difficulties is important for personal growth and has the power to magnify and deepen our sense of meaning in life. Famously and succinctly, Nietzsche wrote, "What does not kill me, makes me stronger." Elsewhere, he elaborated:

> *Examine the lives of the best and most fruitful people and peoples and ask yourselves whether a tree that is supposed to grow to a proud height can dispense with bad weather and storms; whether misfortune and external resistance, some kinds of hatred, jealousy, stubbornness, mistrust, hardness, avarice, and violence do not belong among the favorable conditions without which any great growth even of virtue is scarcely possible. The poison of which weaker natures perish strengthens the strong—nor do they call it poison.*

The pursuit of happiness to the avoidance or exclusion of all pain, risk, and challenge is, ironically, also the pursuit of boredom and dullness. Strive to be happy, but also be mindful not to shield yourself from suffering to such an extreme that your ability to experience intense emotions dulls or atrophies for lack of challenge or exercise, or, worse yet, you find yourself unprepared and lacking the resilience, grit, and emotional maturity to cope with unexpected adversities.

When misfortune or challenge come into your life, don't make it your default priority to evade or deny them. Consider their implications, necessity, and importance. If they are meaningless or unnecessary, then by all means try to avoid or ignore them. But if they are hurdles you must overcome to find greater meaning or accomplishments, be ready and willing to endure them with grit and dignity so they don't make you jaded, bitter, or depressed and sully the rest of your experiences. For better or worse, the magnitude and depth of any accomplishment are correlated with the degrees of effort and difficulty leading up to it.

In what may seem anathema in this sheltering age of safe spaces and trigger warnings, Nietzsche wrote:

> *To those human beings who are of any concern to me I wish suffering, desolation, sickness, ill-treatment, indignities—I wish that they should not remain unfamiliar with profound self-contempt, the torture of self-mistrust, the wretchedness of the vanquished: I have no pity for them, because I wish them the only thing that can prove today whether one is worth anything or not—that one endures.*

Consider that it's not just philosophers and artists who have testified to the value of perseverance, resilience, and grit. For example, celebrated neuroscientist Antonio Damasio wrote, "Pain, suffering, and the realization of death are especially empowering, more so I believe than well-being and pleasure." And psychologist Kay Redfield Jamison, who suffers from bipolar disorder, said, "I believe that curiosity, wonder, and passion are defining qualities of imaginative minds and great teachers; that restlessness and discontent are vital things; and that intense experience and suffering instruct us in ways less intense emotions can never do."

Likely, you are familiar with the myth of the suffering artist. While it is true that many artists are happy with their lives and work, it is also true that rates of depression and other emotional disorders are higher among artists than they are within the general population. One possible explanation for this is that heightened creativity may be correlated with individual differences in the production and effects of the neurotransmitter dopamine. As Daniel Z. Lieberman and Michael E. Long put it in their book *The Molecule of More*:

> *The hyperactive dopamine systems of creative geniuses put them at risk of mental illness.... For some, it doesn't matter. The joy of creation is the most intense joy they know, whether they are artists, scientists, prophets, or entrepreneurs. Whatever their calling, they never stop working. What they care about most is their passion for creation, discovery, or enlightenment. They never relax, never stop to enjoy the good things they have.... They serve the public well. But no matter how rich, famous, or successful they become, they're almost never happy, certainly never satisfied.*

Despite common perceptions, dopamine is not directly associated with happiness, but rather with motivation. People who are "highly dopaminergic" experience very high motivation to constantly strive for novel things (recall that novelty is the first criterion in the definition of creativity). Sometimes, this striving is so powerful that people lose entirely the capacity to be happy; they are never satisfied with what they have because their brains compel them to keep chasing after the "next thing." As Lieberman and Long put it, "Living our lives in the abstract, unreal, dopaminergic world of future possibilities comes at a cost, and that cost is happiness."

If you are not by nature a happy person, you may well be highly dopaminergic. If that is the case, feeling frustrated or unworthy because you can't "just be happy" or because an outsider looking at your life—what you have, what you do, how you live—may

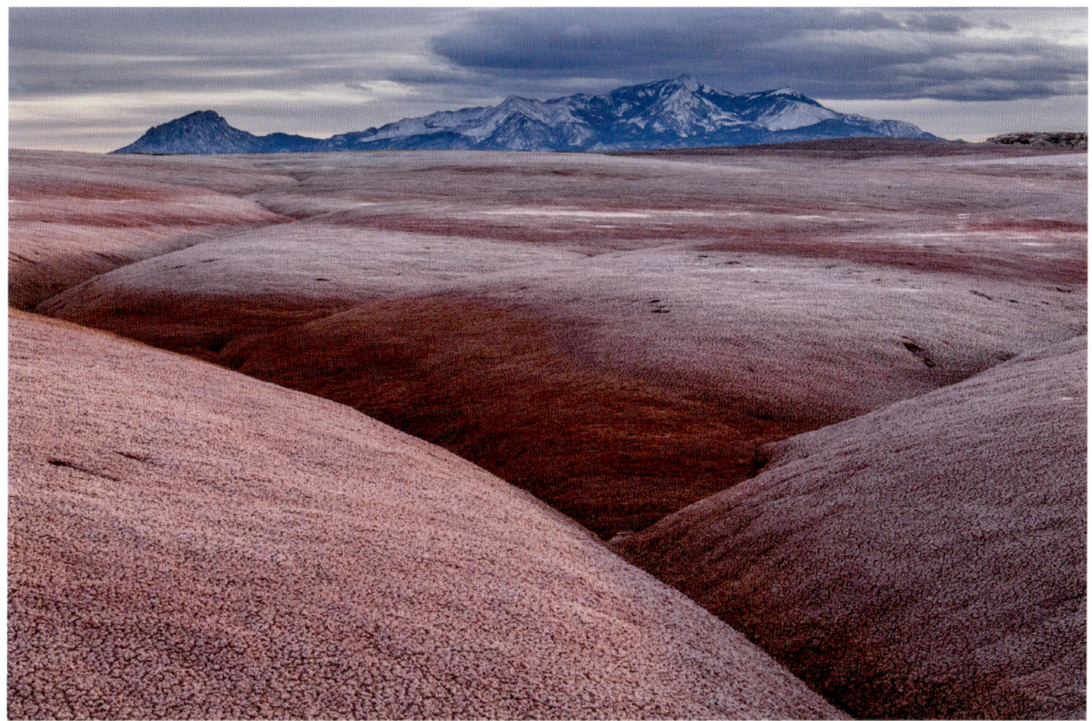

proclaim that you "should be happy" is self-defeating. If you are highly creative, it may indicate that your brain's neuronal wiring is not tuned for happiness. But even if you are not capable of the kind of happiness that other people experience, you may still strive for eudaemonia—the feeling of flourishing and contentment—and few things can reward you with eudaemonia more than artmaking. In this sense, art can be your therapy, medicine, or solace, even if you are chronically unhappy.

Never compare your happiness with others' or feel guilty or unworthy for feeling unhappy when you ostensibly "should be happy." If you are capable of happiness, consider yourself fortunate in that sense. If you are not, make your peace with the knowledge that your life may still be profoundly meaningful without happiness. In some ways, your life may even become *more* meaningful in the absence of happiness. This is because of the effect that Nietzsche described: finding meaning in enduring and persevering unhappy states.

Becoming what you are, as Nietzsche advised, means—among other things—recognizing whether "a happy person" is, or can be, part of what you are. If it is not, striving for it may be futile and frustrating. Strive always for meaning, but don't necessarily expect it to come solely from happiness.

SET VAGUE, OPEN-ENDED GOALS

He who has a why to live can bear almost any how.

—FRIEDRICH NIETZSCHE

What do you want to accomplish in life? It may seem that by virtue of each of us being unique, there will be a great diversity of answers to such a broad, open-ended question. In fact, this is not the case. A growing proportion of young people strive primarily to become wealthy.[33] A 2017 survey of children and teenagers conducted by the travel company First Choice found that three-quarters of them wanted a career in online video (with "YouTuber" coming in first at 34.2 percent).[34]

Some surveys have even shown paradoxical inconsistencies among people's top life goals. For example, a 2008 Pew survey[35] showed that most Americans considered it very important to "have enough free time to do things you want to do" (67 percent), while at the same time also prized highly "being successful in a career" and "having children" (each coming in at 61 percent). Although I am not speaking from experience, I suspect that striving for all three is almost certain to result in frustration and dissatisfaction.

---

[33] According to a 2012 article published in the journal *Psychology Today*, "In the [UCLA] American Freshman survey, the proportion of students who said being wealthy was very important to them increased from 45 percent for baby boomers (surveyed between 1966 and 1978) to 70 percent for Generation Xers (surveyed between 1979 and 1999) and 75 percent for millennials (surveyed between 2000 and 2009)."

[34] See a summary of this and similar surveys here: https://www.cnbc.com/2019/08/02/forget-law-school-these-kids-want-to-be-a-youtube-star.html

[35] See: https://www.pewresearch.org/short-reads/2008/07/09/free-time-middle-americas-top-priority/

In various corporate environments, a common approach for setting employee goals encourages the use of the mnemonic S.M.A.R.T, coined by George T. Doran. The letters stand for Specific, Measurable, Assignable, Realistic, and Time-Related. No doubt, this is a useful strategy for squeezing more productivity from corporate employees, considered literally as "human resources" (i.e., in a similar way to manufacturing supplies, capital, time, and other insentient resources), rather than as living, feeling, creative, adventurous, curious, emotional, imaginative, and unique individuals.

If you are unfortunate enough to have to depend for your livelihood on complying with such dehumanizing practices when at work, I suggest you make a conscious effort to put them out of your mind when you leave the office (unless, of course, it is to joke about them or to prompt other people to recognize the ruthless irony behind them). As a strategy for setting goals in life and art, however, perhaps Realistic is the only S.M.A.R.T criterion worth preserving, and even that only in measure, since in many cases you may have no way to know whether a given goal is realistic until you try it. Unlike professional goals, goals in life and art should align with such rewards as satisfaction, eudaemonia, flow, awe, love, wisdom, peace, interest—not productivity. These rewards, in turn, are not always measurable or quantifiable and not always reduceable to well-defined assignments. Some produce their effect over prolonged periods, and some may even become more powerful and meaningful the more time you put into them, rather than striving for a timely completion. When it comes to goals in life and art, you almost never know in advance what goal will yield the greatest rewards until you become inspired to pursue it, or give it a try, or even abandon a previous goal so you may dedicate more of your time to a new calling. Clearly, the S.M.A.R.T strategy is not the right one for setting such goals.

It is the nature of creative ideas that they sometimes materialize in "aha!" moments, in sudden realizations, in unpredictable bouts of inspiration that cannot be planned for. In fact, planning may prevent you from experiencing such moments by dominating your attention and time, leaving no room for new ideas or for the leisurely, mindful attitude of a "beginner's mind" (the Zen concept known as *Shoshin*, or, more formally, *cognitive disinhibition*), which is the state of mind most likely to produce creative ideas.

In art and life, it may seem that you are better off not setting hard goals at all, and instead just waiting for unforeseen opportunities. I propose that there is, in fact, one universal goal we must all strive for—each in our own way—which is this: to someday look back upon the life we had lived with satisfaction, with the knowledge that we have made the most of the gifts and opportunities given to us. As Thoreau put it, "Every man is tasked to make his life, even in its details, worthy of the contemplation of his most

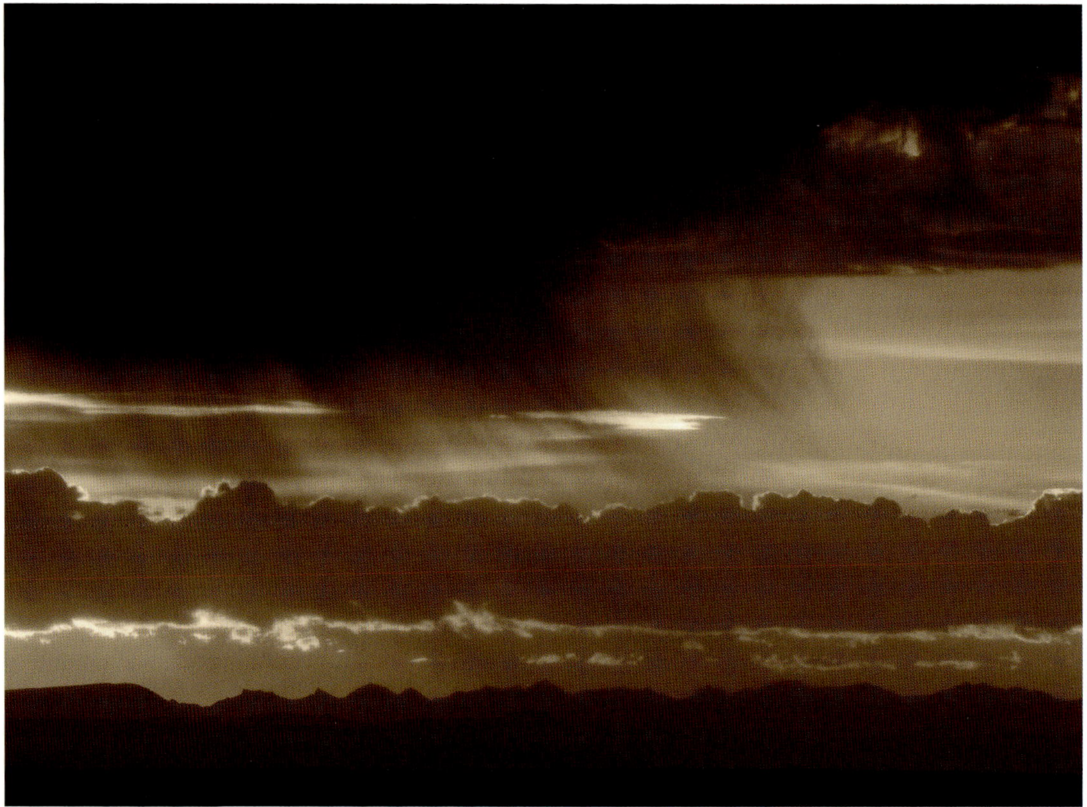

elevated and critical hour." No other measure, whether in the form of material accomplishment or other people's estimates of us, can ultimately compensate for a life lived in boredom, regret, or dissatisfaction.

My advice: Set for yourself whatever decisive short-term goals you need to sustain your life and lifestyle, but leave long-term goals vague and open-ended, to be decided as you encounter opportunities and gain deeper knowledge about the world and about who you are. See how other people's decisions turned out for them, and defer big decisions—where to live, whether to start a family, whether to commit to a career—until you gain more confidence that your choice will be fitting and rewarding to you. Keep yourself on a course, but don't assume from the start that this course will necessarily be the best and final one. Leave room for new opportunities and ideas and allow your older, wiser self as much freedom as you can to make his or her choices.

When you *do* find a goal you feel confident will make your life better, and believe may be within your abilities to achieve, even if it involves risk and effort, give it your all! Many who pursued such noble goals, even if they failed to achieve them, later realized

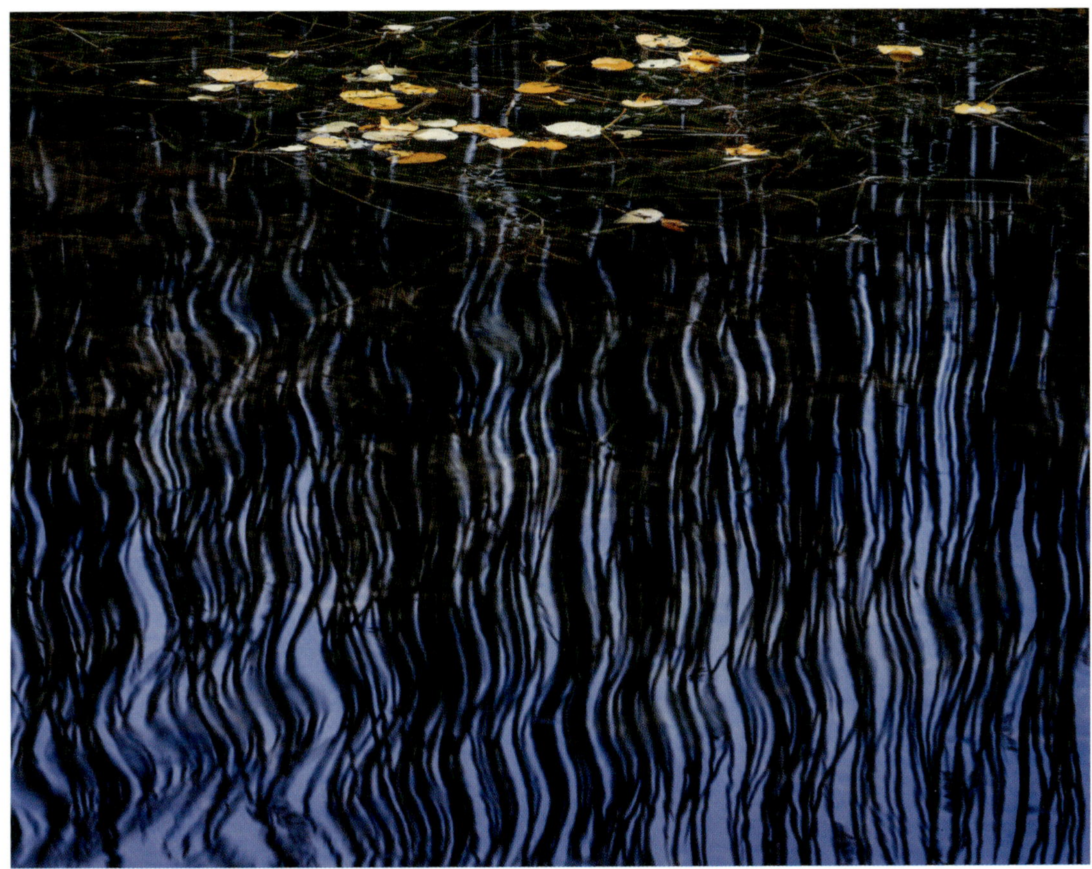

that the experience of pursuing them was profoundly meaningful, life-altering, and worth the time, effort, and risks. As Nietzsche advised in his characteristically dramatic way, "Set for yourself goals, high and noble goals, and perish in pursuit of them! I know of no better life purpose than to perish in pursuing the great and the impossible: *animae magnae prodigus.*"[36] The implication is clear: A life lived in the constant pursuit of meaningful goals is, itself, highly rewarding; not necessarily the achievement of any preconceived goal.

"The most regretful people on earth," wrote Pulitzer Prize–winning poet Mary Oliver, "are those who felt the call to creative work, who felt their own creative power restive and uprising, and gave to it neither power nor time." Since creative epiphanies may arise at any time, sticking with preconceived goals when inspiration pulls you in

---

[36] Latin expression, originally by Horace, meaning "prodigal of a great soul," best read in this context as: be relentless in pursuing what you consider as the highest and noblest values.

a different direction may in some cases make accomplishing the original goal a detriment: a self-imposed fetter that could result in regret for distracting you from a higher calling that you did not know about at the outset.

Don't read the above to mean that you should avoid setting goals for yourself. Aimlessness is a sure path to boredom and frustration. It is important, however, to set your long-term goals such that you will not be worse off for pursuing them. If nothing else, by setting for yourself open-ended goals, you will also set yourself down the path of a "hero's journey,"[37] and you will know the pride that comes from living authentically. Better still, studies suggest that people who diversify their interests, allow for ongoing course corrections, and do not lock themselves into a narrow life path too early are more likely to achieve uncommon success. This may be explained in various ways, the most obvious being simple statistics: The more things you try, the more likely you are to fail, but also the more likely you are to make breakthroughs you could not have known were possible in advance.

What might such vague, open-ended, long-term goals be? A few ideas: Strive to never be bored. Strive to be as self-sufficient as you can be, both materially and psychologically. Strive to keep refining your skills, to broaden and deepen your knowledge and understanding of the world and yourself. Strive for meaningful experiences (and not necessarily for wealth or popularity, which cease to correlate with happiness beyond a certain point). Strive to be kind—human psychology is shaped such that kindness rewards the giver, not just the receiver of kindness. Strive for happiness in the form eudaemonia, rather than flashier but ultimately less satisfying forms. Strive to make peace with your circumstances and personality—the things you can't change. Strive for the courage to live authentically to the degree you can. Strive to feel grateful for any gift—both material and experiential—that comes your way. Strive to be awed often. Strive to be original and expressive in your artistic work. Strive to never stop learning. Strive to make meaningful connections with all lives—human and nonhuman—places, and things. Strive to understand complex concepts and ideas. Strive to be well read. Strive to form meaningful memories. Strive to be interesting to yourself and to others. Strive to behold—not just make—great art, in any form, as a matter of course.

None of these goals have measurable progress indicators nor achievable end products. They are not time-bound, and they don't require you to be accountable to anyone but yourself. They may take on many forms and you may decide to change them as time goes by, as you grow wiser, and as your circumstances change. Their rewards come from merely striving to live up to them day in and day out.

---

[37] Also known as *monomyth*, the hero's journey is a storytelling pattern involving a hero who departs from ordinary life, encounters great challenges and discoveries, and returns triumphant and enlightened.

AVOID UNPRODUCTIVE COMPETITION

Competition is enjoyable only when it is a means to perfect
one's skills; when it becomes an end in itself, it ceases to
be fun.

—MIHALY CSIKSZENTMIHALYI

The important and only vital question is, how much greater,
finer, am I than I was yesterday?

—EDWARD WESTON

Contests in various forms—competitions, juried exhibitions, magazine submissions, etc.—are common in art. Opinions about the usefulness of competitions as means for artistic growth (notwithstanding other benefits they may have) span a wide gamut. Some consider participating in contests as useful motivations to excel, some as benign fun, some as harmful distraction that leads to conformity and to stunting an artist's creative growth. Likewise, judges and juries of art contests may be chosen by a broad range of criteria—popularity, financial success, industry standing, academic qualifications, affiliation with certain institutions, brands, or philanthropists, or seniority within some community (e.g., photographic societies or clubs).

The sheer diversity of competitive venues and the inconsistency of qualifications demanded of jurors suggest that labels such as "award-winning," despite being common among artists, are largely meaningless without also considering the nature and prestige of the contest they won, the number and quality of competing entries, the qualifications, objectivity, and philosophy of the judges, the decision criteria applied, and so on.

As a rule, I recommend avoiding competition except early on in your artistic endeavors, when feedback from jurors may reveal flaws or shortfalls in your technique, or when competition may help establish a reputation and an audience for your work. Beyond these goals, further competition may distract you from more rewarding aspects of art and may, sometimes without you realizing it, influence your work in undesirable ways.

Competitions can feel rewarding, especially if you do well in them. This is why they can be dangerous. Competition rewards artists for pleasing jurors, not for being creative or expressive. In this way, competitions incentivize artists to create work that aims for low common denominators—popularity, simplicity, conformity with prevailing styles and expectations, etc. Competitions also bias viewers who may believe implicitly that jurors possess expertise entitling them to declare some artworks as

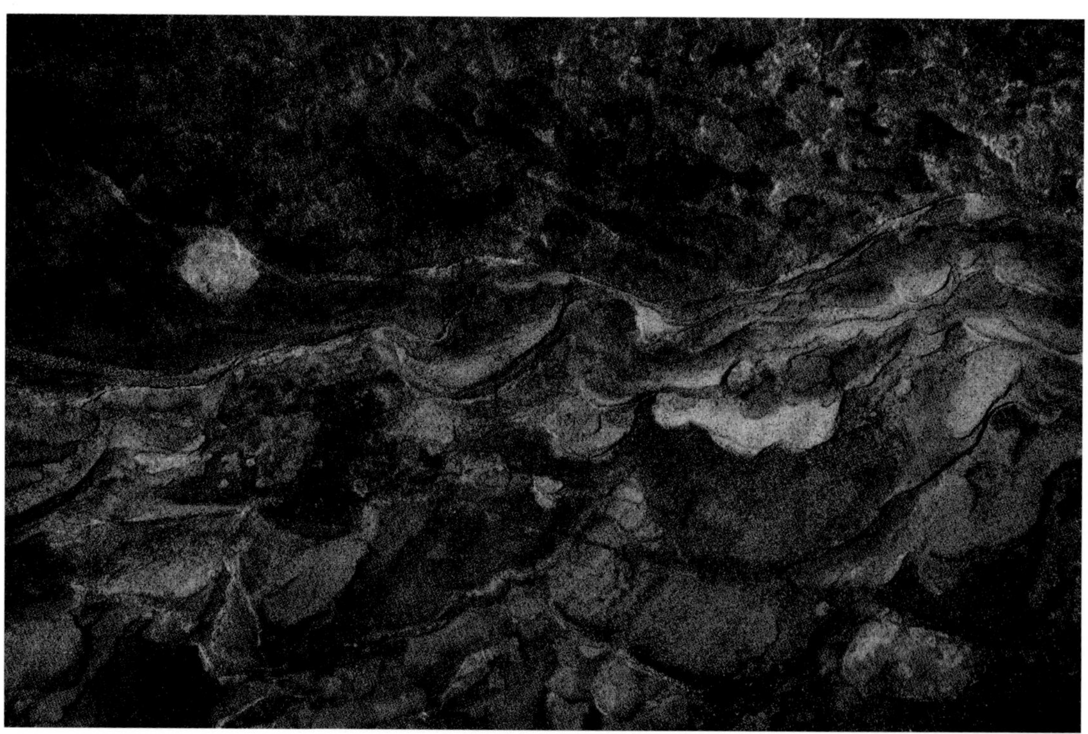

"better" than others. Most often, this is not the case. In fact, much of what we consider today as the most important and venerable art in history was not well received by the art elites of their day, forcing some of the greatest artists in history to compete not against other artists, but against shortsightedness and prejudice, often on the part of so-called "experts."

In 1757, David Hume published a seminal article on aesthetics titled "Of the Standard of Taste," detailing his thoughts regarding desirable qualifications in a person trusted to judge art on behalf of the public—to be a tastemaker. Acknowledging that "it is natural for us to seek a Standard of Taste," and conceding that "there is a species of philosophy, which cuts off all hopes of success in such an attempt," Hume nonetheless declared: "It is impossible to continue in the practice of contemplating any order of beauty, without being frequently obliged to form comparisons between the several species and degrees of excellence, and estimating their proportion to each other."

According to Hume, the ultimate judge of art is history, not any person. While some works of art may be popular during certain periods and/or among certain audiences, the measure of truly great art is that it survives the test of time and appeals to audiences beyond just the contemporaries or cohorts of its maker. But how can we tell *today* whether any given work may ultimately prove itself worthy in hindsight of having been considered as great art? More specifically, who can we turn to today to estimate most reliably what—and to what degree—specific artworks may meet the criteria that will someday qualify them as timeless?

In comparing works of art, Hume suggested, we must first separate judgment from sentiment. Sentiment, being subjective and having no reference to anything beyond the sensibilities of an individual person, is always right for that person. On the other hand, judgment, being rooted in objective understanding, rather than in subjective preference, may be right or wrong in a universal sense, even if we may not know which one until history later reveals it to us.

Who, then, are those venerated people possessing such deep understanding of art that history will most likely affirm their judgments in time? According to Hume, they are people who possess a "strong sense, united to delicate sentiment, improved by practice, perfected by comparison, and cleared of all prejudice."

"Strong sense" means subject-matter expertise. But such expertise alone, according to Hume, is not enough. Those we should consider as qualified to judge art are not just people who happen to possess factual knowledge about certain genres of art, but those whose expertise was also honed by repeated practice over a prolonged span of time; who are sensitive to delicate nuances that others may miss or not know to look for; whose knowledge is not just deep, but is also broad beyond the confines of any one style, discipline, or period (or a handful of styles, disciplines, and periods); and who can be trusted to judge artworks ruthlessly and objectively, without any preference to specific artists, subjects, or styles, without ideological prejudice, and without subjective bias.

Do you know any such people? I don't. Even if they exist, it is likely that there are very few of them—far fewer than there are art competitions, suggesting that the great majority of these competitions are, by necessity, judged by people who lack some qualification, knowledge, or objectivity, making their judgment at best subjective or misinformed, and at worst unfair and unhelpful. Hume would have agreed. He wrote, "But where are such critics to be found? By what marks are they to be known? How distinguish them from pretenders?" He then conceded, "These questions are embarrassing; and seem to throw us back into the same uncertainty, from which ... we have endeavoured to extricate ourselves."

I mention Hume not only because he was a brilliant thinker, but also because, in reading his thoughts, most people tend to miss two important aspects: 1) He wrote specifically about judgment of beauty (aesthetic appeal), and not about judgment of other qualities of art, such as creativity or expression; and 2) He tried to find a common denominator for what society—viewers of art—should consider as a "standard of good taste." He didn't suggest that artists should avoid experimentation and innovation, or that they should compromise their own joy in making art to conform to this standard.

Hume could not have predicted how our understanding of art would evolve after his time. A great revolution in art occurred in the late 1800s—a century after Hume's passing—with the advent of impressionism, followed by a succession of movements now loosely considered as modern art. Practically all pioneering artists in these modern styles were initially shunned and ridiculed by prominent art critics and art institutions. Some were even denied entry into the most prestigious art venues of their time.

In 1918, when modern art was already well established and art became broadly accepted as more than just a term referring to beautiful depictions of familiar motifs, Bertrand Russell published his book *Proposed Roads to Freedom*, where he wrote, "It is impossible for art, or any of the higher creative activities, to flourish under any system which requires that the artist shall prove his competence to some body of authorities before he is allowed to follow his impulse. Any really great artist is almost sure to be thought incompetent by those among his seniors who would be generally regarded as best qualified to form an opinion."

What did Russell mean by "really great artist" (presumably, as distinct from a lesser form of artist)? In a previous book, he characterized an artist as a person who loves "distinctive individuality." He also believed that art must be an expression of

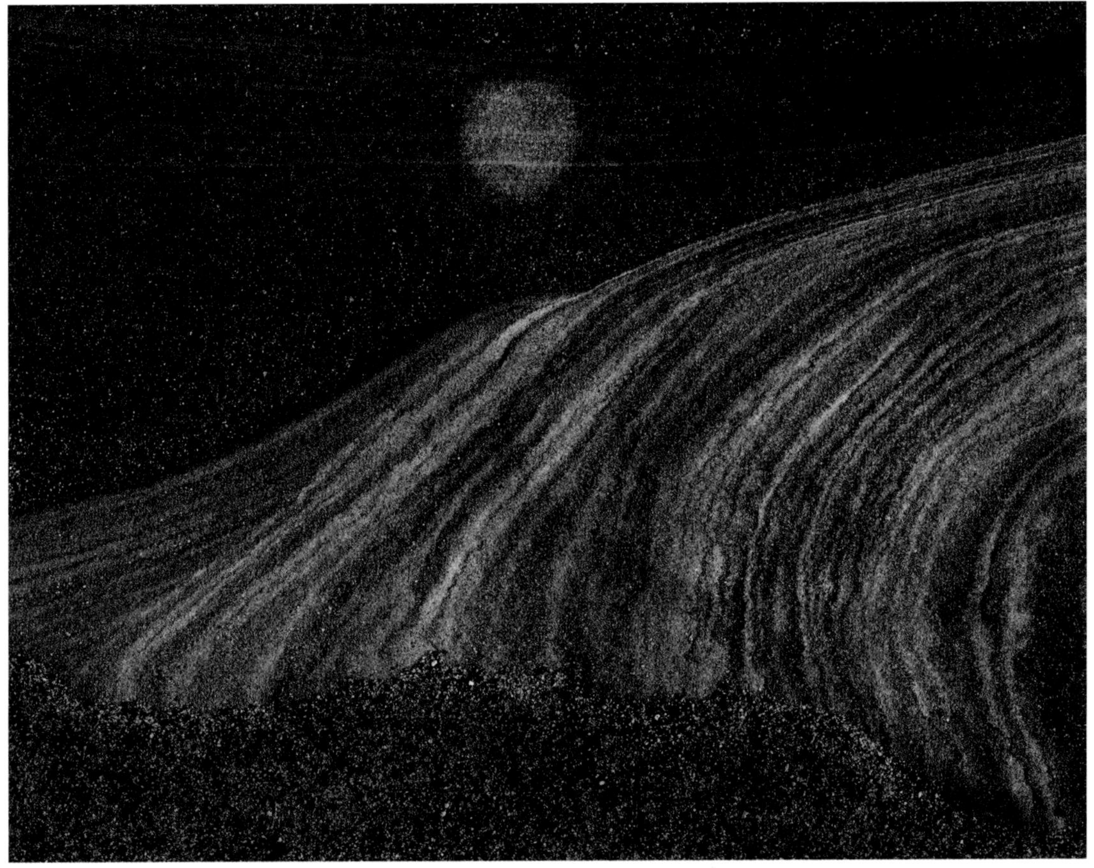

this individuality. In his words, "Art springs from a wild and anarchic side of human nature." Anarchy implies doing things freely and voluntarily, not in deference to anyone else's judgment or to rules imposed by any organization or authority figure.

In his 1923 book *The Art Spirit*, Robert Henri proposed that the very idea of competition is incompatible with artistic expression. He wrote, "The pernicious influence of the prize and medal giving in art is so great that it should be stopped." He added, "To award prizes is to attempt to control the course of another man's work. It is a bid to have him do what you will approve. It affects not only the one who wins the award, but all those who in any measure strive for it." Like Russell, Henri also doubted the ability of judges and juries—or anyone other than the artist—to decide on the merits

of an artwork. He wrote decisively, "History proves that juries in art have been generally wrong."

When the early impressionists began to produce their now-iconic works, the
dominant style in art was realism. The highest authority in art at the time was the
French *Académie des Beaux-Arts* (Academy of Fine Arts), sponsor of the highest venue
for showcasing art: the Paris Salon. In the early 1860s, juries for the Salon rejected
(sometimes in strong and derisive language) several works by pioneering impressionist painters, such as Claude Monet and Édouard Manet. Hearing about the rejections,
French emperor Napoleon III decided that the public had a right to see these works
and judge them for themselves. He established the *Salon des Refusés* (exhibition of the
rejected), which showcased some of the impressionists' works. Later, several of the
early impressionists founded their own society and arranged for their own independent
exhibits, often eliciting mocking critiques in popular press. To make a long story short,
the historical importance we place today on impressionism and its enormous down-
stream effect on so many later art movements should tell you that Russell and Henri
were right—the greatest art experts and juries at that time got it wrong.

Truly creative art—art expressing the uniqueness and extraordinariness of individual artists who may think and create in innovative ways, or who may wish to venture
beyond the zeitgeist of their day—has always faced an uphill battle for acceptance.
As José Ortega y Gasset put it, "Whenever the new Muses present themselves, the
masses bristle." This, in turn, has the unfortunate effect of discouraging innovation
and encouraging artists to stay within the narrow boundaries of what is already known
to be popular. As Marshall McLuhan put it, "Competition is based on the principle of
conformity."

"What I must do is all that concerns me, not what the people think," wrote Ralph
Waldo Emerson in his essay "Self-Reliance." He continued, "This rule, equally arduous
in actual and in intellectual life, may serve for the whole distinction between greatness
and meanness. It is the harder because you will always find those who think they know
what is your duty better than you know it." In another essay, "Heroism," Emerson
wrote, "when you have chosen your part, abide by it, and do not weakly try to recon-
cile yourself with the world. The heroic cannot be the common, nor the common the
heroic." (To the point of this book, a thesaurus will confirm that "common" is synonymous with "ordinary"—the opposite of "extraordinary.")

Another reason ranking in a competition is meaningless is because not all people
are equally disposed to creativity or personal expression, nor do all people have the
same amount of time and resources to dedicate to their art, the same degrees of experience and knowledge, or the same goals and motivations driving their work. Unlike

people running a marathon or spelling difficult words, it's very rare that all competitors in an art contest will have comparable degrees of experience and aesthetic sensibilities, which makes *all* judgment in art a subjective matter. To say that a work that won an art contest is unequivocally better art than any entry that didn't win or wasn't even in the running, or that the creator of an award-winning work is a better artist than another who didn't win a contest, is a meaningless statement.

So, who gets to judge art? If you create your art for others, then others get to judge it. If you create art for yourself, seeking to elevate the quality of your experiences and to express your own values and sensibilities, then there is only one person qualified to judge the worth of your work: you. If others misjudge or misunderstand what you do or why you do it, then, as Norman Mailer put it, "With the pride of the artist, you must blow against the walls of every power that exists the small trumpet of your defiance."

If ultimately you are the only person qualified to judge your work by the criteria you wish for it to be judged, then the only person you should care about competing with is also the only other artist you can know for certain understands and strives for these same criteria: your own past self.

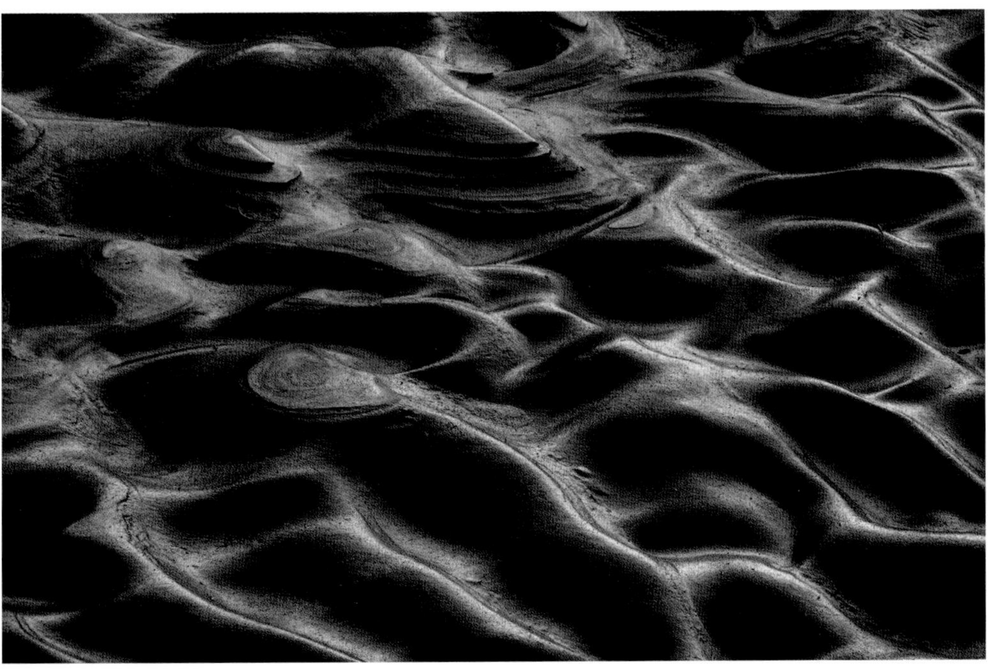

SEEK AWE

> He who can no longer pause to wonder and stand rapt in
> awe, is as good as dead; his eyes are closed.

—ALBERT EINSTEIN

Would it surprise you to know that the words "awesome" and "awful" both come from the same origin: the Old English word *ege*, meaning "terror"? Both words relate also to the powerful emotion of awe, characterized in psychologist Robert Plutchik's "wheel of emotions" as the most extreme combination of amazement and terror. Common to many definitions of awe is the emergent emotional effect of two elements: a sense of deep reverence or fascination, and a sense of existential fear. Predisposition to awe is known from studies to be correlated with certain personality traits—most notably, openness to experience.

Experiencing awe is known to elicit a profound sense of meaning in life. In a paper by two prominent psychologists, Dacher Keltner and Jonathan Haidt,[38] the authors wrote, "Fleeting and rare, experiences of awe can change the course of a life in profound and permanent ways." In the same paper, they characterized awe as a "family" of "emotional experiences that involve perceived vastness and a need for accommodation, whether in response to a charismatic leader, a grand vista, or a symphony."

Now consider that so many things characterized as "awesome"—awesome artwork; awesome trips; awesome jobs; owning an awesome vehicle, camera, or home—despite being rooted in the experience of awe, may also be had without this experience.

---

[38] Dacher Keltner & Jonathan Haidt (2003) Approaching awe, a moral, spiritual, and aesthetic emotion, Cognition and Emotion, 17:2, 297-314, DOI: 10.1080/02699930302297

But why would you want to? The difference between awesomeness arising from awe and awesomeness used just as a figure of speech is akin to the difference between being gifted a trophy and earning one. The profound sense of meaning I mention above comes from *experiencing* awe, not from having or impressing others with awesome things.

Sometimes when I describe my approach to art and life, someone will comment sarcastically, "what's wrong with just taking it easy and having fun?" My answer, even if not always expressed out loud, is this: If you think your easy fun is more rewarding than my (serious, often uncomfortable, and sometimes outright terrifying) awe, then the joke is on you.

By my experience, just one taste of true awe will leave you with a lifelong yearning to experience it again, as often as you can. In his book *Awe: The New Science of Everyday Wonder and How It Can Transform Your Life*, Keltner wrote, "How does awe transform us? By quieting the nagging, self-critical, overbearing, status-conscious voice of our self, or ego, and empowering us to collaborate, to open our minds to wonders, and to see the deep patterns of life." Moreover, he suggested that you don't have to take existential risks to experience awe. You can shape your life and attitude so you may experience what he termed "everyday awe," which may arise from such things as "the strength, courage, and kindness of others; collective movement in actions like dance and sports; nature; music; art and visual design; mystical encounters; encountering life and death; and big ideas or epiphanies."

"In our studies," Keltner wrote, "people who find more everyday awe show evidence of living with wonder. They are more open to new ideas. To what is unknown. To what language can't describe. To the absurd. To seeking new knowledge. To experience itself, for example of sound, or color, or bodily sensation, or the directions thought might take during dreams or meditation. To the strengths and virtues of other people. It should not surprise that people who feel even five minutes a day of everyday awe are more curious about art, music, poetry, new scientific discoveries, philosophy, and questions about life and death. They feel more comfortable with mysteries, with that which cannot be explained."

Who wouldn't want that?

There are people who know awe and people who don't. Strive to be the former.

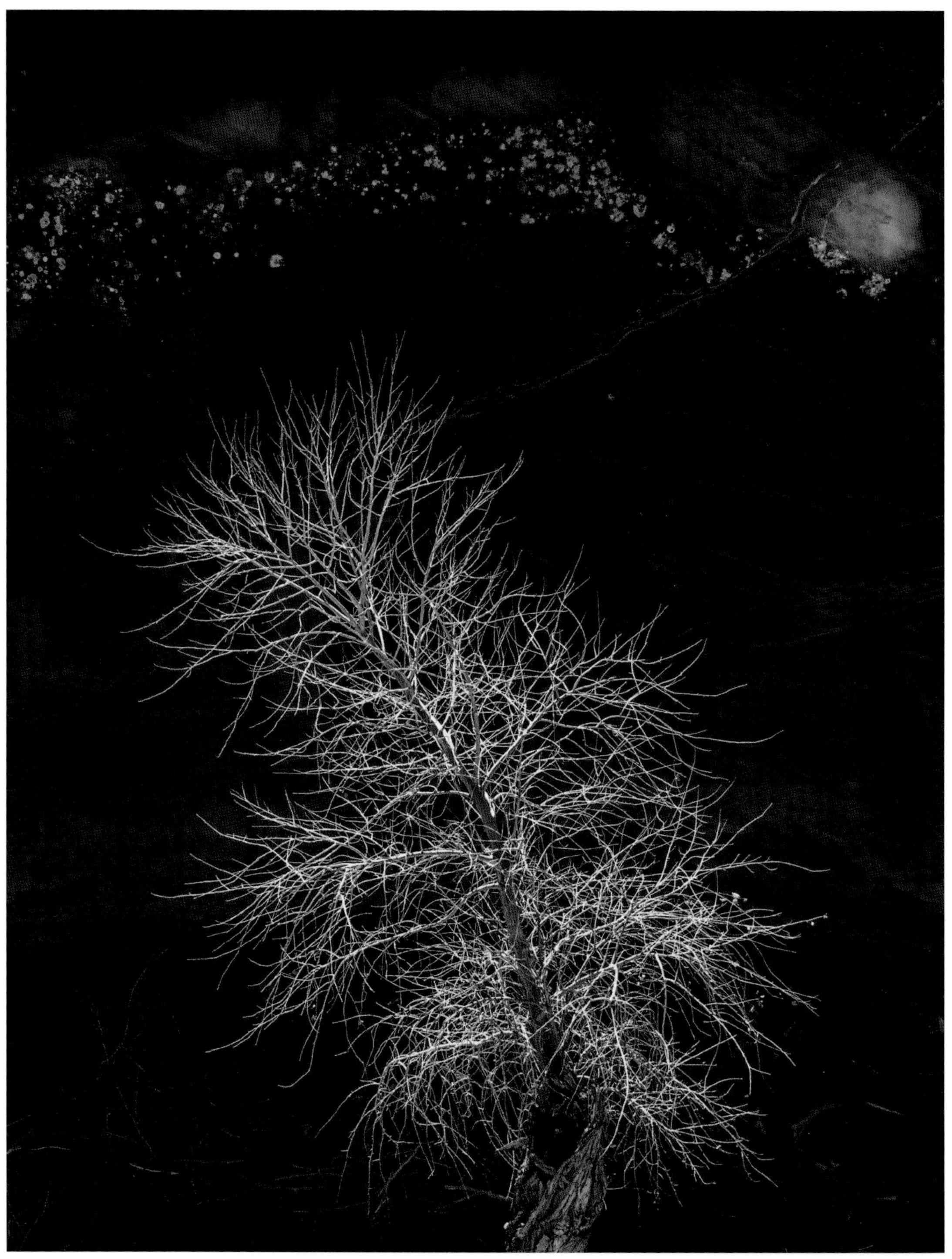

TALK TO YOURSELF

Might your bitter pain not be the voice of destiny, might that
voice not become sweet once you understand it?

—HERMANN HESSE

In my photography classes, when I explain the idea of self-expression in art, I start with this favorite quotation from John Szarkowski: "It isn't what a picture is *of*, it is what it is *about*." (Italics mine) I use the term "concept" to refer to the thing that an image is about. I then qualify that it is not important whether the concept can be described in words. Images, like music and any other form of artistic expression, may convey meanings, ideas, and states of mind beyond what any spoken or written language can, in the same way that every language has some terms, expressions, or euphemisms that can't be translated perfectly to any other language.

The important thing is not to be able to explain an artwork's concept in words, but for you, the artist, to grok—to know intuitively but unambiguously—what your concept is, even if you can't explain it to others, and to use this intuitive knowledge to guide your work: your choices of materials, styles, colors, and all other aspects that are within your control. With each choice, ask yourself whether it fits with and expresses your concept or distracts from it—a conversation only you can have with yourself, being that you are the only person who fully understands what it is you wish to express. At times, you may even hear your inner voice suggesting, without conscious prompting, changes or improvements, perhaps even creative epiphanies pointing you to pursue a different, better, concept. Without this internal dialog, you may become too focused on your original intent and miss these opportunities.

Have you ever found yourself wondering, "should I have another piece of cake?" "Is now the right time to bring up this-or-that topic in conversation?" "Should I buy this item?" Or, "is this really what I want to do?" Consider for a moment who it is you are "speaking" with. We assume wrongly that each of us is, or has, a unified self—a singular, indivisible, "I." Many experiments in neuroscience and psychology have proven this perception wrong. Perhaps most famous are the so-called "split brain" experiments conducted by Roger Sperry and Michael Gazzaniga, in which patients whose brain hemispheres have become separated, by accident or to treat certain conditions such as epilepsy, seem to exhibit different or even conflicting knowledge and preferences when presented with questions or information targeted to one hemisphere or the other. Similarly, our perceptions of who we are and the world around us result from a process known in neuroscience as *binding*, which involves integrating neural information from multiple sources to create a unified perception. As Walt Whitman observed, "I contain multitudes." This is true for any "I."

The process of binding is largely subconscious and beyond your ability to control; but to a degree, you also have conscious access to some information stored in your brain that may not factor automatically into your default perceptions. One way to tap into this knowledge is to consciously ask yourself questions such as I suggest above— to have the "multitudes" you contain talk to each other.

Take as a simple example a photographer standing before an impressive view. Intuitively, this photographer may want to reach for the camera and begin snapping away, or perhaps strive consciously (and regrettably) to apply some "rule" of composition. Think instead how much more useful information this photographer may gain by pondering consciously questions such as, "what am I trying to express?" "What in the scene contributes to or distracts from what I wish to express?" "Am I standing in the best possible spot?" "Will my image be more effective if I include or exclude this-or-that element?" "How will I process this image later?"

The most effective form of inner conversation, if you wish to ensure you are being honest with yourself, is what's known in philosophy as the Socratic method, named after Socrates, who was in the habit of accosting people at random, calling them out on important questions or on things they said, and leading them—by a series of questions—to realize that they have not thought the matter through well enough.

Socratic dialogs don't always end in finding "right" answers, but they are invaluable to transcending biases, confronting doubts, and identifying what information you may be missing and need to learn to gain a deeper understanding of any subject. As a strategy for debate, the Socratic method may get you into trouble if you use it to challenge random people about touchy subjects (to wit, Socrates was put on trial and sentenced to death for doing so); but if you use it to debate yourself—with the goal of avoiding your own blind spots, prejudices, and gaps in knowledge—the worst you may experience is (perhaps severe) discomfort. On the other hand, you will never be in doubt about the good intentions of any party in the debate, as all of them are—in one sense or another—you, even though not all of them may be aware of their inborn irrationalities and prejudices. As Richard Feynman wrote, "The first principle is that you must not fool yourself—and you are the easiest person to fool."

Another way to think about the value of talking to yourself is in the sense of narrating your life—taking an active role in authoring your own story. Although it may not seem obvious to you, the stories your subconscious mind weaves on its own are not the only possible ones, nor are they necessarily the correct ones. I speak from painful personal experience here. In my late forties, I received a diagnosis of a mental condition I never knew I had. As a result, I had new explanations for many events in my life that I used to believe I understood well and attributed to conscious choices on my part. It was humbling, jarring, and profoundly liberating to me to realize in hindsight how much of my life path and the stories I told myself were, in fact, expressions of this disorder. With this knowledge, and with further studies in various methods of psychotherapy (especially Cognitive Behavior Therapy), I was able to become, at least to a degree, my own therapist. (Note that I am in no way suggesting that this approach is a good substitute for consulting with a trained therapist, only that it may have significant benefits.)

Talking to yourself—asking yourself questions, even if they are uncomfortable; verifying that your choices are true to your goals; taking conscious control of your stories and experiences—can be very useful in times when you are facing important and consequential decisions. Beyond just gaining confidence that you considered all possibilities honestly and recognized potential problems, having a Socratic dialog with yourself will also help you to avoid becoming overwhelmed. By asking yourself questions, you can break down even complex problems into bite-sized chunks, and then have an easier time accepting conclusions that may seem daunting, realizing that, as my least-favorite figure of speech goes, "It is what it is."

Other than Socratic dialogs, another way of communicating with yourself that may yield you even greater benefits is to journal: to write down your questions and thoughts, make notes of your doubts and explanations, and articulate your feelings. Beyond being therapeutic and a good way to make yourself mindful of your inner states, journaling will also help you remember details of your experiences that may escape your mind if you wait too long. (I'll revisit and expand on the benefits of journaling later in this book.)

So, talk to yourself and write down your meditations (i.e., keep a journal, if only as a collection of random shorthand notes). It will make you more self-aware and reveal to you aspects of your experience that you may not be conscious of. It will help you find correlations between the outside world and your own feelings that may help in your art, in keeping yourself honest, realistic, and humble, and in reminding you to be grateful for what you have. And in later years, it will allow you to recall your experiences, to "compare notes" with your former self, perhaps even to retell your stories in better ways using acquired knowledge and understanding.

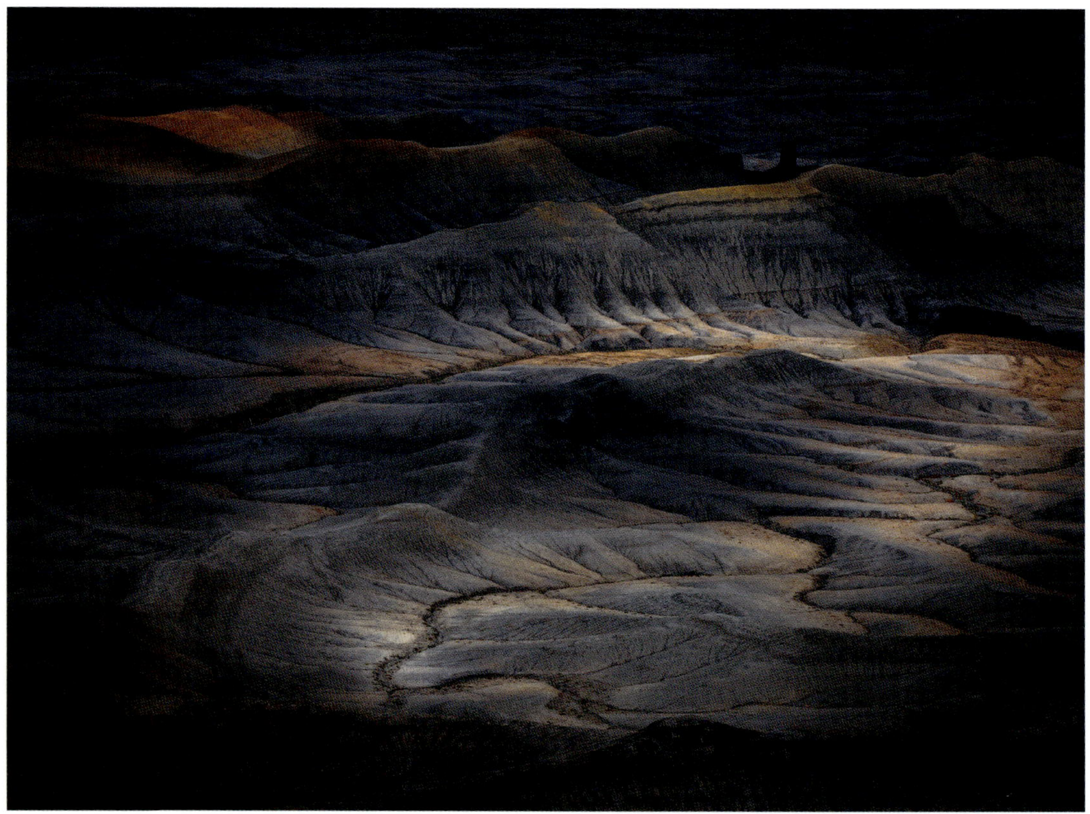

PRACTICE DIVERGENT AND DISINHIBITED THINKING

Genius, in truth, means little more than the faculty of
perceiving in an unhabitual way.

—WILLIAM JAMES

As far as my own experience is concerned, I sometimes begin
a drawing with no preconceived problem to solve, with only
the desire to use pencil on paper, and make lines, tones, and
shapes with no conscious aim; but as my mind takes in what
is so produced, a point arrives where some idea becomes
conscious and crystallizes, and then a control and ordering
begin to take place.

—HENRY MOORE

In most cases, when we take on a task, we reach for tools, methods, and materials we
are already familiar with, or at least know about. In other words, we approach most
problems—whether preparing a dish, mixing pigments, outlining an article, or deciding the proper exposure parameters for a photograph—with known solutions. With
practice, we hone our skills, learn from our mistakes, and find resources to consult
when faced with tasks that are beyond our abilities. This approach to problem solving
is known as *convergent thinking*, defined in the *APA Dictionary of Psychology* as, "critical
thinking in which an individual uses linear, logical steps to analyze a number of already

formulated solutions to a problem to determine the correct one or the one that is most likely to be successful."

Convergent thinking works well for most problems we try to solve—problems we can analyze and break into a series of tasks, which we can tackle in known ways. Where convergent thinking is of no help, however, is when we strive to come up with creative ideas—things that have not been done before, and that we may not know are even possible until we try. Coming up with creative ideas and with creative ways to implement them requires a different approach: *divergent thinking*.

The *APA Dictionary of Psychology* defines divergent thinking as, "creative thinking in which an individual solves a problem or reaches a decision using strategies that *deviate from commonly used or previously taught strategies*." (Italics mine) Put more simply, divergent thinking is about letting go of known patterns, templates, rules, recipes, or any other strategy already known in advance. Instead, divergent thinkers may combine already-known concepts in new ways (this is known as "conceptual blending"), experiment with using tools and materials in uncommon ways, or forcing yourself consciously to consider possibilities that may not be intuitive or already proven.

In artistic work—whether visual, written, audible, or any other—we may prompt divergent ideas by employing metaphors or symbols rather than focusing on explicit depictions or known expressions; by consciously freeing ourselves to experiment with colors, wordings, angles of view, rhythms, or anything else within our control and abilities, and seeing where it may lead us, even if we can't say in advance what the outcome will be or whether it will be successful. Once we arrive at a possible creative idea by way of divergent thinking and decide "hey, let's try this," then it's time to refocus attention and switch to convergent thinking, to using known tools and techniques to see if the idea will lead to anything useful.

Planning your creations in advance is the opposite of divergent thinking. It leaves little or no room for creative, unexpected, surprising ideas to bubble up for consideration and experimentation. If you are pursuing a planned outcome, even if a creative idea pops into your mind, you may feel beholden to your original plan and dismiss the new idea without giving it a try or considering it seriously.

Planning is useful to a creative artist only *after* conceiving an original idea. Planning a predictable outcome before experiencing a creative epiphany is known as preconception. As Dorothea Lange wrote, "To know ahead of time what you're looking for means you're then only photographing your preconceptions, which is very limiting." My advice: Even if you are in the habit of planning your creations (and as long as you did not commit to delivering your work to a client), always consider your plans as tentative. Allow space for new ideas to emerge spontaneously, and be willing to deviate

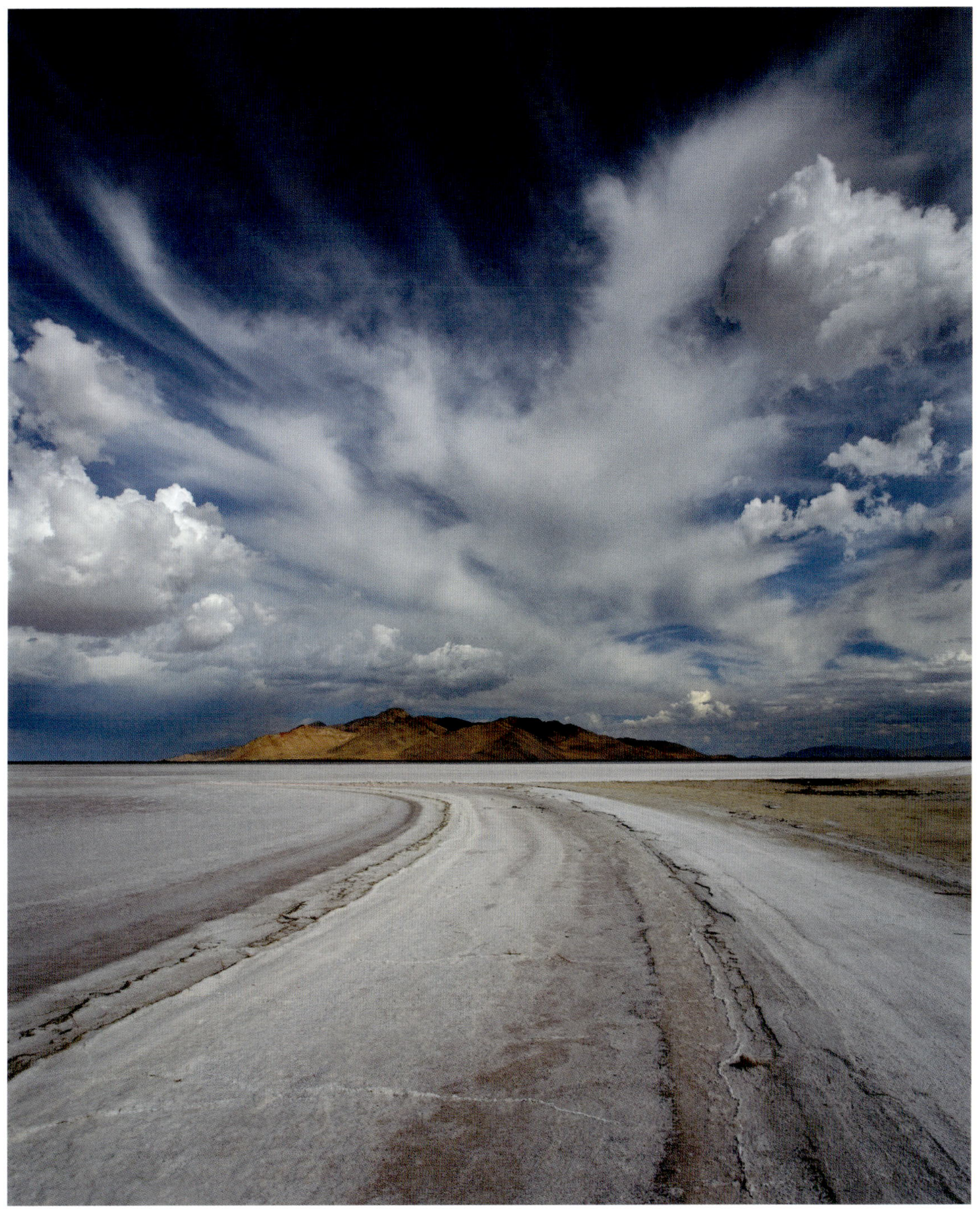

from—or entirely discard—your preconceptions if a more interesting possibility presents itself.

Divergent thinking comes more naturally to some (especially to those who score high on the personality trait of openness to experience), but like any cognitive skill, it can be improved and become more intuitive with practice. At the outset, one of the more difficult aspects of divergent thinking to adopt is to consciously allow for new ideas to form and enter your consciousness. What I mean by "allow" is to be willing to break with previous habits, styles, expectations, and routines—even those that have proven reliably successful in other scenarios—to consciously make mental space for thinking about new possibilities and resist your instinct to reach for obvious solutions. The term for this freeing up of attention, loosening hard-wired boundaries of what is "right" or "acceptable," being willing to combine seemingly unrelated concepts, and broadening the range of possibilities you'll consider is *cognitive disinhibition*—i.e., avoidance of inhibiting your mind, instead allowing it to roam freely, to consider any conceivable idea that may lead to a creative breakthrough.

"Coincidences always happen if you keep your mind open," wrote Werner Herzog, "while storyboards remain the instruments of cowards who do not trust in their own imagination and who are slaves of a matrix.... *If you get used to planning your shots based solely on aesthetics, you are never that far from kitsch.*" (Italics mine)

Edward Weston wrote, "*The moment* presents and suggests what to do, and how to do it." (Italics mine) Note "the moment"—not a preconceived plan, not a guidebook, not a social media influencer, not the contrived rules of some contest you may consider entering, and not what you feel other people will or will not like or approve of. The moment is the sum of all the dimensions of your experience as it happens: what you see, feel, think, imagine, and want to express when inspiration strikes you and a creative moment occurs. No moment is exactly like any other moment. Each makes possible ideas that have not been considered or expressed before.

The enemy of divergent thinking is distraction. Divergent thinking demands cognitive resources—attention, openness, imagination, knowledge, conscious awareness of what is in your environment and of your inner states. The more of these resources you invest in the task of conceiving new ideas, the more of these ideas you will have and the greater the odds that one of them will lead to a creative "aha!" moment. Alas, we live in a world full of distractions competing for and usurping these same cognitive resources. As Andrew Smart explained in his book *Autopilot*:

> *When your brain is bombarded with stimuli like emails, phone calls, text messages, Facebook updates, errands, driving around, talking to*

*your boss, checking your to-do list, etc., it is kept busy responding to
what neuroscientist Scott Makeig, director of the Swartz Center for
Computational Neuroscience in La Jolla, California, calls 'the challenge
of the moment.' Clearly, it is very important to be able to respond to the
moment. Sometimes our survival depends on the ability to successfully
meet this challenge. However, if that moment becomes every minute of
every day of every month of every year, your brain has no time left over
to make novel connections between seemingly unrelated things, find patterns, and have new ideas. In other words, to be creative.*

The dire implication is that in our time it's not enough to strive to become a divergent thinker; you also need to tackle the difficult task of ridding yourself of a common
attention-destroying addiction: the addiction to social technology. Beyond any benefit
that overcoming this addiction may yield in the realm of creative artmaking, consider
also the greater danger of this addiction to your quality of life. As a recent study[39] characterized it:

*With the growth of the Internet use over the last two decades, there has
been an increase in its usages as well as in the frequency of experienced
dysfunctions related to its overuse. Users report loss of control over their
Internet use, social problems as well as school and/or occupational difficulties. Public health concerns are emerging concerning the propensity
of compulsive Internet use developing into pathological behaviors.*

This is a big part of the reason creativity has been declining measurably in recent
years. As individuals, we may be powerless to reverse the trend or to avoid the greater
social implications of living in a world where most people are no longer able to pay
focused attention to such tasks as reading a book, savoring a piece of expressive music,
or conceiving novel artworks. However, there is no denying that making the effort—no
matter how daunting or difficult it may seem—to free yourself of this addiction will
make your life more meaningful and rewarding, and by extension also increase your
capacity for and satisfaction in making creative art.

---

[39] Das A, Sharma MK, Thamilselvan P, Marimuthu P. Technology Addiction among Treatment Seekers for Psychological Problems:
Implication for Screening in Mental Health Setting. Indian J Psychol Med. 2017 Jan-Feb, 39(1):21-27. doi: 10.4103/0253-7176.198939.
PMID: 28250554; PMCID: PMC5329986.

J. P. Guilford—who coined the term "divergent thinking"—also proposed a model for measuring it, which he titled the *Alternate Uses Task* (AUT). AUT breaks down divergent thinking into four distinct aspects:

- *Fluency*: The ability to come up with many possible solutions to a given problem in real time, without advance planning.

- *Originality*: The ability to come up with novel and previously unknown solutions, not just with solutions you already knew about.

- *Flexibility*: The ability to consider a wide range of solutions, not just those that seem most obvious.

- *Elaboration*: The ability to take a solution from abstract idea to practical implementation—i.e., to switch consciously to convergent thinking once a plausible idea is found through divergent thinking.

The AUT breakdown is useful in helping us become better divergent thinkers. For example, if you are faced with a given situation (say, coming up with a creative composition for a photograph) but can only think of one or two options, you have a fluency problem. Likewise, if you can only imagine possibilities that look like other images you have seen before (say, only wide-angle, near-far compositions), you have an originality problem. If you do manage to come up with multiple solutions, but they are generally within the narrow bounds of things you already know how to do (say, only black-and-white square compositions rendered in high contrast), you have a flexibility problem. And if you managed to come up with a good creative idea but can't think of how to implement it, you have an elaboration problem. With this knowledge, you will gain insight into what skills you may wish to train and improve—by deliberate repetition and by progressively raising your challenge level once you become comfortable.

In all cases, the more often you make yourself aware of these problems and push yourself to do better, the easier you will find it to come up with divergent ideas, and the more creative possibilities will naturally occur to you. Paraphrasing an old Funkadelic song title: free your mind ... and your art will follow.

Sometimes, the only way to discover who you are or what life you should lead is to do less planning and more living—to burst the double bubble of comfort and convention and just do stuff, even if you don't know precisely where it's going to lead, because you don't know precisely where it's going to lead. This might sound risky—and you know what? It is. It's really risky. But the greater risk is to choose false certainty over genuine ambiguity. The greater risk is to fear failure more than mediocrity. The greater risk is to pursue a path only because it's the first path you decided to pursue.

—DANIEL PINK

Planning is very useful when you have a desired outcome in mind and know the steps needed to accomplish it. Put another way, a plan is the product of convergent thinking. While conceiving a plan may require a degree of creativity, implementing it is a decidedly uncreative activity. Consequently, when it comes to creative activities such as artmaking, *when* you come up with your plan can be as important as *whether* you come up with a plan. What I mean by this is that if you plan the production of an artwork too early—before experiencing a creative epiphany or a feeling you wish to express artistically—you eliminate (or at least severely diminish) the role of creativity in your work and its associated rewards.

Planning is also a form of preconception. Preconception, taken literally, means deciding on a concept for your artwork in advance, rather than allowing a concept

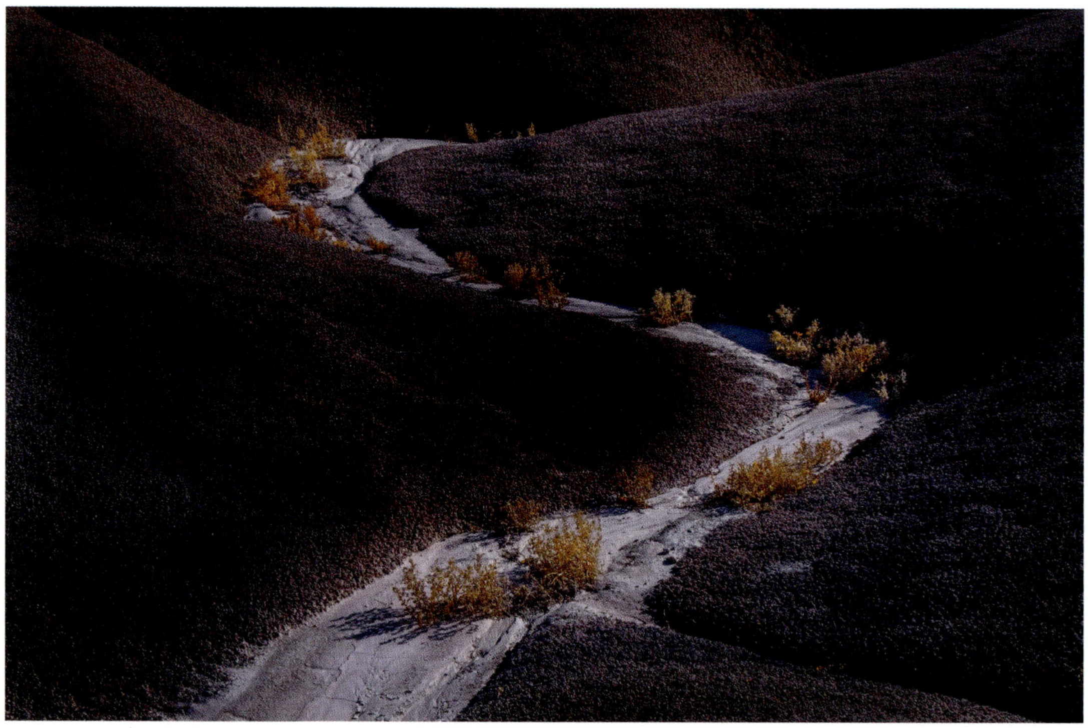

to emerge organically, in real time, in response to an experience or a feeling. In this sense, planning can also be considered a hindrance to self-expression: You can't know in advance when inspiration will strike you, or what feelings you may experience and wish to express at some future time. This is another reason why planning too early— before having a genuine, meaningful feeling you wish to express—comes at the risk of eliminating or diminishing your capacity to be self-expressive, again robbing you of the rewards associated with self-expression.

My suggestion: Defer planning until after you have had a meaningful experience or feeling—a concept—worth expressing, and after you have considered multiple possible ways to express it. This is the essence of *visualization*: having a sense—a mental representation—of what you wish to create, conceived in real time. Only then, with this visualization in mind, should you make a plan to realize your idea.

Just as important, given that it's the nature of creative ideas to pop into your head seemingly at random, be prepared to abandon or deviate from your plans if more interesting or rewarding possibilities present themselves. Make it a point to remain open to new experiences—discoveries, unforeseen encounters, unanticipated feelings—even if you are already in the process of implementing a plan—rather than locking yourself completely into a preconceived plan and closing yourself off to other, perhaps better, possibilities. Vincent van Gogh described this attitude, which had led him to make some of the most original and venerable art we know of. He wrote:

> *If I do nothing, if I study nothing, if I cease searching, then, woe is me, I am lost. That is how I look at it—keep going, keep going come what may. But what is your final goal, you may ask. That goal will become clearer, will emerge slowly but surely, much as the rough draught turns into a sketch, and the sketch into a painting through the serious work done on it, through the elaboration of the original vague idea and through the consolidation of the first fleeting and passing thought.*

Likewise, pioneering science fiction writer Isaac Asimov stated, "To succeed, planning alone is insufficient. One must improvise as well."

Consider that oftentimes in art the worst outcome of a preconceived plan is to achieve exactly what you planned, and not even consider what other—better, more creative, more expressive, more meaningful, more adventurous—opportunities you may have denied yourself unwittingly by not allowing for other possibilities to emerge and be considered as you go. This may also be true if you try to plan your life too early or too far ahead. Consider that your older self likely will be wiser and more experienced than you are at the time you make any plan. If you plan too strictly or make consequential decisions too early, you may deny this older, wiser version of you the freedom to make better choices later in life—choices founded in greater knowledge and understanding of yourself and of the world than you have today. Plan only as much as necessary, and only when you feel sufficiently confident in what you wish to accomplish.

WORK TO LIVE

> Much that we take for granted about the desirability of work
> is ... not adapted to the modern world. Modern technique
> has made it possible for leisure, within limits, to be not the
> prerogative of small privileged classes, but a right evenly
> distributed throughout the community. The morality of work is
> the morality of slaves, and the modern world has no need of
> slavery.
>
> —BERTRAND RUSSELL

Before becoming a full-time artist and writer, I spent about two decades working various jobs, both as an employee and as an independent business owner. Like most people, I took it for granted that I had to strive constantly for more income and pursue any opportunity to increase my material prosperity. I also took it for granted that I had to implicitly accept trading as much of my time—my living moments, private experiences, interests outside my professional duties and preoccupations—for more earnings, more responsibilities, more fame and popularity, more (newer, better, shinier) "stuff," because it's "just the way things are." It is not.

I don't lament (too much) my career-driven years. I've always had to earn an income and was fortunate to realize at an early age the importance of saving and investing some of it for later years. I consider that period in my life as part of the cost of entry for the life I live now and the freedoms it affords me to set my own schedule, pursue a variety of interests and experiences (most of which do not generate income), live where I wish to live, and speak my mind freely without having to worry too much about jeopardizing my livelihood. Also, I recognize that even if I did have the means to support myself without having to pursue a professional career, there's a good chance I would not have used them wisely in my younger years, lacking the maturity and insights I have gained since. Although I often felt miserable in various workplaces, and painfully bored with so much meaningless professional work, those became powerful motivators for me to seek meaning and opportunities beyond the workaday life.

The adage "time is money" is, to a large degree and in many contexts, true in the sense that you may trade money for time and time for money. However, it misses an important point, which is this: When it comes to the value of money, economists differentiate between *nominal* value (absolute value, measured in standard units of currency) and *real* value (the subjectively determined benefit you get from the things you may purchase with a given amount of money). The value of time also may be measured in nominal units (either earned or forfeited), but its real value depends on what you do with it. This is why studies show that, beyond a certain level of income, having additional money ceases to correlate with increases in happiness or satisfaction. In fact, there are many scenarios in which, after already earning a certain base level of income, the "marginal cost of money"—the amount of time, wellness, and discretionary activities you must give up to earn an additional unit of income—may become negative; rather than add to your overall happiness and satisfaction, it may diminish them. I suspect that, like most people, this is not news to you. I also suspect that, like most people, you may not have given serious consideration to the question of where that point of diminishing returns may be for you—how much income you *truly* need to live meaningfully; the point beyond which spending more of your living moments on unfulfilling work for the sake of greater wealth becomes self-defeating.

William Blake wrote, "You never know what is enough, until you know what is more than enough." Similarly, Kurt Vonnegut described a time when he and fellow author Joseph Heller attended a party at the lavish home of a wealthy person. Jokingly, Vonnegut asked Heller how he felt when realizing that the party's host likely made more money on the previous day than Heller earned in forty years from the sales of his famous novel *Catch-22*. Heller responded, "I have something he can never have." "What's that, Joe?" asked Vonnegut. Heller replied, "The knowledge that I've got enough."

"No one can have whatever he wants," wrote Seneca, "What he can do is not want what he doesn't have, and cheerfully enjoy what comes his way." No doubt, this is easier said than done. And yet, it can be done; and, once done, you will have accomplished Heller's eminently valuable "one thing": the knowledge that you have enough. Having enough means having freedom—the freedom to pursue what you wish to do

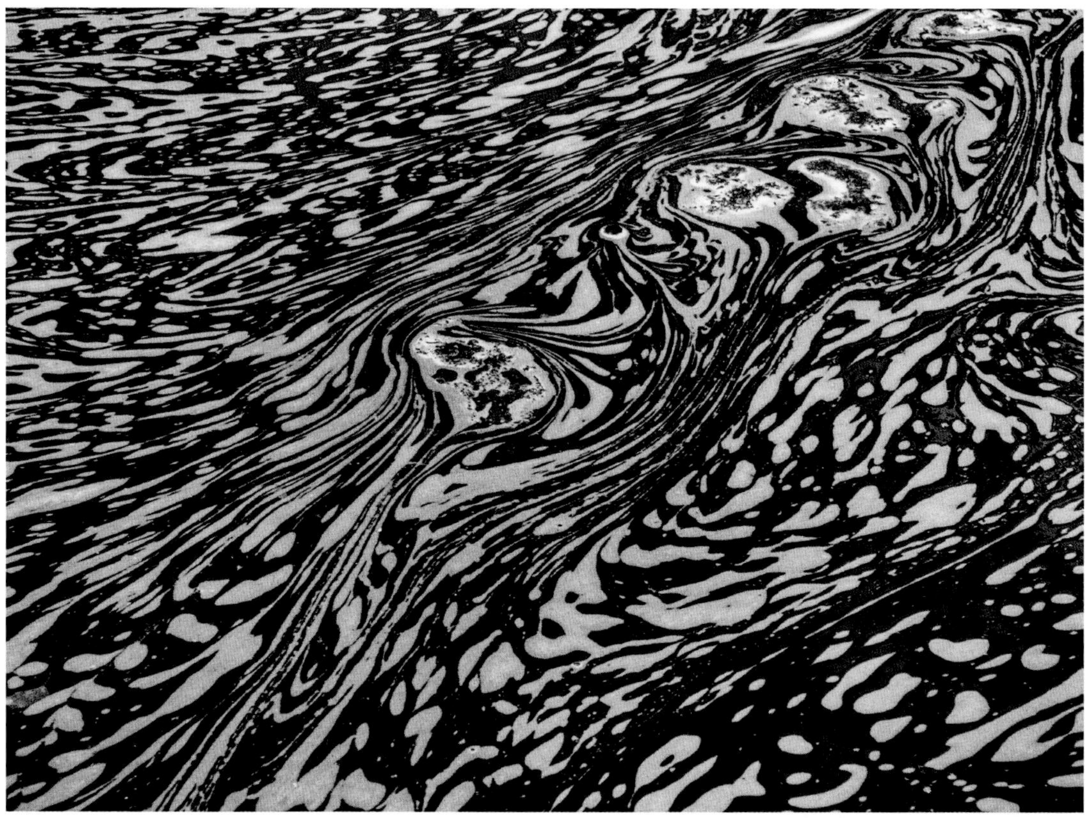

rather than what you must do to make ends meet. As Seneca put it, "If you set a high value on liberty, you must set a low value on everything else."

What may not be obvious is the role that art can play in your life based on where you are relative to the point of feeling you have enough. Up to that point, art may help you persevere and balance out the drudgeries of stressful, boring, or meaningless work with moments of beauty and elevated experiences. As John Ruskin put it, "Life without industry is guilt, and industry without art is brutality." After that point, however, art may take a more prominent role in your life and soothe the anxiety that comes from having to decide for yourself how to put your time to good use—the anxiety that Kierkegaard described as "the dizziness of freedom."

If you are fortunate to be among the minority of people who are genuinely satisfied with their professional pursuits, recognizing the point of enough and the rewards of art are still important in this sense: Beyond the point of enough, you may free yourself to practice your work, not as a job but as an art. By this I mean that beyond the point of having enough, you may free yourself to consider creative ideas in your professional pursuits, dedicate some of your time to teaching and mentoring others, and focus on the most rewarding and meaningful aspects of your work, rather than strive for more senior or stressful positions.

Bertrand Russell asked, "What will be the good of the conquest of leisure and health, if no one remembers how to use them?" When you have art, you will know exactly what to do with your leisure and how to put it to the best uses possible. By this I don't just mean filling your time creating or beholding art, but also, as I suggested earlier in the book,[40] striving to become a more interested, and more interesting, person.

---

[40] See page 99.

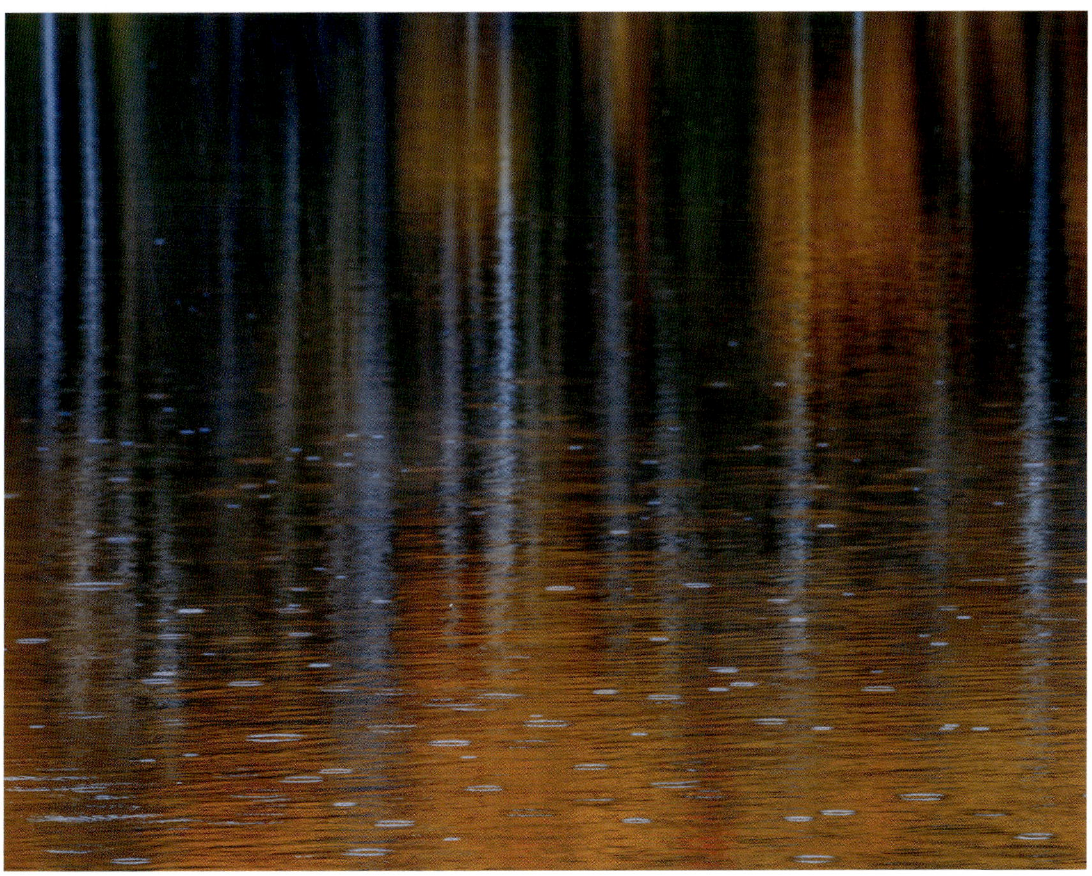

2.3. EXPRESS WHO YOU ARE

I have never found anywhere, in the domain of art, that you don't have to walk to. (There is quite an array of jets, buses and hacks which you can ride to Success; but that is a different destination.) It is a pretty wild country. There are, of course, roads. Great artists make the roads; good teachers and good companions can point them out. But there ain't no free rides, baby. No hitchhiking. And if you want to strike out in any new direction—you go alone.

—URSULA K. LE GUIN

In the previous sections, I advised you to first learn and become who you are, then use this knowledge of yourself to choose—to the best of your ability and freedom—a life that best fits this unique and extraordinary person. Along the way, I also suggested that art may help you in both these tasks: the task of learning who you are, and the task of living as you are.

Art may complement, enrich, and elevate your life in many ways. As a beholder of art, you may benefit from introducing beauty—aesthetic experiences—into your life. In beholding great art in any medium you may also find respite from suffering and from the mundane challenges of life. Therefore, strive to become not just a maker of art, but also a connoisseur of art: a person able to understand, relate to, and find value in a broad range of artforms, not just those you practice yourself, nor those that are obvious or aim no higher than to be superficially appealing. With apologies for what may be an obvious tautology, the more forms of art you know how to derive value from, the more value you will gain from having art be a part of your life.

As a maker of art, you may introduce into your life realms of experience and meaning beyond just enjoying art made by others. You may gain material benefits from art if you find ways to sell your work; you may gain social benefits from art if you commune with fellow artists or win fame and admiration for your art; you may satisfy your ego by winning contests against other artists. Still, all these rewards are extrinsic—provided by other people. As I explain earlier in the book,[41] scientific studies and many accounts of great artists reveal that the greatest rewards to be found in making art are the inner—intrinsic—ones. Intrinsic rewards arise from approaching art with the aim of being creative (i.e., produce work that is original and nonobvious) and expressive (i.e., strive to impart your emotions—not just pleasing appearances—in your work).

Creativity in practice translates to this: Learn from and be inspired by others, but don't plagiarize; strive to imagine new possibilities; don't stop at what is safe, easy, or obvious. Expression in practice is a bit more complex since it involves not only honesty and effort, but also technique. How do you express certain feelings (perhaps even feelings for which there are no words) in visuals or soundwaves or sculpted shapes?

The answer: You may learn some of it from others, but as of the time of this writing, we—the human species—have no decisive scientific explanation (at least not beyond a rudimentary understanding of simplistic concepts) for how art "works" to express complex emotions. This, dear reader, is not a downside of art, but the opposite; it is what makes art mysterious, exciting, and adventurous. It means that no matter what your knowledge or skill level is, you may—by use of your imagination alone—discover new ways of making art, expressing things in art, and deriving value from art. You may also discover new roles that art may play in your life and in others' lives that have not yet been conceived. But these discoveries are only possible if you use your own imagination and strive to find and express in your work your own original, authentic feelings and ideas.

In this final section of the book, I offer you advice for thinking about how to go about expressing who you are and what you feel in your artwork.

---

[41] See page 128.

SHOULD YOU BECOME A PROFESSIONAL ARTIST?

The idea of an art detached from its creator is not only
outmoded; it is false.

—ALBERT CAMUS

I'm often asked for advice on how to become a "professional landscape photographer."
Alas, the best I can do for anyone asking is to recommend some useful resources
and encourage them to discover their own way, rather than attempt to mimic mine.
Artists—professional or not—are not fungible. If you wish to become an artist, odds
are you already know the kind of art you wish to make. However, if you wish to become
a *professional* artist, you must also decide what kind of professional you wish to be.
Your answer will likely be different from mine, and perhaps different from any other
professional artist's.

What does it mean to be a professional artist? That's a bit like asking what it means
to be a doctor. Without further qualification, people may intuitively assume it means
one thing—which it sometimes does, but not always. If you've watched enough com-
edy shows, you likely have seen some version of a scene where a person with a doctoral
degree in a field other than medicine is asked to offer medical advice and responds
irritably, "I'm not that kind of doctor." Likewise, I sometimes find myself having no better answer to some questions about professional photography than, "I'm not that kind
of photographer."

On the morning before writing this essay, I went for a long drive in the desert, taking a "day off" after spending two weeks alone in a campsite at the edge of a
sparse aspen grove on the high slopes of a desert mountain, where I spent most of the

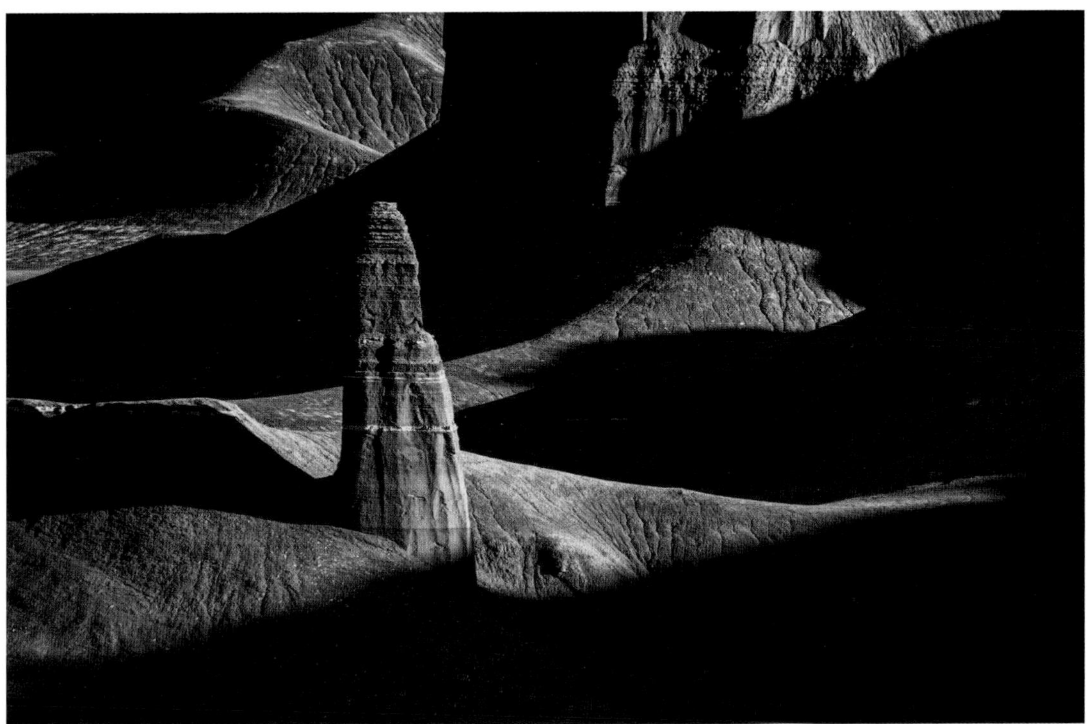

previous days working on this very book. A powerful thunderstorm swept over the area while I was away from my camp, rendering the dirt road leading up the mountain inaccessible. I took an alternate route to a paved road and decided to head home for a night and use the opportunity to resupply. Earlier this morning, the damaged part of the road was regraded, allowing safe passage, and I was able to return to my camp, where I am now working and where I intend to spend another week writing and photographing before heading home again to catch up on some office chores, after which I will decide where to go next, and for how long.

Each day at camp, after spending a few hours writing, I go for walks or spend some time reading. On my recent walks, I have savored the beauty of an unusually prolific wildflower season, communed with various wildlife, and made a few photographs. In the evening hours I cook good dinners, then eat them sitting outside by a fragrant campfire. As darkness falls, I listen to music and lounge in my camp chair, sometimes for hours, gazing into the night sky, rapt in thoughts.

Although each of my outings is unique in some ways and never entirely planned, the time I have spent at this campsite so far and the experiences it has afforded me are not uncommon. This, to me, is not a "photo trip," or any other kind of trip. This is how I have lived and worked for many years now: my version of being a "professional artist."

It's a life I could not have had if it was not for my reclusive nature and my comfort spending prolonged periods of time alone in remote natural settings, if I had a family to support, or if my business affairs required frequent in-person interactions with clients, colleagues, or other people. This is why when someone asks me for advice on being a "professional artist," I assume they likely have a different idea of what it means than I do. Being a professional artist means making aesthetic objects and selling them for a living. It applies equally to a painter exhibiting high-priced pieces in prestigious galleries, a person making independent films to promote social justice, or a person selling homemade jewelry at art fairs or chainsaw-carved bears by the side of a forest road. This is to say that there are many and diverse ways to become a professional—one who makes a living in art. In my experience, most independent professional artists discovered their own ways to becoming one.

Please don't take any of the above—including my description of my cherished times in nature and my freedom to roam—to mean that my life as a professional artist is filled with perpetual bliss and is free of struggles. It is not. Also, please don't take any of it to mean that you should envy me or want to be like me. You should not. It took me a long time to find a lifestyle that fits my personality and enables me to earn enough to sustain my modest material needs. If you sincerely wish to become a professional artist, I suggest you design your own life to fit *your* personality and needs. Don't expect to fit yourself to any existing template, nor that all your plans and attempts will prove successful.

If the life of a professional artist (whatever that means to you) is not within your reach, consider careers other than art, if only for the time being. I have. For two decades I made my living in various "regular" jobs, always prepared when opportunities for more meaningful living came my way. I am a professional artist today not because it was always obvious to me that this is what I wanted to be, nor because I followed a prescribed and reproducible path, but because working in other professions and living other lives did not satisfy me and I kept trying different things until I found something that worked.

One bit of advice I have for guiding your life, both personal and professional, is to not start by choosing a label ("professional artist" or any other) and then seek ways to shoehorn your life into it. Instead, consider first what you have to work with—your personality, knowledge, abilities, resources, commitments, opportunities, circumstances, interests, needs, aspirations—and then find a way of life and/or a vocation within those parameters that is most meaningful to you, whatever that ends up being. Figure out the label later. If the world considered me a "desert rat" or an "outdoor bum" instead of a "professional artist," but other aspects of my life remained as they are, it wouldn't bother me in the least.

When I decided to give professional landscape photography a try, I knew a few things about "the business," but most of what I knew was not relevant to what I wanted to get out of becoming a professional photographer. Most professionals I knew at the time were stock photographers, which I did not want to be. However, as more photographers began to use the internet and a new economy was starting to emerge, I had an inkling that I might be able to earn an income as a photographer, not by selling photographs but by becoming a "photographers' photographer"—by writing and photographing with the goal of inspiring other photographers to find beauty and meaning in photography and in nature, even if they never wished to become professionals themselves. Thankfully, my instincts proved right.

With that said, however, if I had to start fresh today and the only professional artists I knew of were popular internet influencers, I would not have wanted to be that, either. No matter how lucrative it may be or how tempting the fame, being a public figure, spending my time incessantly building up a following, and earning an income from advertising and promoting consumerism is not a good fit for my personality, the ways I wish to use my time, and my ethical distaste for certain practices of online advertisers.

I was lucky to have established my reputation, practice, and lifestyle in a time of transition. I've never had to earn a living in whatever the prevailing definition of "professional photographer" was at any time. I got into the profession when one definition of the term was becoming obsolete, and the next one was not yet established. This freed me to carve my own niche somewhere in between. In fairness, this should disqualify me from giving advice to aspiring professionals. The best professional advice I have to offer from personal experience is, alas, not a very practical one. It is this: Try to earn a living in a way that will allow you to live a rewarding and meaningful life and require you to make as few compromises as you must, and hope you get lucky. Don't expect to be able to make a plan that will pan out exactly as you intended. Learn and adjust as you go. Don't be afraid to make mistakes you can recover from, even if difficult.

While "get lucky" may seem facetious or simplistic, there are some bits of practical advice I can offer sincerely to those who hope to do so: Work hard, even if you're not sure you'll succeed. Research and learn as much as you can about the opportunities open to you, even if they seem far-fetched or outside the norm. Make sure you do what you do for the right reasons (i.e., not just because you want fame or a paycheck; if that's all you want, there are easier ways than becoming a professional artist to get there). Live

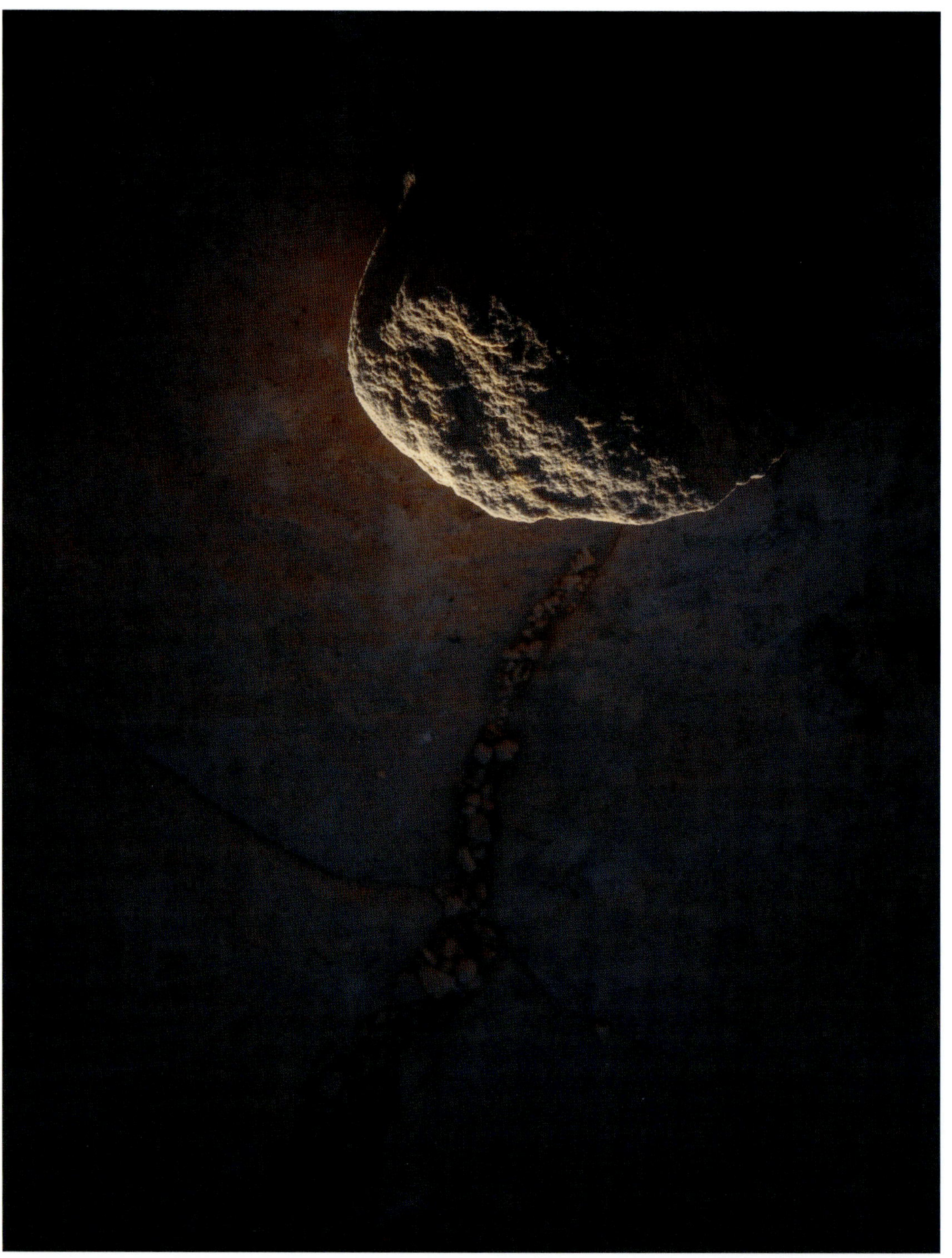

frugally and resist getting on the "hedonic treadmill." Don't commit to things or situations that may have long-term implications if you are not sure that's what you really want to do with the rest of your life. Don't get so caught up in your daily routines that you lose sight of the "long game." Become comfortable with the possibility of failure or having to change course. Consider everything you spend time or money on in light of its opportunity cost—what else you might do with that same time or money, and whether there may be better ways to use them. Be willing to disregard critics, naysayers, or even experts if you are convinced they are wrong. While these may not guarantee luck, they absolutely will increase your odds of getting lucky. Just as important, they will help you find out what getting lucky means to you (and perhaps only to you).

~ ~ ~

If you ask around or listen to other professional artists describing their modes of work, you will find that we don't all do what we do in the same ways, for the same reasons, or even with the same philosophy. Speaking from my experience, I know of many professional landscape photographers who are content spending relatively little time in nature. Many only go into scenic locations on short and carefully planned trips, just to photograph them, and spend little or no time experiencing them—camping, hiking, learning about their natural histories; communing with them; being mindful and respectful of, and knowledgeable about, their communities of life; forming intimate relationships with them over time; getting to experience them at all times of the day or year; seeking inspiration in them; or finding creative ways to express their own relationships with and experience of them. For me, these are essential aspects of being a naturalist, in addition to being an expressive artist—aspects without which photographing these places will be meaningless to me, and thus pointless. For other professionals in my field, this is not the case.

Many professional photographers are content visiting known locations they have no intimate, personal familiarity with, repeating other people's compositions rather than striving to be creative and expressive. Many are enamored with the mechanics of the medium, and care less about expressing themselves in it. Some love being public figures, centers of attention, community leaders, brand loyalists, or shrewd marketers. Some present themselves as professional photographers even if they only earn a small part of their income in photography and dedicate most of their working time to other professions. I am none of these things.

I don't mean to criticize anyone else's ways or definitions of what it means to be a professional artist. I only mean to say that, despite producing similar products, what these professionals do is not what I do: I am not "that kind of photographer."

~ ~ ~

The distinction of making similar products despite taking different approaches is an important one. Despite having different modes of work and being driven by different motivations, some artists produce similar-looking works, and consumers may not be able to tell just by looking at these works what kind of artist produced them or for what reasons. This may fairly be irrelevant to some consumers (e.g., if they are happy with how a picture they bought looks on their living room wall or on the cover of their corporate report); however, it may be extremely relevant to other consumers (e.g., if they wish to purchase a piece of creative, expressive art and want to know that it is an original creation conveying genuine emotions rather than copied from someone else). In either case, the fact that your art may be just as appealing to consumers as art made by someone driven by different motivations, or who may not place much value on creativity or originality as you do, should not matter to you in choosing what kind of artist—or professional—you want to be.

Your choice should be rooted in one consideration only: which kind seems most meaningful to *you*—the kind that has the greatest potential to enrich and elevate your own life; the kind that yields you the most satisfying experiences and lifestyle; the kind you may look back on in your elder years with pride and satisfaction, and congratulate yourself for having had the courage and wisdom to strive to become.

~ ~ ~

Years ago, I came across this quotation, attributed to the painter Chuck Close: "Inspiration is for amateurs—the rest of us just show up and get to work." I immediately disagreed with it. I have been a professional artist for many years. I have never created any meaningful artwork except when I feel inspired. Being one who becomes bored quickly with things that fail to hold my interest and to make my life meaningful, I can also say that if, at any time during my career, I felt like I had lost my capacity for inspiration, or couldn't sustain myself without resorting to making art without inspiration, I would have given up on art as a career a long time ago.

Close's statement only proves one thing—that art is not a one-size-fits-all endeavor; that each of us, if we are sufficiently dedicated and courageous, finds our own way in art. What works for one artist may not work for another. In fact, the very opposite of what works for one may work best for another.

If your primary motivation is to earn a living by your work, surely there are better vocational choices than to become a professional artist. Also, if you practice your art primarily for the intrinsic rewards that come with creative self-expression, you may still reap these rewards without ever selling a single piece. As Alfred Stieglitz wrote:

> *Let me here call attention to one of the most universally popular mistakes that have to do with photography—that of classing supposedly excellent work as professional, and using the term amateur to convey the idea of immature productions and to excuse atrociously poor photographs. As a matter of fact nearly all the greatest work is being, and has always been done, by those who are following photography for the love of it, and not merely for financial reasons. As the name implies, an amateur is one who works for love; and viewed in this light the incorrectness of the popular classification is readily apparent.*

Some esteemed professionals likewise recognized the value of maintaining the attitude of amateurs: of doing their work, before anything else, for the love of it, to express themselves creatively and to sustain themselves emotionally, not just financially. For example, Alfred Eisenstaedt wrote, "Once the amateur's naive approach and humble willingness to learn fades away, the creative spirit of good photography dies with it. Every professional should remain always in his heart an amateur." Likewise, Brassaï said in a lecture, "To keep from going stale you must forget your professional outlook and rediscover the virginal eye of the amateur." Even Ansel Adams advised one aspiring young photographer who wrote him for advice, "Photography as a profession is a grim business with terrific competition. Frankly, I advise most people to approach it as an avocation. Many of the greatest photographers were 'amateurs' in the sense that they did not make their living from the art." This is true in media other than photography, too. To wit, the great jazz pianist Bill Evans said, "I would often rely more on the judgement of a sensitive layman than that of a professional, since the professional, because of his constant involvement with the mechanics of music, must fight to preserve the naivety that the layman already possesses."

My advice: Don't assume that becoming a professional artist will necessarily make your art better or more rewarding. It may—but only if you find a way to align your professional work with the kind of art you wish to produce and the personal benefits you wish to gain by it, beyond just making an income. This attitude has guided my own decision to focus my professional work on teaching and writing about art, rather than on selling finished pieces. This has allowed me to retain both my creative freedom and the freedoms that come with self-employment.

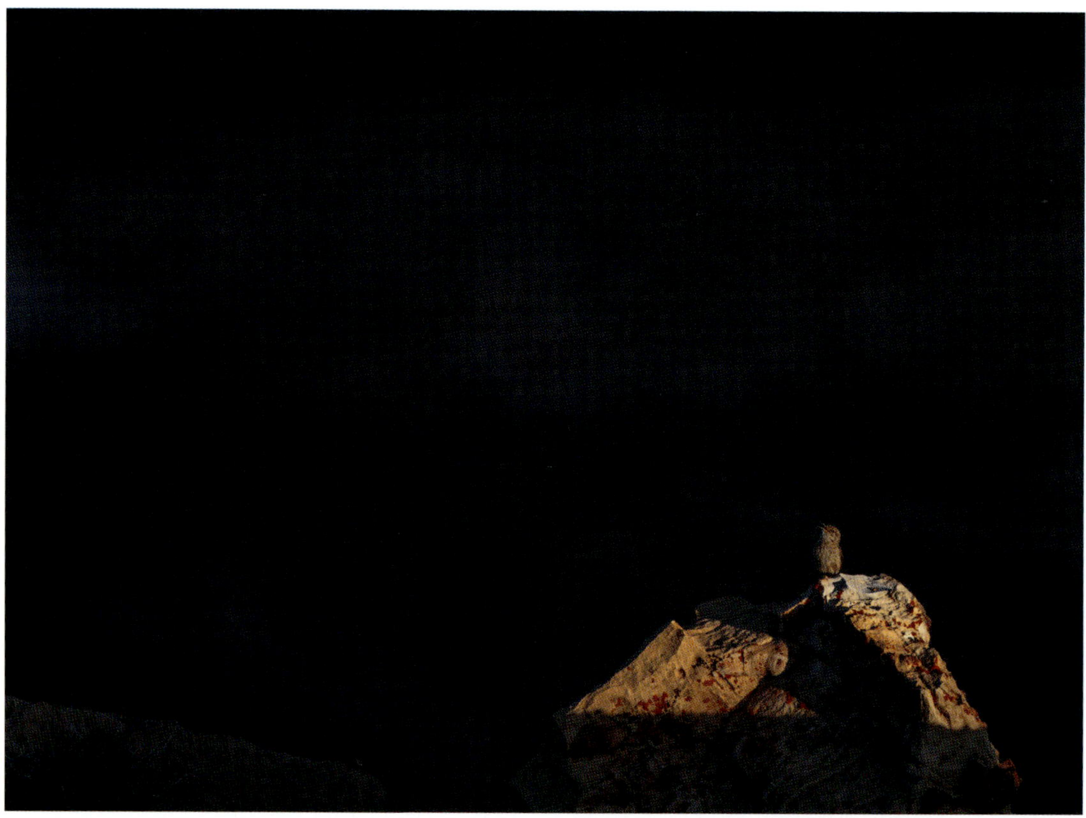

FREE YOURSELF CREATIVELY

> It is true that some artists or critics in certain periods have tried to formulate laws of their art; but it always turned out that poor artists did not achieve anything when trying to apply these laws, while great masters could break them and yet achieve a new kind of harmony no one had thought of before.... The truth is that it is impossible to lay down rules of this kind because one can never know in advance what effect the artist may wish to achieve.
>
> —E. H. GOMBRICH

In a 2010 IBM survey of more than 1,500 Chief Executive Officers (CEOs), creativity ranked as the most desirable quality in new hires. A similar study, conducted in 2017 by PwC,[42] found that "77% of CEOs find it difficult to get the creativity and innovation skills they need." At the same time, many corporate environments promote such hackneyed slogans as, "There is no 'I' in 'team,'" or "One team, one dream," not realizing that these platitudes stand in direct contrast to nurturing creativity. Perhaps if those who chant such slogans pursued their own silly logic, they might notice that while there is no "I" in "team," there are two of them in "creativity," and no less than four of them in "individualism." There are also "I"s in "imagination," "inspiration," "innovation," "independence," "ideas," and "expression."

Of course, we should not get in the habit of inferring any important meaning from linguistic accidents. Studies show that while groups (in corporate or academic

---

[42] See: https://www.pwc.com/gx/en/ceo-survey/2017/deep-dives/ceo-survey-global-talent.pdf

environments) may indeed be essential to vetting and implementing creative ideas, these ideas usually originate in the minds of creative individuals: the indispensable "I"s that *must* exist (and be allowed the freedom and independence to imagine novel ideas) within any team that aspires to creative achievement.

In art, individuality is even more important than it is in most jobs. It is rare for a group of artists to work together as a close-knit team when conceiving new ideas. Even a great orchestra performs scores written by individual composers. While some artists band together to promote certain concepts, to make individual contributions to larger projects, or to participate in group exhibits, the artwork itself is generally conceived by individuals. A good example of this is a defiant manifesto representing the ethos of a movement known as abstract expressionism, written in 1943 by Mark Rothko and Adolph Gottlieb in response to criticism of their (and others') work in the *New York Times*. Among other points in the manifesto, they wrote:

1. *To us art is an adventure into an unknown world, which can be explored only by those willing to take the risk.*

2. *This world of imagination is fancy-free and violently opposed to common sense.*

3. *It is our function as artists to make the spectator see the world our way—not his way.*

Now try to imagine employees in a corporate or academic environment making such declarations about their work. Of course, despite collaborating to declare their shared values, Rothko and Gottlieb created their own original artworks.

As an artist, you must allow for and defend your own creative ideas and guide your work by your own values and goals, not by the opinions of anyone else. Whereas some corporate, military, or academic environments may rightfully demand that you adhere to certain processes, requirements, or hierarchy or command, this is decidedly not the case in art. As Bertrand Russell wrote, "It is not by any system, but by freedom alone, that art can flourish."

To be creative is to be original. This is not in dispute, as some may think; it is baked into the formal definition of the term "creativity." Artwork that merely depicts reality or that is created according to any externally imposed guidelines may still be art (even good art), but it is not *creative* art, meaning that such work, no matter how beautiful or successful, will not reward you with the inner personal benefits of creative expression.

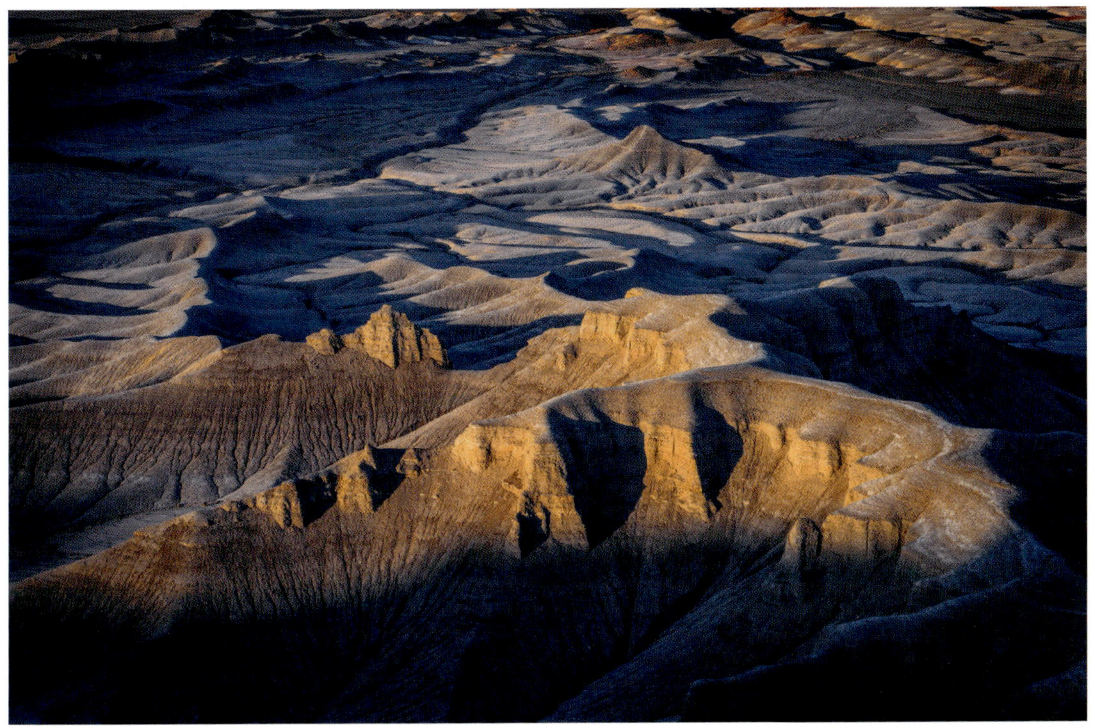

"Any wholesale creed in art is dangerous," wrote D. H. Lawrence. Of all artistic media, this is perhaps most true in photography, where departure from strict realistic representation, despite being common and expected in visual art for well over 150 years, is still often met with dogmatic antagonism. As Edward Steichen, whose work spanned multiple photographic styles, admonished:

> *The most precious factor in the creative life of an artist in any medium is freedom. Totalitarian, political, or national ideologies that seek to direct or channel the arts are pernicious; they can strangle the work of individual artists and cripple their own culture. They are not, however, the only things that hamper an artist's freedom. It can also be curtailed by commercial conditions or by the theories of aesthetics ordained by various groups, cults, cliques, or 'isms.' But it seems to me that the most damaging restrictions on an artist's liberty are self-imposed. So often,*

Defend your right and freedom to be creative, whatever that means to you, no matter what medium you work in, and regardless of what anyone else might deem appropriate or acceptable. "Only those who will risk going too far," wrote T. S. Eliot, "can possibly find out how far one can go." "Without freedom, no art," wrote Albert Camus, "art lives only on the restraints it imposes on itself, and dies of all others."

Rollo May wrote, "It is the dogmatic beliefs and rigid customs which resist new creativity." He attributed the lack of creativity in our time specifically to a decline in creative courage. In his book *Man's Search for Himself*, May wrote, "Our particular problem in the present day ... is an overwhelming tendency toward conformity" adding, "The hallmark of courage in our age of conformity is the capacity to stand on one's own convictions—not obstinately or defiantly (these are expressions of defensiveness not courage) nor as a gesture of retaliation, but simply because these are what one believes. It is as though one were saying through one's actions, 'This is my self, my being.'"

When it comes to making art, as Paul Strand wrote, "There is no such thing as THE way; there is only for each individual, his or her way, which in the last analysis, each one must find for himself in photography and in living." As practical advice, Strand offered this: "You may see and be affected by other people's ways, you may even use them to find your own, but you will have eventually to free yourself of them."

EXPRESS YOURSELF

> Art, which demands such tremendous labor-sacrifices from the people, which stunts human lives and transgresses against human love, is not only not a thing clearly and firmly defined, but is understood in such contradictory ways by its own devotees that it is difficult to say what is meant by art, and especially what is good, useful art,—art for the sake of which we might condone such sacrifices as are being offered at its shrine.
>
> —LEO TOLSTOY

Tolstoy defined art as "a human activity, consisting in this, that one person consciously, by certain external signs, conveys to others *feelings he has experienced*, and other people are affected by these feelings and *live them over in themselves*." (Italics mine) About three decades later, Alfred Stieglitz wrote,[43] "What is of greatest importance is to hold the moment, to record something so completely that those who see it will *relive an experience of what had been expressed*." (Italics mine) The implication in both cases is that a work of art created according to these philosophies must start with an experience the artist has had, found to be significant and worth expressing, and wished to communicate it to others.

Put another way, although possible and perhaps even lucrative, it is pointless to create a work of art that suggests to viewers an experience the artist manufactured for

---

[43] Stieglitz famously referred to the effect of designing photographs such that they communicate the photographer's feelings to viewers as "equivalence." See page 42.

aesthetic appeal or popular acceptance, but did not actually have. This commitment of artists to experience first, then express their experience in art, is found not only in visual media, but also in writing, as expressed by Robert Frost: "No tears in the writer, no tears in the reader. No surprise in the writer, no surprise in the reader."

It is worth qualifying that "experience" may refer to anything the artist has felt and was inspired by. It applies equally to a harrowing adventure, witnessing a majestic feat of nature, or having a profound idea or revelation while sipping coffee in the comfort of your own home. The resulting artwork may be realistic or fictional, or anything in between. The important point is not the circumstances of the experience, nor relaying its exact details to a viewer, but rather striving to convey to the viewer the nature and intensity of the emotions inspired by the experience.

If art is concerned primarily with the transmission of feelings, then, as Tolstoy put it, "Little can imitation, realism, serve, as many people think, as a measure of the quality of art. Imitation cannot be such a measure; for the chief characteristic of art is *the infection of others with the feelings the artist has experienced*, and infection with a feeling is not only not identical with description of the accessories of what is transmitted, but is usually *hindered by superfluous details*." (Italics mine) Stieglitz likely would have agreed with Tolstoy. His idea of equivalence referred specifically to the expression of feelings—not of appearances. He hoped that people who saw his "equivalent" photographs would feel, in his words, "freer to think about the relationships in the pictures than about the subject matter for its own sake."

Conveying your own thoughts and feelings in art is referred to as self-expression, as I explained earlier in the book.[44] Many artworks and genres in art today are decidedly not self-expressive. This doesn't necessarily make such works "bad" art, but it does detach them from the authentic, inner personal experiences of their makers. While such artworks may still be good and important art and may serve many useful purposes, if your goal in art is to elevate your own life—the depth, intensity, and richness of your own experiences—it makes sense that you will want to maintain a direct relationship between your life experiences and your art (i.e., be self-expressive).

Despite perhaps contradicting Tolstoy's and Stieglitz's assertions, aiming to make self-expressive art is no guarantee of—and should not depend upon—whether or to what degree your viewers will understand what you intended to express. This is because the impression that any person may receive from art depends on both objective and subjective factors. No matter how much you know about the former, you cannot know the latter. You have no way of knowing what history, knowledge, beliefs, biases, and preconceptions—what Gombrich referred to as the "beholder's share" of an

---

[44] See page 61.

artistic experience—each viewer may bring to the experience of witnessing your work. Your concern, therefore, is and can only be to do the best you can in contributing your "artist's share."

Alas, Stieglitz's idea of a perfect equivalence between an artist's experience and the experience of a viewer is, in truth, naïve, and at best, partly tenable. Thus, the primary reason to pursue self-expression is not, as it might seem, to convey (in the equally naïve wording of Minor White) "specific and known feelings" to another person, but to elevate and deepen *your own* creative experience by focusing on, intensifying, and seeking novel ways to express your feelings. If others later understand, relate to, or appreciate what you attempted to express, consider it a bonus, not a goal.

Tolstoy wrote, "One of the chief conditions of artistic creation is the complete freedom of the artist from every kind of preconceived demand." In this, he is in the good company of many other notable artists and thinkers—for example, Oscar Wilde, who (a few years before Tolstoy) wrote:

> *Whenever a community or a powerful section of a community, or a government of any kind, attempts to dictate to the artist what he is to do, Art either entirely vanishes, or becomes stereotyped, or degenerates into a low and ignoble form of craft. A work of art is the unique result of a unique temperament. Its beauty comes from the fact that the author is what he is. It has nothing to do with the fact that other people want what they want.... Art is the most intense mode of Individualism that the world has known. I am inclined to say that it is the only real mode of Individualism that the world has known.*

If your goal is to be a self-expressive artist, don't limit yourself arbitrarily to any style, genre, objective realism, or anyone else's idea of purism or tradition unless you have a good reason to do so, no matter who may be offended by it. By "good reason," I mean a reason rooted in your own aesthetic sensibilities, your own judgment of how to best express your own feelings, your own understanding of what art is (at least the kind of art you wish to create), and the role you wish for art to play in your life.

By this characterization, we can also say that a "bad reason" is attempting to conform with other people's demands, prejudices, judgments, or expectations when they are unnecessary or at odds with your own and that you are free to disengage from, at least in your artistic pursuits. If that means that certain communities, publications, pundits, or jurists will reject or fail to appreciate your work for what it is, consider it a small price to pay for being authentic in your art: true to your own values, motivations, aesthetic sensibilities, and philosophy. Certainly, you will not be the first nor the last artist to find themselves at odds with others—even with a majority of others and even with people or institutions in positions of authority or those widely considered as experts. In fact, it's fair to say that most artists we consider today as "the greats" have faced such resistance and misunderstanding, at least at some periods in their careers.

In art, self-expression is a higher goal than strict realistic depiction. However, self-expression and realism are not necessarily in contradiction. It's just that realism should not—in any medium—be considered a *sine qua non* (essential condition) for art. Realistic appearances can absolutely be used expressively (i.e., in ways that convey subjective meaning and feelings, rather than just what things look like objectively). In fact, one of the first artists to take issue with being dubbed a realist was the French painter Gustave Courbet, who is formally considered a realist painter. In an open letter he titled *Realist Manifesto*, he wrote:

> *The title of Realist was thrust upon me just as the title of Romantic was imposed upon the men of 1830. Titles have never given a true idea of things: if it were otherwise, the works would be unnecessary.... I simply wanted to draw forth from a complete acquaintance with tradition the reasoned and independent consciousness of my own individuality.*

If your aim is to express your authentic feelings and meanings, it is important to understand that what you think and feel may be *inspired by* what you see, but it is not *synonymous with*, nor entirely contained in, what you see. Put another way, your goal in self-expression must be to state, "here's something that expresses what I felt," and not necessarily, "here's an exact depiction of what I saw." Both may be considered in their own way as "truth," but not in the same sense. "This question of realism," wrote Robert Louis Stevenson, "let it then be clearly understood, regards not in the least degree the fundamental truth, but only the technical method, of a work of art. Be as ideal or as abstract as you please, you will be none the less veracious."

The pursuit of self-expression (i.e., striving to convey your own authentic, subjective feelings in your art) comes with benefits that go beyond just what artworks—what products—you create. To be self-expressive, you must first experience the things you wish to convey—be inspired, make yourself conscious of and attentive to emotions, thoughts, and meanings associated with or arising from your experiences. This, in essence, means being constantly mindful of what is happening outside and within

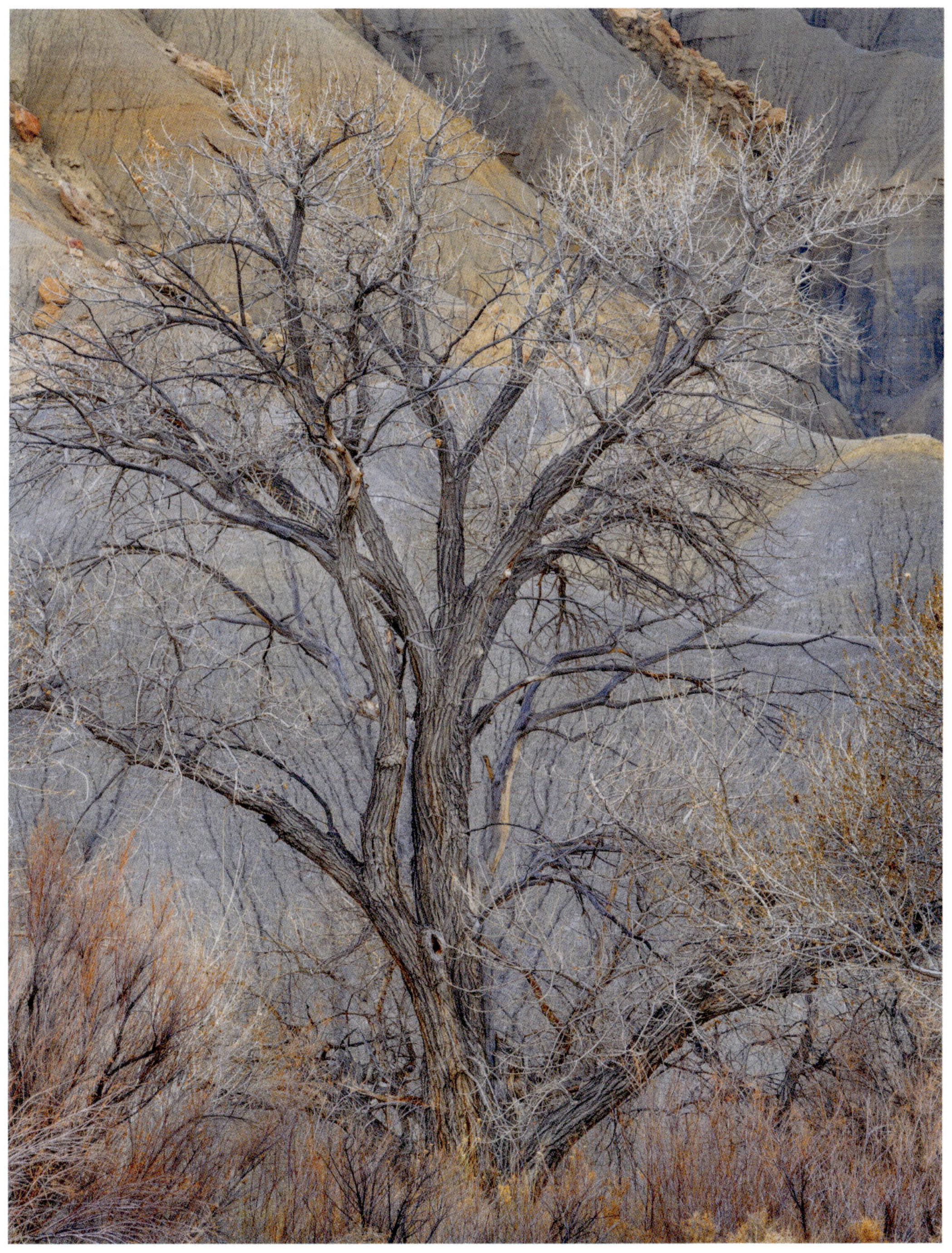

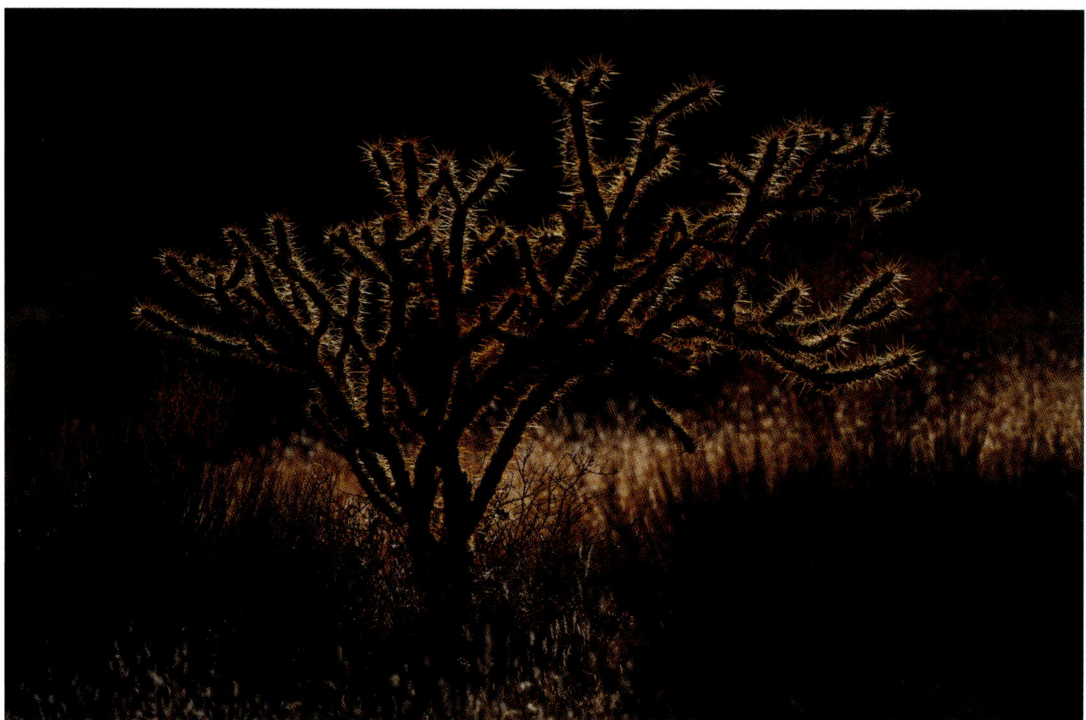

you, which comes with benefits I explained earlier in the book[45]—primarily deepening your experiences as they happen, including those that may not necessarily culminate in artistic expression. Also, the more unique and personal your experiences, the more unique (and therefore creative) your art will be, with all the benefits that come from exercising and continually improving the cognitive skills associated with creative thinking, again extending to situations beyond just artmaking.

Another long-term benefit of making self-expressive art is that, in time, your body of work will come to reflect what Paul Strand described as "a record of your living," meaning not just a record of your travels or of themes you saw in other people's work and ventured to imitate, but a record of your Living—with a capital "L"—the multidimensional tapestry of your inner and outer life: what you saw, felt, thought, sensed, intuited, believed, created, and found meaningful in the course of years or decades. Albert Camus described this idea of art as a "record of living" in his book *The Myth of Sisyphus*. He wrote:

---

[45] See page 141.

Too often the work of a creator is looked upon as a series of isolated testimonies.... A profound thought is in a constant state of becoming; it adopts the experience of a life and assumes its shape. Likewise, a man's sole creation is strengthened in its successive and multiple aspects: his works. One after another, they complement one another, correct or overtake one another, contradict one another too.

Consider that to a random viewer, artworks may seem like expressions of inner experiences even if in truth they are not (i.e., just because a work may be expressive doesn't mean it is necessarily *self*-expressive). This leads some artists to assume that if a viewer believes a work is expressive of a meaningful experience, that's a good enough alternative to actually having had such an experience. The silliness of this mode of thinking becomes apparent when you apply it to other scenarios. Convincing people to believe erroneously that you climbed Mt. Everest is hardly the same as having actually climbed Mt. Everest. Showing people a picture of you holding a trophy or a medal you did not earn and allowing them to believe you had is hardly the same as having performed the feat for which such honors are awarded.

If your goal is to elevate your own life by artistic work, then what is the point of making art that elicits powerful emotions in other people if you did not experience these same (and preferably greater) emotions yourself? What is the point of making an epic picture if you did not have an epic experience? What is the point of making others believe you've found a moment of private inspiration in some beautiful natural place if in truth you stood at a popular viewpoint with people and cars buzzing around you? What is the point of impressing others with your beautiful images if you did not have a deeply moving aesthetic experience of your own? What is the point of having people celebrate you as a creative artist if much of your portfolio consists of imitations and derivations of other people's art?

To be self-expressive is to be authentic. It is to have—before anything else—authentic experiences, both in conceiving your art (seeking and finding inspiration and creative ideas) and in the process of creating your art (honing your skills, contemplating what you wish to express and how you may express it, experiencing flow, experimenting, learning). Jumping to the final stage—the finished artwork—without thoroughly exhausting the inner rewards to be found in living, thinking, and creating artfully may still yield you "good" art by some characterizations, perhaps even income and fame, but in doing so, you will only be depriving yourself of more satisfying experiences.

> In the journal I do not just express myself more openly than I
> could to any person; I create myself.

—SUSAN SONTAG

Earlier in this book[46] I characterized mindfulness as the ability to consciously focus your attention entirely on things (both within you and in the world outside of you) happening in the present moment—to the deliberate exclusion of all things not relevant to your immediate experience. This is hard to do and even harder to sustain for prolonged periods, but it's a skill you can train and improve by frequent repetition. One way to make yourself mindful is, as I mentioned, a regular daily meditation practice. However, there are other ways to corral your attention and focus it at will on the present moment.[47]

One of these ways is to keep a journal and to write in it often, any time you experience a meaningful thought or feeling. Journal entries don't have to be long narratives; they may be just a line or two and take seconds to write. However, the act of writing a journal entry forces you to pay attention to your experience and think of ways to describe it in words, having the effect of focusing your mind on your immediate experience and suspending thinking about unrelated, distracting things—i.e., to become mindful.

---

[46] See page 141.

[47] Note that although these methods may be effective on their own, they can be even more so if you practice them in addition to a regular meditation practice and other ways of training yourself to control your attention.

Journal entries describe real events, but do so from a subjective perspective. This also happens to be what mindfulness is about: noticing real things (in the world and within you) as they happen, acknowledging their significance and meaning, and deciding consciously whether they are useful. The more frequent and detailed your journal entries, the more the act of writing will demand your attention and help you identify, distill, and express your thoughts, consider them meaningfully (rather than just instinctively, habitually, partially, or dismissively), place them in context of other aspects of your experience, and put them to beneficial use—if not immediately, then later as reminders when reflecting on how you may express them creatively in art or writing.

You may keep a small notepad with you and take notes by hand, or you may use one of many mobile apps available today, some of which also allow you to illustrate your notes with snapshots, augment them with voice memos, record the precise time and location, and add other useful information. Studies show that writing notes by hand is more effective in terms of engaging your cognitive and motor functions than typing them. But generally speaking, the act of pausing to take notes in any form can be beneficial and rewarding, and help train your mind to be more mindful, constantly anticipating[48] the need to describe and record your thoughts and feelings.

~ ~ ~

Marcus Aurelius was perhaps the closest that a human being can get to being king of the world. He was a ruler of the Roman Empire for nearly two decades and had power over the lives of millions of people, command of the world's most powerful fighting force, and access to practically any material good he desired. Unlike so many who consider themselves "leaders" by virtue of holding a position of power, Marcus was also a deep-thinking Stoic philosopher who aspired honestly to being a virtuous person, and a wise, benevolent ruler. To keep himself honest and to seek wisdom, he kept a personal journal (now available to us in various translations under the title *Meditations*). In his journal, Marcus admonished himself often for his failures, examined and questioned his decisions, reminded himself of bits of Stoic wisdom to help strengthen his spirit, contemplated his mortality and the great responsibilities he had, and sought ways to transcend his doubts.

Often, in his *Meditations*, Marcus reminded himself to be mindful—to pay attention to the here and now, and not be distracted by other concerns. For example, in one entry he wrote:

---

[48] Studies in neuroscience sometimes refer to our brains as "prediction machines," constantly processing information to anticipate what we may want or need to do next.

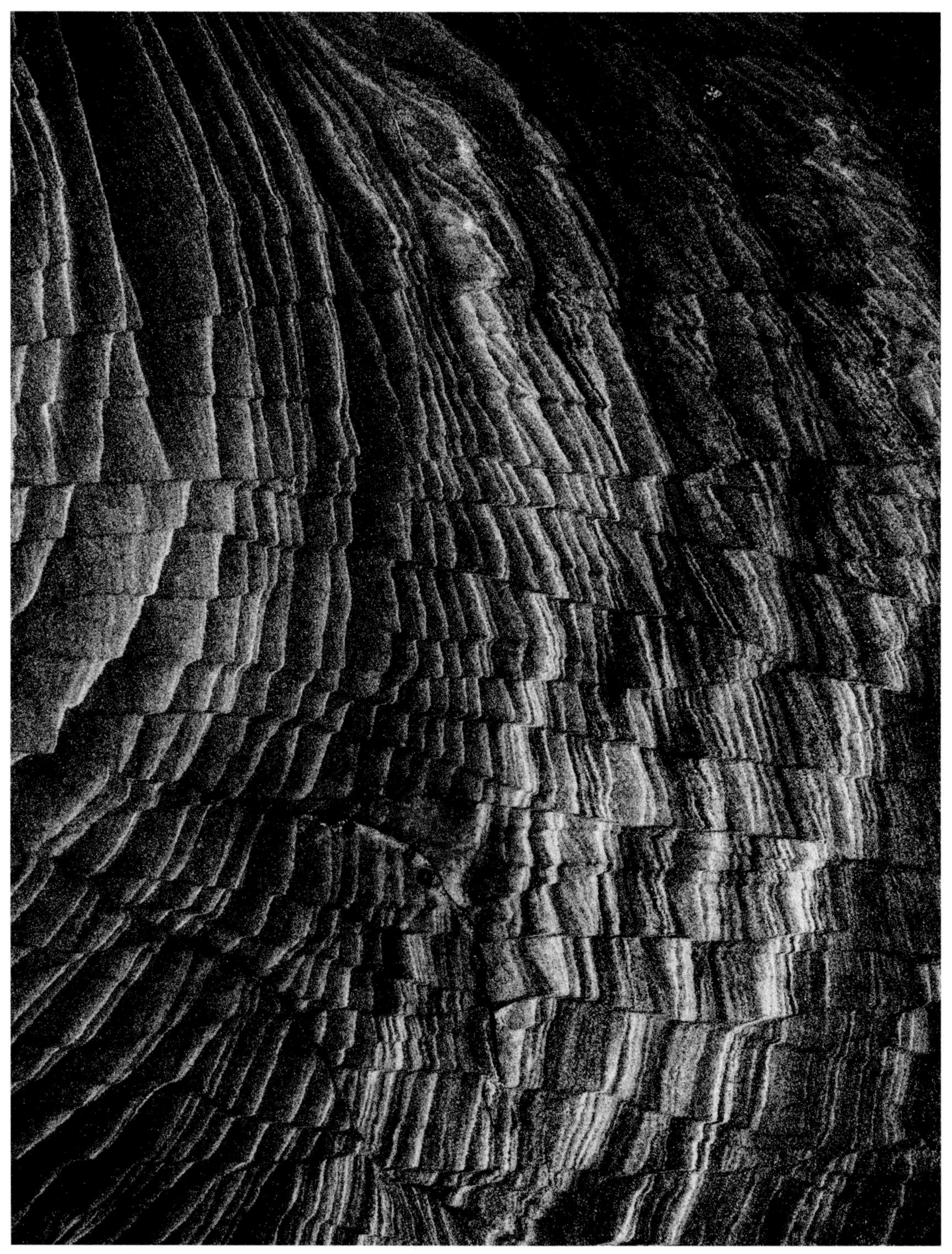

Concentrate every minute ... on doing what's in front of you with precise and genuine seriousness, tenderly, willingly, with justice. And on freeing yourself from all other distractions. Yes, you can—if you do everything as if it were the last thing you were doing in your life, and stop being aimless, stop letting your emotions override what your mind tells you, stop being hypocritical, self-centered, irritable. You see how few things you have to do to live a satisfying and reverent life? If you can manage this, that's all even the gods can ask of you.

By comparison, most of us likely don't have to shoulder the burden of having our decisions and actions affect millions of other lives in addition to facing our own challenges. If one of the world's greatest philosopher kings found journaling helpful in carrying the weight of the world on his shoulders, imagine how powerful it can be in elevating your own life.

My own journal consists mostly of short notes, poems, ideas, and reminders I jot down throughout the day, sometimes just long enough to remind me of something I decided to defer, acknowledging its importance for later contemplation in leisure but not wanting it to distract me from my present experience. Knowing I will revisit my notes at a later time, it is easier for me to let go of nagging thoughts that are not relevant to what I am doing and feeling, assuring myself I will not forget or neglect them, and will give them due attention at a more appropriate time.

Beyond recording significant thoughts as they happen, and confronting my own doubts, shortfalls, limitations, and regrets, I have found journaling to be profoundly useful in my artistic activities too. Recall that being self-expressive in art means expressing your authentic thoughts and feelings in your work. Put another way, to be self-expressive is to portray real events, but to do so—knowingly and unapologetically—from a subjective perspective. This is exactly what we do when we journal—we exercise the same brain circuitry that narrates our life stories and distills and extracts important meanings from them, which, in turn, are also the concepts underlying self-expressive art.

MAKE INVENTORIES

> I have to make a rapid inventory of the universe, just as a man in a dream tries to condone the absurdity of his position by making sure he is dreaming. I have to have all space and all time participate in my emotion, in my mortal love, so that the edge of its mortality is taken off, thus helping me to fight the utter degradation, ridicule, and horror of having developed an infinity of sensation and thought within a finite existence.
>
> —VLADIMIR NABOKOV

Other than keeping a journal, another good method for making yourself mindful and focusing your attention on your present experience is to form a habit of making inventories. I mean this literally: Stop and list—in writing or in your mind—all the things you have to work with, the raw ingredients available to you to create things from. If you are making a photograph, for example, list as many things as you can see within your field of view. If you are writing a poem, list all the metaphors, symbols, objects, adjectives, and other linguistic components that come to your mind when you think about what you wish to express. If you are composing music, look around you for patterns that may inspire rhythms, suggest a specific pitch, or that may correlate with certain notes, chords, or the sounds of certain instruments. Be sure to also take inventory of the thoughts and feelings within you that you may wish to express.

As you make your inventories, do so without judgment. Don't decide right away whether anything is useful or not, whether you may wish to include or exclude it, whether it contributes to or distracts from what you wish to express. Suspend those decisions until after you have gathered a sufficiently rich inventory. Making these judgments too early may prime or bias your mind toward specific outcomes before you know what other outcomes may be possible.

An analogy I use when teaching this method is this: Imagine yourself coming home hungry and tired after a long day's work. Your spouse or partner has already gone to bed and left for you on the kitchen table a loaf of bread and a jar of peanut butter. If this is all you see, that's your dinner. But if you take some time to peek into the cabinets and refrigerator, survey the ingredients and flavorings available to you, perhaps research some possible recipes for these ingredients, you will likely realize you can make a much more satisfying meal than a peanut butter sandwich. Now consider what else you did without even noticing it: You consciously took charge of your attention and applied it toward making yourself aware of your environment and of your feelings. In other words, by consciously deciding to make an inventory, you also made yourself mindful. Then, by examining your inventory and deciding what you can make from it— what ingredients to use or to leave out, and how you may combine these ingredients

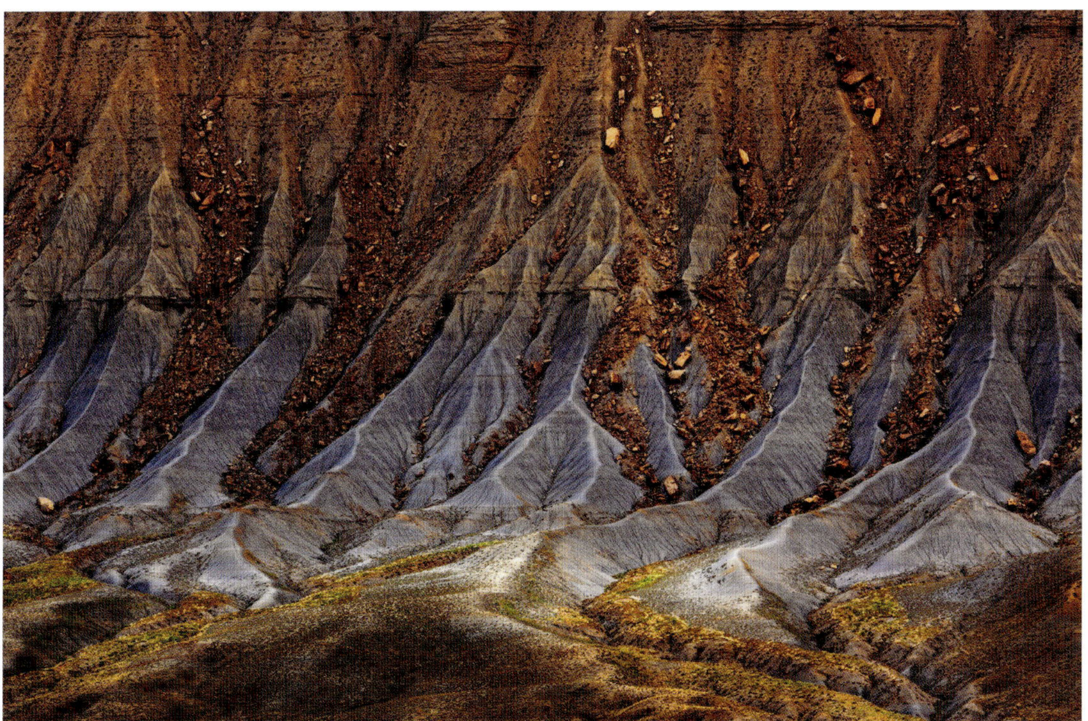

into creative products—you also prolonged your state of mindfulness, and perhaps even set yourself on a path to experiencing flow. If you then proceed to implement your ideas—to apply your tools, to contemplate or even research how to do some things you don't yet know how to do—you will prolong this mindful state even further.

My advice: Make inventory-taking a standard part of your creative process—the first thing you do when inspiration strikes, when something (a feeling, a thought, an encounter) stops you in your tracks or even just suggests the possibility of making a significant, expressive artwork.

If you are a visual artist, a good way to consider what kinds of things you may want to list among your inventory are what's known as the "seven elements of art": lines, shapes, space, values (what photographers may refer to as tonality, brightness, or zones), forms, textures, and colors.

Edward Weston is considered a pioneer of modernism in photography. He was famously prolific and creative. He didn't limit himself in terms of subject matter. Upon receiving a Guggenheim Fellowship along with a grant to fund a photographic project, Weston proclaimed, "My true program is summed up in one word: life. I expect to photograph anything suggested by that word which appeals to me during my fellowship."

Keeping the idea of an inventory in mind, consider this passage Weston wrote in his journal, *The Daybooks of Edward Weston*, describing his first impressions upon arriving in Mexico:

> *Did I visualize what I was to see in my first Mexican port? This is hard to say today—seeing, with stranger's eyes, a stageset: blocks of low houses—a continuous wall of alternate pastel blues, pinks, greens. Down narrow streets Indian boys drove heavy-laden burros; around corners appeared vendors of water or chickens—a half-dozen hanging head down, their legs crossed over a pole, all peeping dolorously.*
>
> *Street stands sold tropical fruits — some new to me and delicious—for instance, the mango is truly nectar. Aguacates—avocados—sold for 5 centavos! There were vehicles for hire, two-wheeled carts and low-swung coaches. In one of these, drawn by a span of horses—decrepit ones I must admit—we drove along the coast at sunset.*

This is an artist trained intuitively in making inventories. Notice how many details he has committed to memory: colors, shapes, the number of chickens and horses, the price of avocados, and so much more. No wonder he was able to conceive photographic compositions so prolifically—he not only had a lot to work with, but he was consciously aware of it all, making all these elements available to him to consider and to compose with.

Likewise, Hermann Hesse described the correlation between noticing—making inventories of—things in your environment and evolving an artistic instinct. He wrote:

> *Accustom yourself every morning to look for a moment at the sky and suddenly you will be aware of the air around you, the scent of morning freshness that is bestowed on you between sleep and labor. You will find every day that the gable of every house has its own particular look, its own special lighting. Pay it some heed and you will have for the rest of the day a remnant of satisfaction and a touch of coexistence with nature. Gradually and without effort the eye trains itself to transmit many small delights, to contemplate nature and the city streets, to appreciate the inexhaustible fun of daily life. From there on to the fully trained artistic eye is the smaller half of the journey; the principal thing is the beginning, the opening of the eyes.*

PREVISUALIZE, VISUALIZE, AND POSTVISUALIZE

I can, and have taught a child of seven to expose, develop,
and print creditably in a few weeks, thanks to the great
manufacturers who have so simplified and made fool-proof
the various steps in picture making: which accounts for the
flood of bad photography by those who think it is an easy
way to "express" themselves. But it is not easy! – not easy to
see on the ground glass the finished print, to mentally carry
that image on through the various processes of finishing to a
final result, and with reasonable surety that the result will be
exactly what one originally saw and felt.

—EDWARD WESTON

The term *visualization*, in the sense of forming a mental image of the finished work
before applying any tools or materials, is generally attributed (at least in photography)
to Ansel Adams. As the story goes, the idea came to Adams in 1927 when he realized
he could predict the effect of a red filter when making his photograph *Monolith, the
Face of Half-Dome*. In truth, it is likely that Adams's epiphany was inspired by his friend
and senior Edward Weston, who described it in some of his journal entries written in
Mexico in 1923.

Adams deserves credit for evolving and formalizing the idea of visualization, making it a central premise of his approach to photography. He opens the first chapter of
his book *The Camera* by defining visualization as "the entire emotional-mental process
of creating a photograph," and as including "the ability to *anticipate a finished image*

before making the exposure." (Italics mine) Implied in Adams's definition is that a visualized photograph *must be* different from the subject as commonly seen (otherwise there
would be no need to visualize an "anticipated image"). He elaborated on this attitude
in several of his later writings and talks. For example, in a 1983 interview, he stated:

> *While the landscapes that I have photographed in Yosemite are recog-*
> *nized by most people and, of course, the subject is an important part*
> *of the pictures, they are not "realistic." Instead, they are an imprint of*
> *my visualization. All of my pictures are optically very accurate—I use*
> *pretty good lenses—but they are quite unrealistic in terms of values. A*
> *more realistic simple snapshot captures the image but misses everything*
> *else. I want a picture to reflect not only the forms but what I had seen*
> *and felt at the moment of exposure.*

Some use the terms *visualization* and *previsualization* interchangeably. I propose it
useful to distinguish between the two: to consider the implications of the "pre" part as
referring to things that precede visualization—things we do in preparation for visualization, and that will make our later visualizations more effective, more productive, and
more expressive.

If visualization is, as Adams expressed, the forming of an anticipated image in
the mind before making an exposure, then previsualization may refer to anything that
comes before that. Taken literally, anything we do before visualizing—whether sipping our morning coffee or brushing our teeth—may be considered as previsualization.
However, among the many activities that may precede visualization, there are certain
attitudes, activities, and modes of thought that, if we apply them consciously and deliberately prior to setting out to make photographs, may have direct, desirable effects on
our later efforts to visualize.

Collectively, the attitudes and practices that may be conducive to better visualization—i.e., useful forms of previsualization—amount to mindfulness: taking conscious
control of our attention and directing it at will toward aspects of our present experience, prompting ourselves deliberately to notice, to become aware, and to take inventory of qualities of our surroundings and inner states—the building blocks available
to us to make expressive photographs. Mindfulness also involves reclaiming attention
away from unproductive distractions—thoughts that are unrelated to our immediate
experience and that may diminish our awareness of things happening in real time and
may sabotage or distract us from our enjoyment of and interest in creative work.

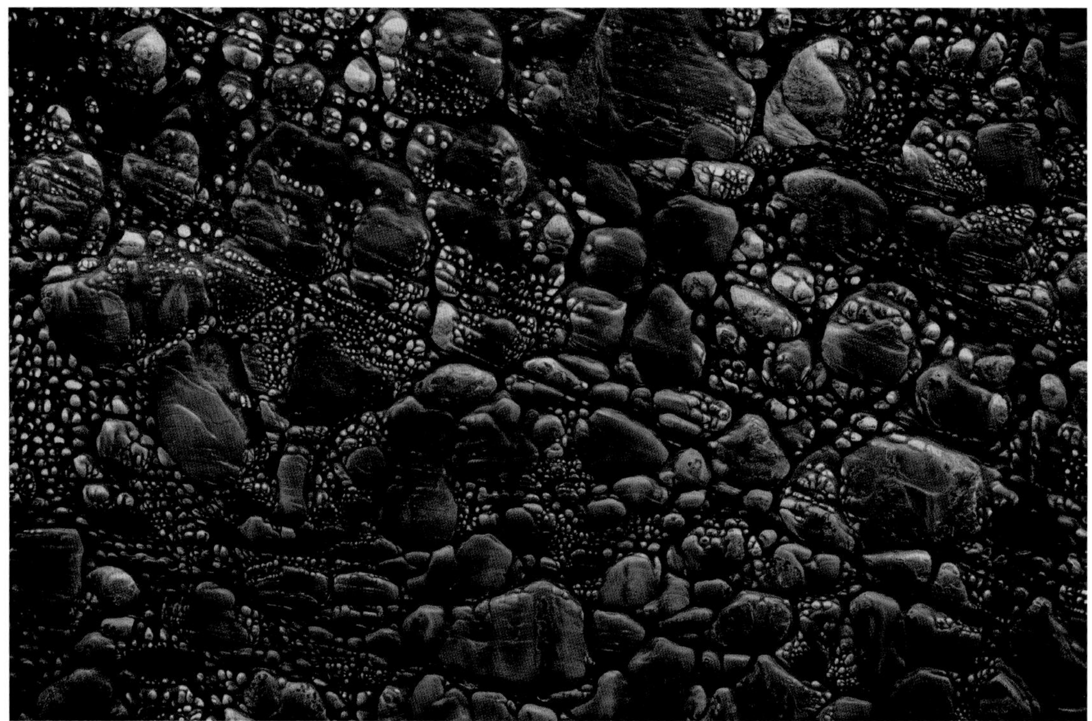

It is folly to think about previsualization in the abstract as something unequivo-cally good or bad. Certainly, previsualization may be a good and useful practice when we consider it in terms of mindfulness, but some forms of previsualization may have the opposite effect. The most insidious and undesirable form of previsualization is preconception: deciding in advance what photographs you'll make at some future time, rather than remaining open and allowing creative ideas to ensue spontaneously from meaningful experiences—epiphanies, chance discoveries, serendipitous strokes of inspiration, powerful emotions. Since we cannot predict how we may feel or what may inspire us at a future time, no preconceived photograph can be considered self-expressive. Worse yet, preconception may bias, limit, or extinguish entirely your ability to conceive novel ideas in real time, in response to experience. Put another way, *when* you previsualize an image—whether in real time or in advance—is just as important as *whether* you previsualize.

When you previsualize by way of making yourself mindful—attentive to details of your environment and experiences as they happen—you "prime" your creative pump and prepare yourself to visualize more effectively when a creative idea presents itself.

Then, and only then, is the time to cease previsualizing (being mindfully and openly aware) and begin visualizing (forming an anticipated image in your mind's eye).

In further credit to Adams, one of the few times he used the term "previsualize," rather than just "visualize," is in reference to concepts—what photographs aim to express. In a 1943 article titled "A Personal Credo," Adams wrote, "A photograph is not an accident—it is a concept. It exists at, or before, the moment of exposure.... From that moment on to the final print, the process is chiefly one of craft; the previsualized photograph is rendered in terms of the final print by a series of processes peculiar to the medium."

In the same sense that previsualization refers to useful things we may do *before* (i.e., in preparation for) visualization, and visualization refers to images we anticipate once we have a concept—an intent—but before making an exposure, some photographers suggested the term "postvisualization" to refer to useful things we may do *after* exposure.

The first to mention the term postvisualization was Minor White, who suggested that when preparing to print a photograph, "a resurgence of the creative state of mind is desirable." In other words, recalling and reliving the creative experience—what we hoped to express (i.e., the concept) at the time we visualized the photograph—may be useful in guiding later (technical) printing decisions.

Jerry Uelsmann offered a different way to think about postvisualization. Uelsmann considered postvisualization as "the willingness on the part of the photographer to *re-visualize the final image* at any point in the entire photographic process." (Italics mine) In other words, rather than allowing our original visualizations to become prescriptive and to dictate all further steps to the final image, Uelsmann acknowledged that it's the nature of creative ideas that they may arise at any time and, when they do, perhaps suggest other—better—ways of finishing our images than we originally conceived.

By remaining open to new possibilities, we may realize after exposure (perhaps when processing or printing, perhaps even years after we thought we were "finished") that the original visualization may not have been the most effective, and allow for further consideration, perhaps even for a new and different visualization of the captured photograph.

Thus, by distinguishing consciously previsualization from visualization and postvisualization, applying each when appropriate and allowing for new creative possibilities, we not only improve our odds of making meaningful creations, but we also create opportunities for further inspiration and creative thinking, as well as for more prolonged, meaningful, and enjoyable artistic experiences.

Away with ideals. Let each individual act spontaneously from the forever incalculable prompting of the creative wellhead within him. There is no universal law.

—D. H. LAWRENCE

Working in projects is, without a doubt, a better and more satisfying way to practice art than to pursue single works. Creating singular works is, without a doubt, a better and more satisfying way to practice art than working in projects.

Each of the statements in the preceding paragraph is false. Certainly, the two cannot coexist. Each of these statements, however, is true and the two are not in contradiction when preceded or followed by the words "for some artists." Which group of "some artists" do you fit into? The answer is in you. By this I mean that the answer is contained in your own unique personality. More specifically, the personality trait of conscientiousness is important in deciding whether working in projects or pursuing individual works will prove more appropriate and rewarding to you than the alternative.

The APA defines conscientiousness as "the tendency to be organized, responsible, and hardworking." Highly conscientious people are industrious, tend to plan their work in detail, and stick to their plans. They are not easily distracted and take great pride and pleasure in achieving their planned goals, even if the work required is tedious or otherwise unenjoyable; even if other, perhaps better, ideas present themselves before the work is finished.

Conversely, people with low conscientiousness tend to be impulsive and easily distracted, take risks, juggle a lot of ideas, and are more concerned with the quality of their immediate experience as they work than with the expectation of future rewards when the work is done. Such people may begin working on an idea with great enthusiasm only to later become distracted or bored and lose interest in the work before completing it.

It may be tempting to conclude that you should aspire to become highly conscientious. However, your degree of conscientiousness is, for the most part, not a matter of choice. Like other personality traits, your degree of conscientiousness is largely determined by genetic predisposition and formative (external) influences. You are what you are, which is why each of the statements at the opening of this essay is only true for some people.

By necessity, high conscientiousness is at least in some ways at odds with creativity. Specifically, conscientiousness is often in competition with another personality trait that is strongly correlated with creativity: openness to experience. People with high openness to experience generally possess what some researchers described as "leaky attention." They tend to have a lot of ideas influenced by a broad range of concepts (i.e., they are good *divergent* thinkers), often overtaking or negating previous ideas. Highly open people tend to be distracted easily and get excited to pursue new possibilities, sometimes to a point where new ideas seem to them more important and worthy of their attention than existing work in progress. This explains why highly creative people are often good at starting things, but are not always disciplined (i.e., conscientious) enough to finish them.

This is not to say that creative people can't also be highly conscientious. In fact, creative people who are fortunate to also have an uncommonly high degree of conscientiousness are those most likely to become commercially successful and widely recognizable. This is because high conscientiousness makes people more productive; it gives them the discipline to see projects to completion, and the tenacity to pursue professional success more vigorously than those with lower conscientiousness, who may consider such things as commerce and popularity as lesser priorities—if not as necessary evils—when compared with their joy in conceiving and pursuing new ideas and experiences, regardless of what anyone else may think (or buy).

Returning to the matter of projects versus single images, it should be obvious by now that project-oriented work—work that demands consistency, resisting the temptation to switch attention to other things, and limiting yourself to working within narrow, preconceived success criteria for the sake of future reward—can be very appealing to highly conscientious people. On the other hand, this mode of work may seem like a tedious chore to those who rank highly on openness to experience, whose desire to try new things may overwhelm their degree of conscientiousness when answering the question "what should I work on now?"

To people whose creative impulses are powerful enough to overcome their conscientious discipline, working on projects may feel like an imposition: something to rebel against rather than something to take pride in. Such persons likely will (perhaps begrudgingly) still act in a conscientious manner in professional, interpersonal, ethical, or other contexts, but it would be much harder for them to reign in their attention and creative urges when some creative "aha!" moment presents itself and inspires them to work on something new rather than set it aside to complete an existing project.

Research shows that, statistically, artists as a group tend to score lower than the average population on conscientiousness, perhaps explaining Mary Oliver's statement: "There is a notion that creative people are absentminded, reckless, heedless of social

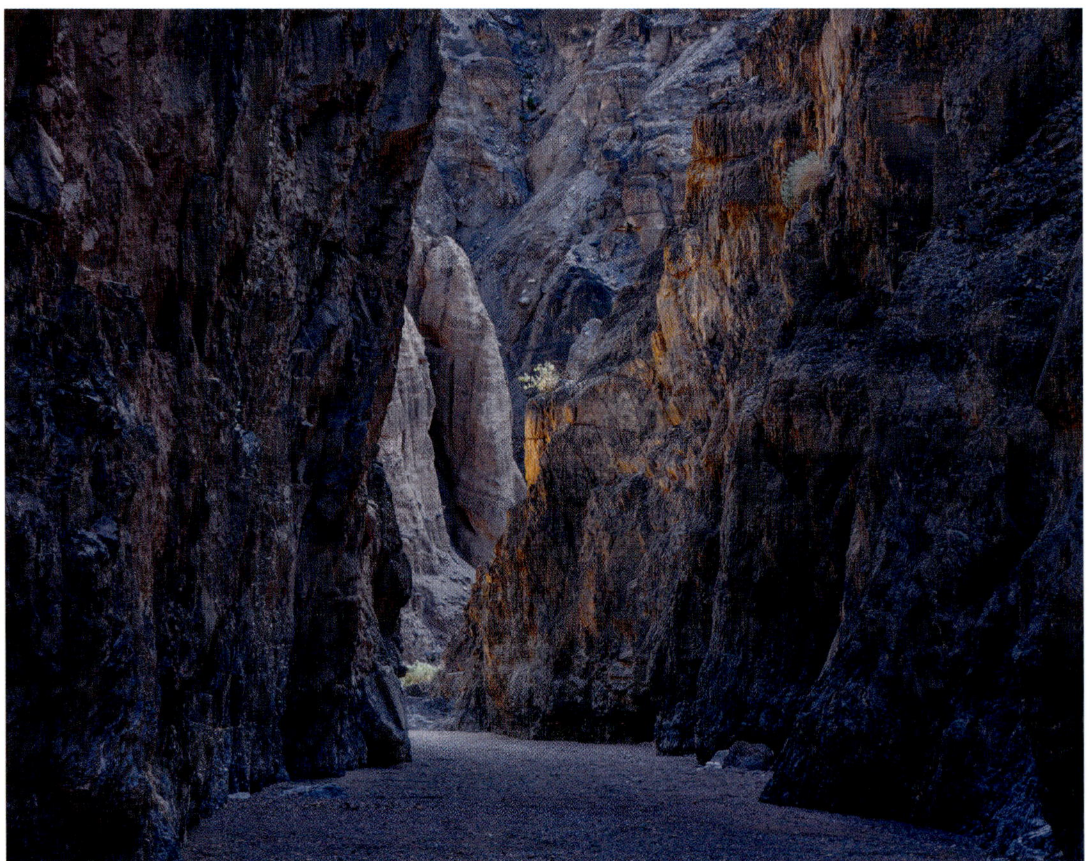

customs and obligations. It is, hopefully, true." This also explains why most artists, past and present, pursued their work one piece at a time, rather than in projects. Often, these individual pieces may seem entirely unrelated to an outside observer. Consider, for example, how different Leonardo da Vinci's *Mona Lisa* is from his *Vitruvian Man*, not to mention he was also an excellent sculptor, scientist, inventor, and musician. Of course, there are also examples for the opposite. For example, Claude Monet made about 250 paintings of waterlilies and around 30 paintings of haystacks.

In a greater sense, we must consider that, given each of us is unique and that we are all mortal, we each work toward one grand project: our life. More specifically, the one project uniting all that we do, whether or not we are conscious of it, is to make the brief slice of time afforded to each of us to be conscious living beings as meaningful as possible. As Albert Camus put it: "Any thought that abandons unity glorifies diversity. And diversity is the home of art."

J. D. Salinger put it more succinctly when he wrote, "An artist's only concern is to shoot for some kind of perfection, and on his own terms, not anyone else's." Perfection on your own terms means perfection according to your own personality. For some, this perfection may be expressed in singular works; for others in thematic collections of works. The point being that, as long as it is considered as an expression of one's personality, one kind of perfection is no less perfect than another kind of perfection.

Earlier in this book,[49] I mentioned that *know thyself* is just the first of three maxims that were engraved above the entrance to the Temple of Apollo in Ancient Greece. The second of these maxims is *nothing to excess*. This advice also, if perhaps in a roundabout way, is related to choosing between committing yourself to projects or remaining open to new ideas and inspirations that may yield singular creations.[50]

For highly conscientious people, the risk of excess may manifest as becoming too involved in a project to a point where they become stressed by their limited capacity to only do so much within a given time, or by the need to leave some things unfinished to meet a deadline or because they cease to be relevant. As a result, such people may overwork themselves to finish a project even when the project is no longer enjoyable to work on, or may even fail to achieve its originally intended purpose. For highly conscientious people, finishing a project may seem the ultimate measure of success, rather than their enjoyment in the process of working on the project, the importance of the finished product, or the realization that one's limited time and resources may be better spent on other things. If you are such a person, I recommend doing what any good

---

[49] See page 69.

[50] For the curious, the third maxim from Apollo's Temple, perhaps not as relevant to the topic of artistic work, can be paraphrased as: "guaranteeing another person's debt leads to ruin."

project manager knows to do: Define the project's success criteria in advance, identify relevant success metrics, and consider them regularly as you go. If during the project it becomes clear that the success criteria can't be met, abandoning a project is a better choice than sinking more effort and resources into it.

For those who are not very conscientious, excess may also be a problem. Specifically, excess of tempting ideas and competing priorities. Coming up with new creative ideas is rewarding and enjoyable, but if you don't finish at least *some* of what you start, you will never be satisfied with your work. Those who do not have the discipline to remain focused on long-term projects may still do well training themselves to focus attention long enough to work on smaller, short-term projects and/or do the best job they can with single works, rather than abandoning them too early when another idea calls.

Being woefully low on conscientiousness, I don't work in projects in the sense of pursuing new works with the goal of grouping them together at some future time. I prefer to live and create one moment at a time, one day at a time, not in constant expectation of some future reward. I do, however, sometimes group works after the fact into a consistent presentation—a portfolio or an exhibit, which is a form of a short-term project but doesn't demand the investment of time and attention that a more complex one might.

Find what works for you. Don't let anyone convince you that either of the statements in the opening paragraph of this essay is absolutely and universally true.

BE A PART OF THE STORY

In order for the artist to have a world to express he must first
be situated in this world, oppressed or oppressing, resigned
or rebellious, a man among men.

—SIMONE DE BEAUVOIR

For much of the time I was "growing up" as a photographer, Galen Rowell was a
household name among outdoor photographers. At the time, it would have seemed
inconceivable that anyone practicing some genre of nature or landscape photography
would not know of Rowell's legendary reputation as an adventurer who would go to
great efforts and incredible athletic feats, often on a moment's notice, to chase after an
opportunity to make a fine photograph.

Alas, Rowell and his wife died in a tragic plane crash shortly before the age of
social media. With no online presence and no family or institutions working to sustain
and promote his legacy, Rowell's reputation has faded in recent years. Many young
photographers today, whose knowledge of their medium comes predominantly from
social media, have not heard of him. Also, as printed editions of his books[51] have sold
out, and alongside a steep, ongoing trend of general decline in reading in recent years,
fewer and fewer people know of his work, philosophy, and teachings. Still, a perusal of
his biography will leave you in little doubt that he lived an exciting and interesting life,
and that he was a deep thinker who sought meaning and strove to excel, not only in his
photographic work, but also in the quality of his experiences: the stories out of which
his photographs were created.

---

[51] At the time of this writing, none of Rowell's books is available for purchase in electronic formats.

Should you be fortunate live to an advanced age and look back on the story of your life, which would you prefer it to be? To have lived a profoundly meaningful and exciting life, rife with stories of adventure, discovery, thrilling times, and transformative experiences, but with the knowledge that few people will know or remember that you had lived such a life; or to have achieved such great fame that your name will likely be remembered long after your passing, despite your life having been largely devoid of meaningful personal triumphs and exciting experiences? For most people, the difference is not a matter of random chance, but a matter of having made deliberate choices in guiding their lives.

One aspect of Rowell's legacy that proved eminently important in my life is his philosophy of "participatory photography," wherein a photographer is not just a passive observer and recorder of scenery, objects, beings, or events, as a photojournalist might be, but rather plays an active role in the unfolding story. Participatory photography may be characterized broadly as "having skin in the game"—facing the raw sensations, challenges, feelings, and risks ensuing from direct contact with and sharing in the experience of what you photograph. Creating photographs in this manner is not about just returning home with some trophies—"good shots"—it's about having the photographic experience be part of a real-life adventure story. One doesn't practice participatory photography solely for the sake of any qualities of the resulting photographs, but for the sake of the quality and depth of the photographer's experience: to make the photographer's own life story more interesting, more exciting, and more meaningful, even if the people who will later view the resulting photograph will know little or nothing of the story of its making.

In contrast with Rowell's participatory philosophy, many photographers take the opposite approach, pursuing good photographs for their own sake, regardless of qualities of the experiences involved in their making (and sometimes making up contrived "hero stories" about these photographs after the fact to boost their appeal). Consider, for example, the story told by Ansel Adams about the making of his famous photograph *Moonrise, Hernandez, New Mexico*.[52] In his book *Examples: The Making of 40 Photographs* (published in 1983, more than forty years after he made the photograph, during which *Moonrise* became one of his best known and bestselling works), Adams tells a story of coming upon "an extraordinary situation—an inevitable photograph," having a "clear visualization" of the image he wanted, then rushing to make an exposure as the light was fading quickly, failing to find his Weston light meter, and triumphantly determining the exposure based on his memorized knowledge of the luminosity value of the moon.

---

[52] Adams is famous for being factual and inexpressive in his titles, rather than using creative titles to influence his viewers' impressions.

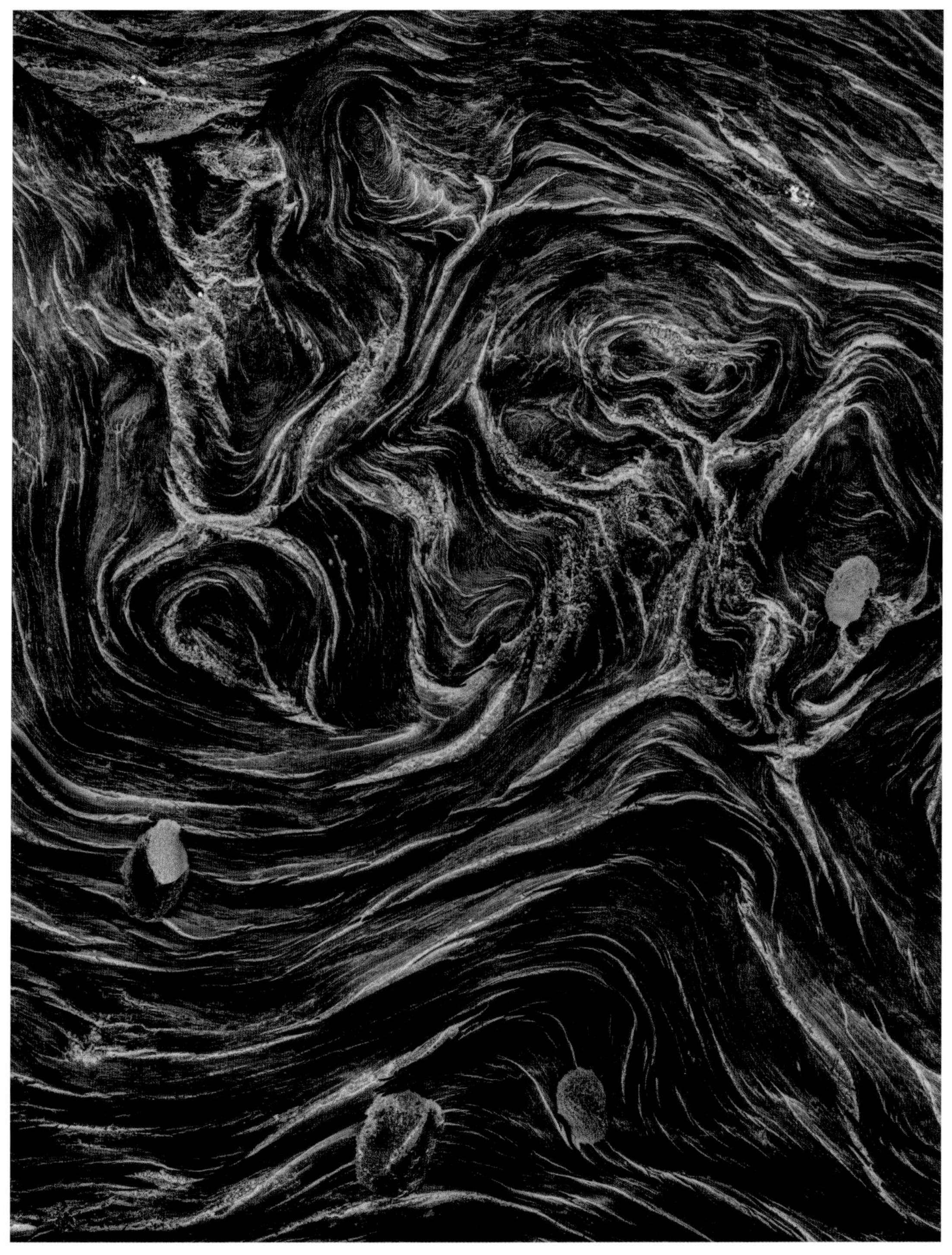

This story contradicts an earlier blurb Adams perhaps forgot he wrote in 1943 (just a couple of years after making the photograph) when *Moonrise* was chosen by Edward Steichen for publication in the magazine *US Camera*. In that original description, Adams referred to the image as "a rather normal photograph" made "after sundown" (i.e., not as the light was changing rapidly), and described in detail how he used his Weston light meter to determine the correct exposure values. Also, his later prints of *Moonrise* look nothing like his earlier attempts, suggesting he could not have had a "clear visualization" of the final photograph when he made it. Clearly, both stories can't be true, and the timing of their publication suggests that the later—more heroic—version is likely a fabrication (i.e., that the real story of the making of *Moonrise* was not the memorable and exciting experience Adams claimed to have had in his later account). It seems unlikely that if that was the true story he would have kept it a secret for four decades and say nothing about it in his original description.

"Every production of an artist," wrote W. Somerset Maugham, "should be the expression of an adventure of his soul." Galen Rowell was a quintessential "adventure photographer" in the sense that he was an exceptionally skilled athlete who climbed great mountains, traversed remote deserts, and endured formidable physical challenges beyond the capacities of most people. However, those are not the only kinds of adventures there are. An adventure is, before anything else, an experience that is unusual, exciting, involving uncertainty and risk—all of which may mean different things to different people, but still yield the same inner states: exhilaration, surprise, trepidation, triumph, perseverance, grit, determination, pushing yourself to your limits (or what you thought your limits were).

Adventures of all kinds, whether they end in success or in disappointment, also give rise to the same aftereffects: feeling lucky and proud for having had the courage to embark on them, learning that you have in you the courage to push your proverbial "envelope," to dare to venture beyond your comfort zone. These things, in turn, lead to increased confidence and personal growth. If nothing else, you come away from an adventure with a good story: an adventure story, a memorable story, a story you will likely return to later in life to realize its significance in the grand anthology of stories of the person you became.

Adventures involve tackling unexpected challenges, but they don't necessarily need to be great physical challenges. Adventures may involve grappling with creative challenges, learning challenges, personal challenges (e.g., overcoming shyness, physical disabilities, discrimination, or other limitations), financial challenges, challenges that require enduring through dark moods or difficult times, challenges involving complex interpersonal or professional relationships, and so on. All forms of adventure have this in common: they require that you participate in them. You must encounter them in person, invest effort in them, persevere them, be moved emotionally by them—not observe them from a distance. They require you to play a part in a story.

"How vain it is," wrote Thoreau in his journal, "to sit down to write if you have not stood up to live." Diarist Anaïs Nin expressed the same sentiment in her own journal. She wrote, "I will not be just a tourist in the world of images, just watching images passing by which I cannot live in, make love to, possess as permanent sources of joy and ecstasy."

My decision, years ago, to become a professional photographer and writer ensued from my desire to not just pursue photogenic subjects, but to live, work, and evolve a deeper knowledge of and relationship with a unique desert region known as the Colorado Plateau. Each time I visited this place before coming to live here, it rewarded me with much more than just pleasing photographs. The more I explored, the more time I spent camping and living among the region's many unique environments, witnessing and communing with the life forms, geology, weather, relics of ancient cultures, the more I felt that this is my home: the place where I feel more comfortable, inspired, moved to think and to feel deeply, than anywhere else. After several such experiences, I fell in love. I wanted these places, these beings, these phenomena to become a part of my story, and I wanted to play a positive role, however small, in theirs.

Most of my photographic and written work was inspired by and created in this environment over a period of decades, in close contact with the things and events that shape it, and that in turn have shaped me. My life here has not always been easy or charmed. But it has been, to borrow Rowell's term, intensely "participatory." My reward: I can now, and for as long as I live, look back on my life as a life of adventure, incredible beauty, and life-enriching experiences. Being the person I am—a naturalist, a reclusive introvert, a passionately curious learner, a deep thinker—no office-bound job, no urban dwelling, no pricey possession, and no amount of fame could have shaped my stories in the same ways or to the same degree as my ability to spend most of my days immersed in the wildness of this place, in solitude, in direct contact with the natural things and phenomena that make it what it is. Also, no place could have yielded me experiences or stories of this magnitude if I could only visit it on occasion, for short periods, seeing only its most obvious, superficial aspects. If I had limited my interest in this or any other place to just photographing it, I would not have had what I consider today to have been the most deeply meaningful and beautiful years of my life.

I urge you to find such a life for yourself, too: not necessarily a life of outdoor adventure as I have, but a life that so fits with and complements who you are that you will someday be able to look back upon it with great pride and satisfaction, knowing

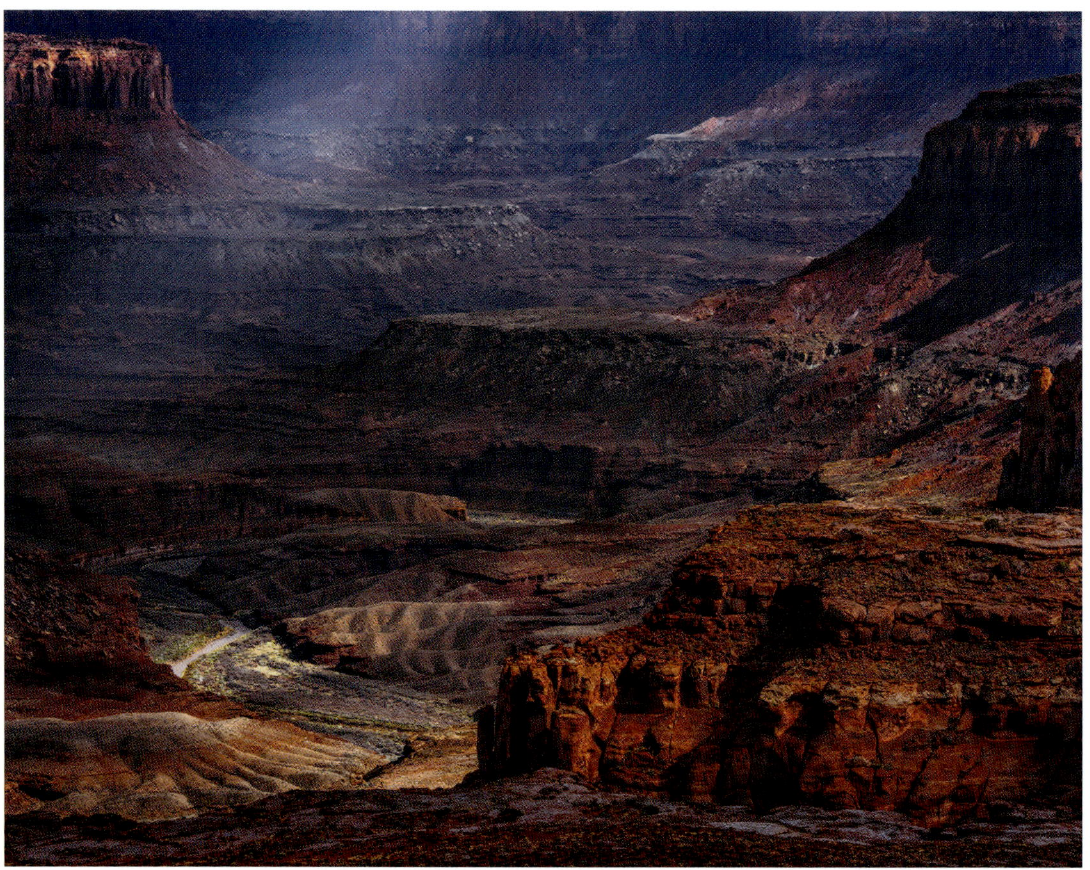

without the slightest doubt or ambiguity that you put your living years to the best possible use—whatever that means, or will come to mean, to you.

The artworks and writings I admire most are those made by artists who have, or have had, interesting and meaningful lives, whether they unfolded in natural settings, in cities, or anywhere else they loved and came to know deeply and obsessively. I feel very much the same as Stieglitz, who wrote, "It is not art in the professionalized sense about which I care, but that which is created sacredly, as a result of a deep inner experience, with all of oneself, and that becomes 'art' in time."

"If your daily life seems poor to you," wrote Rilke, "do not blame that: blame yourself. Tell yourself that you are not poet enough to call forth its riches; because for the creator there is no poverty and no poor and unimportant place." Likewise, Robert Henri wrote, "For an artist to be interesting to us he must have been interesting

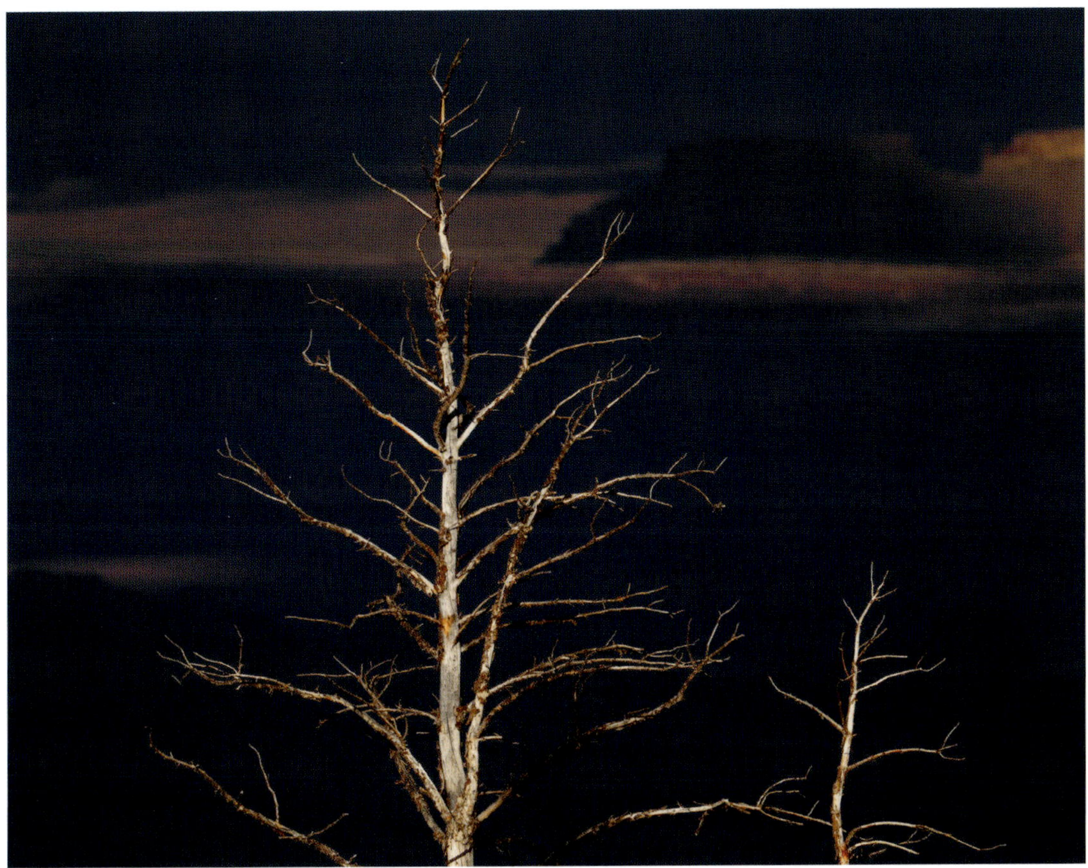

to himself. He must have been capable of intense feeling, and capable of profound contemplation."

Is your life story interesting to you? Does it reward you with intense feelings and move you to profound contemplation? Is your artwork created sacredly, as a result of deep inner experiences? If not, don't wait to lament not having these things in your elder years, when it may be too late to do anything about them. Find a story worth living—your own story—and do your best to live it. Tell others the parts of it that are worth telling, but don't compromise the real story for the sake of impressing others with manufactured myths and confabulations.

"Art," wrote Willa Cather, "springs out of the very stuff that life is made of. Most of our young authors start to write a story and make a few observations from nature to add local color. The results are invariably false and hollow. Art must spring out of the fullness and the richness of life."

BE EXTRAORDINARY

You have to be incorruptible in your art, and to be so in your
art, you have to train yourself to be so in your life.

—PAUL CÉZANNE

To be extraordinary is, in the simplest sense, to not be ordinary. Rest assured, you are
not. Nobody is. But many people, whether they are conscious of it or not, try to be.
To be ordinary is to have no distinctive features, to not stand out as exceptional or
unusual, to not be differentiated.

In his book *Flow: The Psychology of Optimal Experience*, Mihaly Csikszentmihalyi
referred to differentiation as one of two opposing processes that define the self. The
other, complementary, process is integration. Finding a proper balance between
these two processes is essential to becoming a unique, therefore complex person.
Complexity, according to Csikszentmihalyi, comes from the experience of flow. He
explained:

> Following a flow experience, the organization of the self is more complex
> than it had been before. It is by becoming increasingly complex that
> the self might be said to grow. Complexity is the result of two broad
> psychological processes: differentiation and integration. Differentiation
> implies a movement toward uniqueness, toward separating oneself from
> others. Integration refers to its opposite: a union with other people, with
> ideas and entities beyond the self. A complex self is one that succeeds in
> combining these opposite tendencies.

Failing to balance differentiation and integration (i.e., being either too individualistic or too dependent on others) may lead to undesirable consequences. Csikszentmihalyi explained:

> *A self that is only differentiated—not integrated—may attain great individual accomplishments, but risks being mired in self-centered egotism. By the same token, a person whose self is based exclusively on integration will be connected and secure, but lack autonomous individuality. Only when a person invests equal amounts of psychic energy in these two processes and avoids both selfishness and conformity is the self likely to reflect complexity.*

To be ordinary—to conform—is safer and easier than to be extraordinary: an exception. To do what others expect of you is easier than to try new things, defy norms, question beliefs, part with traditions. But too much conformity also comes at a cost—the cost of withholding, hiding, suppressing, even feeling ashamed of the things that make you different, unique, extraordinary: the things that make you, you.

Too much differentiation may amount to selfishness. But selfishness should not be confused with individuality. Individuality is about how you see and express yourself. Selfishness is about how you treat others. "Selfishness," wrote Oscar Wilde, "is not living as one wishes to live, it is asking others to live as one wishes to live." Being true to yourself—being authentic, in the existentialist definition of the term—even if it means finding yourself at odds with your society, is not selfish. Indeed, it is the people who expect you to behave in ways that don't feel authentic to you—to conform unquestioningly to values, traditions, and expressions decided by others—who are the most selfish.

What two things in the world are exactly alike? Only the most basic things: two molecules, two atoms, or two subatomic particles may be structurally indistinguishable. But when it comes to more complex things—whether rocks, trees, house cats, or human beings—no two are ever exactly alike. The most complex structure we know of in the universe(!) is the human brain. Like it or not, having such a brain makes you unique, different from all others—extraordinary.

The questions to ask yourself are these: How will I manifest my extraordinariness in the most useful, meaningful, and satisfying way? How will I embrace the things that make me different from others—my gifts, handicaps, personality traits, quirks, desires, aspirations—and use them in the most adaptive ways (i.e., toward making my life better in the long term)? There are many ways to answer these questions, some more specific, more practical, safer, or easier than others, but all come down to this: choosing and continuously evolving a personal philosophy to guide your life.

Having a personal philosophy doesn't mean adopting some ready-made "ism" and striving to live up to it. In fact, it might mean the opposite: learning what "isms" exist, considering them in the context of who you are, what you know, what seems wisest, worthwhile, and most practical *to you*, and then constructing your own sense of the world—your own values, your own understanding of what will make your life most satisfying, even if it doesn't fit neatly within the confines of a single formal ideology.

Among the things you might use to discover, become, and express your authentic self—the things that make you a unique, differentiated, extraordinary individual—art holds a place of honor. This is because in art you have complete freedom—if you choose to embrace it—to do what is most meaningful to you. Even though it may not always seem that way, any restrictions you impose in your art are self-chosen. Make sure to choose your restrictions for the right reasons, not because other people say it should be so.

Don't think of art as just a fun hobby or just a way of making pleasing objects to entertain or impress others. Art can be much more than that. To think that the purpose of art is only to create artifacts is like saying that the purpose of eating is only to provide your body with nutrients, that the purpose of driving is only to transport yourself from one point to another, or that the purpose of learning is only to gain practical job skills. Art—like food, travel, and learning—can be a source of far greater pleasures, meanings, and opportunities for enriching life than any utilitarian purpose. There is a reason people differ in their choices of art, food, travel destinations, and academic pursuits. The reason is that we are each different—extraordinary—by virtue of *what* we are: the genes and circumstances that decide our personality and physical characteristics, and the unique circumstances that shape each of our individual lives.

You are extraordinary. It's up to you to decide what to do with it—to suppress it and be ordinary, or embrace it and *be extraordinary*. Don't wait too long to decide. With every choice you make, you either bring yourself closer to becoming what you are, living as you are, and expressing who you are, or departing from and suppressing who you are, at the risk of someday discovering you had lived someone else's life, someone who is not you.

You only get one chance to discover and to become yourself: to be extraordinary. Don't let it go to waste.

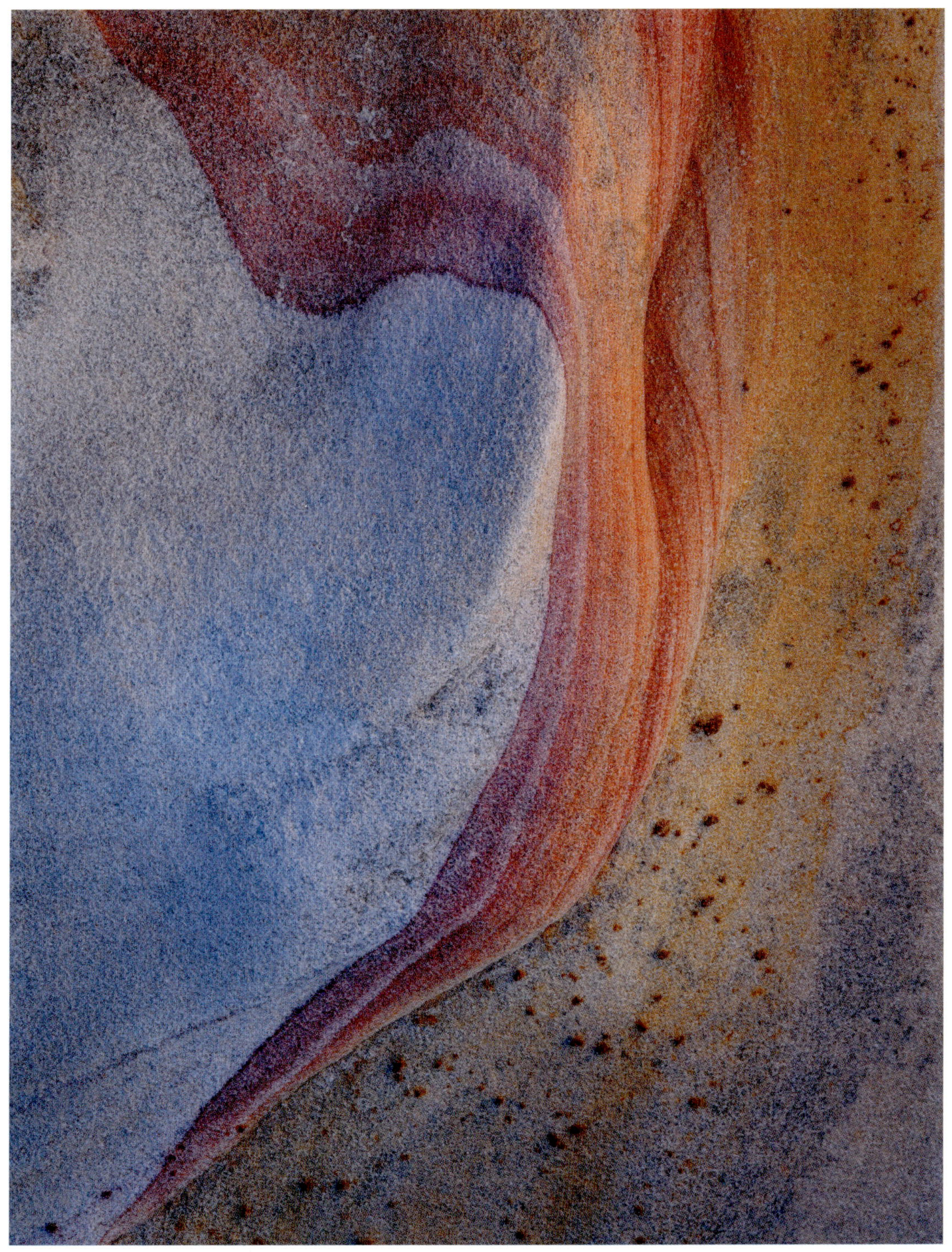

ABOUT THE AUTHOR

As a professional artist and writer, I believe that the practice of creative pursuits not only manifests in the making of art, but also has the ability to enrich life, foster meaningful experiences and contentment, and bring healing through lifelong discovery and adventure.

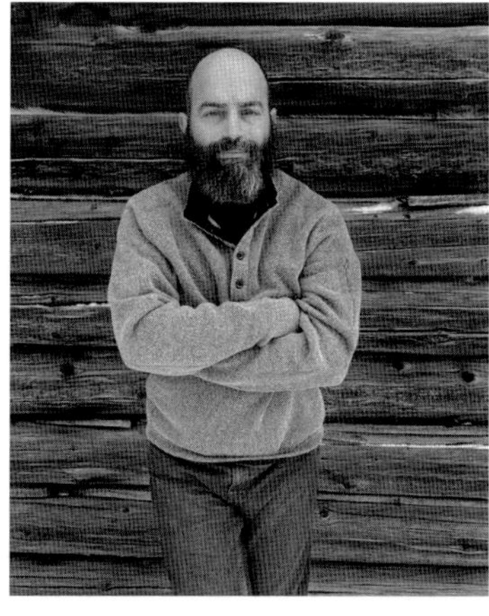

I wish to create images that convey my connection with the wild places of the American West. My images are the result of a complex relationship with these lands that has evolved over many years—through times of bliss and conflict, love and loss, and life changes. In my images, I seek to convey a reverence and gratitude for how these places have shaped my life. My subjects are not just attractive models to me, they are friends and sanctuaries and characters in my own story. I do not consider myself a photographer who creates art, but rather an artist working in the medium of photography.

I am the author of several books. My work has been featured in various publications, including *LensWork Magazine*, *Photograph*, *Outdoor Photographer*, *Popular Photography*, *Digital Photographer*, *Landscape Photography Magazine*, *PhotoLife*, and *On Landscape*, among others.

Guy Tal
www.guytal.com